JERUSALEMWALKS

This series originated with PARISWALKS by
Alison and Sonia Landes. Other titles include:

LONDONWALKS by *Anton Powell*
FLORENCEWALKS by *Anne Holler* (forthcoming)

NITZA ROSOVSKY

Jerusalemwalks

Photographs by
Richard Lindzen and Nitza Rosovsky

A New Republic Book
Holt, Rinehart and Winston
New York

In memory of my mother
Leah Berman Brown

Published by Holt, Rinehart and Winston
383 Madison Avenue, New York, New York 10017.

Published simultaneously in Canada by Holt, Rinehart and
Winston of Canada, Limited.

Library of Congress Cataloging in Publication Data

Rosovsky, Nitza.
  Jerusalemwalks.
  "A New republic book."
  Includes index.
  1. Jerusalem—Description—Tours. I. Title.
DS109.R68   915.694'4   81-4274   AACR2
ISBN Hardbound: 0-03-060077-4
ISBN Paperback: 0-03-060078-2 (An Owl Book)

Designer: Jacqueline Schuman
Maps by David Lindroth
Printed in the United States of America
3 5 7 9 10 8 6 4 2

Photographic Credits
Richard Lindzen: pp. 6, 22, 32, 40–41, 43, 51, 64–65, 81, 87, 108–9,
127, 139, 158, 167, 171, 173, 186, 241, 265, 266, and 273.
Nitza Rosovsky: frontispiece, pp. 66, 94–95, 99, 105, 110, 132, 146,
148, 181, 188, 195, 206, 218–19, 224, 228, 255, 261, and 262.

ISBN 0-03-060077-4 HARDBOUND
ISBN 0-03-060078-2 PAPERBACK

Contents

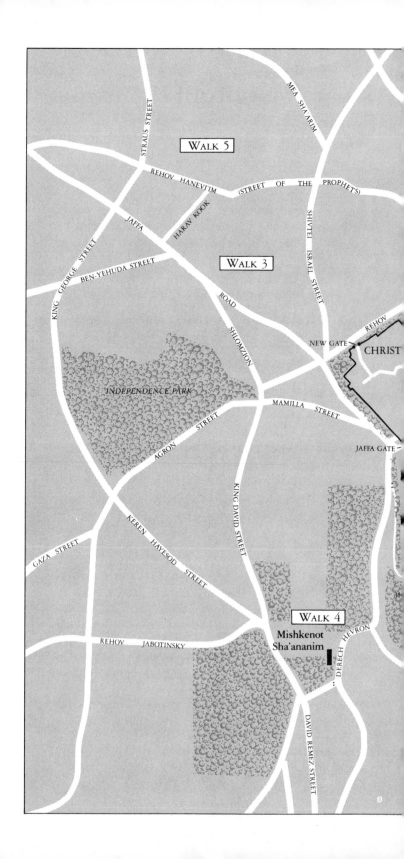

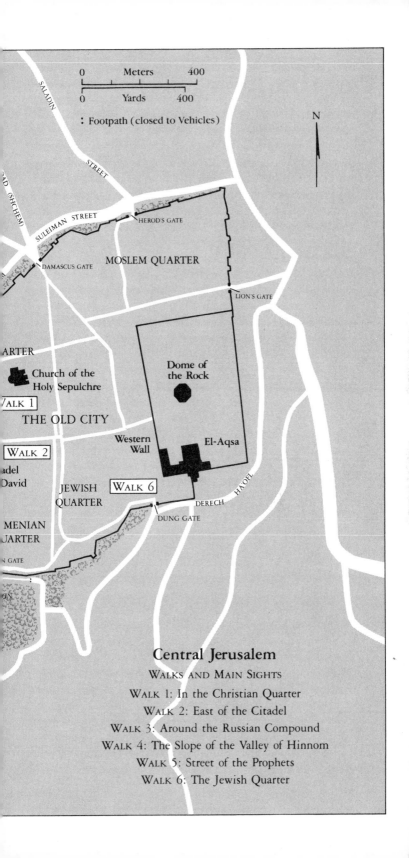

Central Jerusalem

WALKS AND MAIN SIGHTS

WALK 1: In the Christian Quarter
WALK 2: East of the Citadel
WALK 3: Around the Russian Compound
WALK 4: The Slope of the Valley of Hinnom
WALK 5: Street of the Prophets
WALK 6: The Jewish Quarter

Acknowledgments

In March 1978, my friend Martin Peretz asked me to write *Jerusalemwalks*. For the pleasure that working on this book has brought me I shall always remain indebted to Marty.

Many helped make this book possible: family and friends who provided nourishment for body and soul during my various stays in Jerusalem, the distinguished "streetwalkers" who tested the walks and supplied corrections and observations, and all those who showered me with their favorite guidebooks to different cities. Most of all I wish to thank the people of my native city who shared their knowledge of and their love for Jerusalem with me: an Armenian merchant in the bazaar, a Moslem grave digger, a Supreme Court judge, and many, many others. It was a heartening sign in a period of political turmoil.

Staff members of various institutions provided invaluable assistance, and every door in Jerusalem seemed to open when I explained what I was trying to do: at the Albright Institute of Archaeological Research, Hebrew University, the Islamic Archaeological Department, the Israel Exploration Society, the Israel Museum, the Jerusalem Foundation, the Jerusalem Institute of Management, the Jerusalem Municipal Historical Archives, Yad Yitzhak Ben Zvi, and at Harvard University's Widener Library and Semitic Museum.

Special thanks are due to Dr. and Mrs. Nahum Goldman and to Elsa Wyser for their hospitality. One summer I spent several weeks at Mishkenot Sha'ananim, a truly unforgettable experience.

For their individual help I wish to thank Zvi Bazak, Michael Barbour, Charles Berlin, Ruth Cheshin, Oleg Grabar, Rafi Grafman, Walid Khalidi, Stephen Urice, and especially Mayor Teddy Kollek. Yehoshua Ben-Arieh, whose work has brought nineteenth-century Jerusalem back to life, has been most generous with his time. Meron Benvenisti, who probably knows the city better than anyone else, has helped with many suggestions. Every façade properly described in the following pages has benefited from the stern eye and humorous pen of Naomi Miller who walked and read most of the book. Magen Broshi patiently answered endless questions, and read parts of the manuscript. I particularly want to thank him for his impeccable standards and for his kind comments. Naturally, I take sole responsibility for all remaining errors in the book; Mujir ed-Din probably said it

Acknowledgments

best about Jerusalem when he wrote, circa 1500 A.D.: "It was, perhaps, built by the founder of the school, but Allah knows best."

The editor of this book, Marc Granetz, struggled long with my creative spelling and with sentences based on the strictest rules of Hebrew grammar. It is to his credit that we are still friends.

My guide and mentor, coauthor of *Pariswalks* and "godmother" of the *Walks* series, is Sonia Landes. For three years she listened to me, advised and encouraged me, and eventually walked half of this book. Her remarks improved the prose and shortened the length of the walks.

Finally, I wish to thank my family: Leah for her enthusiasm, Judy for walking and editorializing, Michael for politely listening to too many Jerusalem tales, and Henry: "For whither thou goest, I will go; and where thou lodgest, I will lodge"—even away from Jerusalem.

JERUSALEMWALKS

Introduction

Why is this book different from all other books? More
has been written about the Holy City than about any
other place in the world; is there really a need for one
more volume, for another Jerusalem guide?

Many guidebooks attempt to cover the whole city,
and because there is so much to see they discuss mostly the important landmarks and only occasionally
mention a quaint bazaar or side street. From the Holy
Place of your choice they will lead you to museums,
monuments, and tombs. In a few pages they will try to
cram four thousand years of history. Often, as a result
of an overdose of information, exhausted tourists are
seen wandering around with a glazed look in their
eyes, saturated with dates and dynasties, hoping never
to see another Herodian wall.

Jerusalemwalks proposes a different approach that
can, perhaps, be called "micro-sight-seeing." Rather
than show you more than you can absorb or enjoy, it
offers an intimate, close-up look at a few small sections
of the city. Six walks are presented in this book, each
one lasting approximately two and a half hours and
averaging about one mile in length. The walks will en-
able you to stroll through back alleys, climb onto hidden rooftops, explore old residential neighborhoods,
and eat in out-of-the-way places. You will have a
chance to examine minute details on the façades of
private houses and public toilets, or gaze at grand vistas from the top of the highest bell towers. You will
learn how to bargain in the markets and how to sip
Turkish coffee. From clues hidden in archaeological
sites, and with the help of your imagination, you'll discover some of the splendor of bygone days. Even the
most ordinary places will reveal their secrets once you
know how to read their stories. A concise, in-depth
history of a certain event may help you remember the
significance of an era, an important individual, or the
architecture of an entire period. You'll become familiar
with both the "Heavenly City"—*Yerushalayim shel
ma'alah*, in Hebrew—and with the everyday one—

Yerushalayim shel matah—where people live, eat, pray, love, hate, sin, and dream.

Much has been said about the meaning of the city where the roots of the Judeo-Christian heritage of Western society lie. To Jews Jerusalem has always been the symbol of national and religious freedom, the city that the Messiah will enter at the End of the Days. To Christians it is the place where Jesus died for the sins of mankind and where the Second Coming will occur. It is the third holiest city to Islam, whence Mohammed departed on his Night Journey and to which he will return on the Day of Judgment. It is the City upon the Hill, the hope of better days yet to come. "For out of Zion shall go forth the Law, and the word of the Lord from Jerusalem," said Isaiah (2:3). Ir Hakodesh to the Jews, el-Quds to the Arabs, the Holy City has stirred such passion in the hearts of men that at times her lovers preferred to see her destroyed rather than possessed by somebody else. In forty centuries the city has been ravaged and besieged nearly as many times.

A tremendous body of literature exists about Jerusalem and anyone who tries to add to it must be aware of the debt owed to those whose previous work has contributed to our contemporary knowledge. One writes in the shadow of giants, from the Biblical prophets to present-day scholars. Thus it was with fear and trepidation that I first put pen to paper. Sometimes I wondered, "Who am I to write about Jerusalem?" My only solace comes in the form of a Hassidic tale about two *Mithnagdim* who were walking down the street. Said one: "I have thought and thought and have reached the conclusion that in the eyes of the Almighty I must be a *gornisht*, a nothing." "Amazing!" said the other; "I have been pondering the very question, and have arrived at the same conclusion. In the eyes of God I too am a nothing." A Hassid who was walking behind them joined the conversation: "Gentlemen, I couldn't help but overhear you, and I want you to know that by some incredible coincidence I have also thought of God and the universe and decided that in God's eyes I too must be a nothing, a *gornisht*." "Ha," said one *Mithnaged* to the other. "Who is he to think that he is a nothing?"

I was born and brought up in Jerusalem. My mother

was an avid walker and ever since I can remember Saturdays were devoted to explorations. Between my father's and grandfather's patients and my other grandfather's customers, we seemed to know everyone. Our family had lived in the country for many generations and we had a relative on every street—or so I thought, as I was dragged to remote corners on dutiful calls. Thus I know the city well, and although I live elsewhere now, I come back frequently and I will always think of myself as a Jerusalemite. It is my favorite place, my beloved city, and I would like to share with you the exhilaration I feel when I walk down the winding lanes and smell the aroma of the spices in the bazaar, or catch a glimpse of the oft-depicted mountains that surround the city.

But first, a few technical points about the book. As the printer's ink begins to dry on any guidebook, parts are already out-of-date. This is especially true of Jerusalem, where building and renewal projects are constantly undertaken. It is hoped that the walker will not be unduly inconvenienced by such inevitable changes. Maps have been slightly simplified for the sake of clarity. A chronology of historical events ends the "Information and Advice" section. The city's history is long, complicated, and interesting, and many good books have been written about it.

The only consistent thing about Hebrew and Arabic transliterations are their inconsistencies, even when one tries to follow certain general rules. *Revolt in the Desert* opens with a "Publisher's Note," in which two pages of correspondence with T. E. Lawrence show the proofreader's exasperation. (Q. "Jedha, the she camel, was Jedhah on slip 40." A. "She was a splendid beast.") Lawrence explains: "There are some 'scientific systems' of transliteration, helpful to people who know enough Arabic not to need helping, but a washout for the world. I spell my names anyhow, to show what rot the systems are." Street signs, placed by successive administrations, vary. A street may be called by different names in Hebrew and in Arabic; the English street signs may give different names at different intersections; even the same name may be differently spelled. In the Old City, the definite article in Arabic appears as *el* on signs, a Jordanian legacy. Although *al* is now preferred by American scholars, *el* has been used throughout the book. When standard English texts were not available, I took the liberty to attempt my own translations. The Masoretic Text was used for quotations from the Old Testament, the King James Version for quotations from the New Testament.

War and destruction have left little of Biblical Jerusalem; there are no palaces in the City of the Great King. With the exception of the Dome of the Rock, Jerusalem boasts few magnificent buildings. Ruled from the distant capitals of foreign empires, the city, as well as the country, was poor and neglected. In the 1530s the Ottomans rebuilt the Wall, then let the Holy City sink back into oblivion until, by the year 1800, only nine thousand people were living here. Herman Melville called her a "barbarous city"; Mark Twain found Jerusalem "mournful and dreary and lifeless. . . . I would not desire to live here." It was not until the 1860s that the city began to spread outside the Wall; the Old City remains close to the downtown area of modern Jerusalem. This compactness makes Jerusalem an ideal city for walking, and walking is the ideal way to see a city. The six walks in this book are equally divided between the Old City and the new. They are within an area of two square miles and within walking distance of many major hotels. They were selected for their history, location, accessibility, and continuity—that is, where interesting sites could be found next to each other. My own competence—or perhaps, in cases, lack of it—in dealing with languages and certain areas was also a factor in choosing the walks I did.

As mentioned before, the average walk is about one mile long, and, depending on your pace and on the amount of time you spend dawdling in shops or restaurants, should take approximately two and a half hours. It is a good idea to read a walk before setting out. In several places in the book there are lengthy historical descriptions; I try to direct you to a sheltered spot where you can read quietly, though this is not always possible.

Walk 1 is mostly within the covered alleys of the Old City and can be taken even on hot or rainy days. A few of the shops will be closed on Sunday. Parts of Walk 2 are also sheltered but it begins outside the Wall, where it can get hot in the middle of a summer day. It ends near the Dome of the Rock and el-Aqsa

Mosque, and if you wish to visit those places, remember that they are closed to non-Moslems on Friday. Walk 3, through downtown, is most peaceful on Saturday, when there is little traffic, but many of the sites will be closed, as will the restaurants. Walk 4 covers more ground, physically, than the others, but a short version is given. If you wish to enter the Herodian tomb, take along a flashlight or matches. As you'll be outdoors most of the time, the walk is ideal for a late afternoon. You can end it by watching the last rays of the setting sun linger over the Old City Wall. Walk 5 takes you through residential streets where you can glimpse many private courtyards; I hope you will respect the privacy of the residents. Walk 6 breaks my own rule of covering mostly ordinary places. It deals with historic sites in the Jewish Quarter, which is still in the process of reconstruction. On Friday afternoons, as hundreds of people go down to the Western Wall, a unique atmosphere envelops the quarter; it is a good time for the walk.

This book discusses mainly the city's history and its architecture. Many other things contribute to the magic that is Jerusalem. When the light changes, the Jerusalem-stone buildings take on different hues, from ocher to amber, and the city turns golden. After a rainstorm wild flowers bloom in the valleys, the domes sparkle, the Wall gleams. Unexpected views open up as you walk; the very names of the streets recall the city's rich heritage. The citizens, who love Jerusalem in their own different ways, will enrich your visit; meet them, talk to them. Remember, though, that for them the Holy City is not only a shrine but also home, so bear with them and ignore the seeming lack of reverence or the dirt you may encounter. In the end, the shape of your Jerusalem will be determined by the emotions you experience as you walk in the footsteps of history. If you make your own discoveries on the walks and wish to share them, I will be glad to hear from you. In the words of the Psalms: "Walk about Zion, and go round about her, count the towers thereof. Mark ye well her ramparts, traverse her palaces, that ye may tell it to the generation following."

Information and Advice

Before You Go

Israel government information offices can be found in many major cities, such as New York, Chicago, Los Angeles, Atlanta, London, and Toronto. You can also get information through Israeli consulates, El Al Airlines, and, of course, your travel agent.

With a valid passport, citizens of most countries can enter Israel without visas and stay for three months. No vaccination certificates are required. If you plan to take a small appliance with you, note that the electric current is 220 volts.

If you go in summer, take light, washable clothes. Evenings can get very cool in Jerusalem, so bring along a jacket or a heavy sweater. A sun hat is a must, sunglasses useful. It does not rain in Israel in summer; in winter, a light coat or a lined raincoat is advisable. Houses are not well heated, so pack some woolens. In spring and fall temperatures vary, so wear several layers that you can peel off. And don't forget your most comfortable shoes.

Major credit cards and traveler's checks are accepted in most hotels, restaurants, and shops that deal with tourists. (See "Money and Banking.")

General Information

Free—and friendly—information is provided by the Government and Municipal Tourist Offices, located at 24 King George Street, tel. 241281/2; Omar Square, next to Jaffa Gate, tel. 282295/6; and 34 Jaffa Road, tel. 228844. Hours are Sunday through Thursday, 8:00 A.M.–6:00 P.M.; Friday and holiday eves, 8:00 to 2:00 or 3:00. The office within Jaffa Gate is also open on Saturday from 10:00 to 2:00. At the tourist offices you can usually get maps of the city, and many free publications that list weekly events: *Hello Israel*, *This Week in Jerusalem*, *Where to go and what to do*, and others. These publications are also available at many hotels. At certain hours of the day most large hotels have volunteers who are there to help tourists.

The Jerusalem Post is published daily, except Saturday. The Friday edition lists many of the following week's activities. For up-to-date details call 241197 after 6:00 P.M.

Tickets for both cultural and sports events can be obtained at Ben Na'im, 38 Jaffa Road, tel. 224008 (Walk 3), or at Cahana, 1 Rehov Herbert Samuel, tel. 222831 (off Zion Square, which you pass on Walk 3 and where Walk 5 begins).

Language may be a problem at times, although almost all public signs are written in Hebrew, Arabic, and English. Many people speak some English, especially those in the tourist industry.

Accommodations

A travel agent is the best adviser: prices vary and reservations are best made in advance. Although the rate of inflation in Israel is among the highest in the world, hotels there are cheaper than in Europe and your dollar buys a lot.

The following hotels are just a small sample of those available in Jerusalem. Elegant and expensive are the King David Hotel, the Plaza, and the Hilton (which is somewhat less central). The Intercontinental, on the Mount of Olives, is also a first-class hotel. Somewhat less expensive are the Moriah, Kings, President, and Ariel; in the same price range but away from the center of town are the Holyland, Ramada-Shalom, and Tadmor. In East Jerusalem the American Colony is a fine, old hotel. Two pleasant and inexpensive places to stay are St. Andrew's Hospice and Notre Dame Hospice.

If you want to write for information, remember that the mail is slow, and it can take an airmail letter a month to go one way. You can get information from the Israel Hotel Association, 8 Agrippas Street, Jerusalem, tel. 222815. The following are also located in Jerusalem: Israel Youth Hostel Association, P.O. Box 1075, 3 Dorot Rishonim Street, tel. 225925; Israel Student Tourist Association, 5 Eliashar Street, tel. 231418; Christian Information Center, Omar Square.

Several agents specialize in renting apartments in Jerusalem: Dahaf, 43 Jaffa Road, tel. 233941; Sheal, 7 Hillel Street, tel. 226919; and Apartotel, 214 Jaffa Road, tel. 531221.

Transportation

Walking is the best way to get to know any city. In Jerusalem, the center city is very compact: all six walks in this book are within an area of two square miles, so your feet are the best vehicle. The natives are friendly and curious, and will offer to help you even before you are lost.

City buses run from 5:30 A.M. to sometime between 10:00 P.M. and midnight. (In West Jerusalem there is no bus service on Friday afternoons, Saturdays, and Jewish holidays.) The buses are cheap, frequent, and crowded—especially during rush hour. Taxis are not inexpensive because the cost of gasoline is so high, but since distances are short, one rarely pays more than a few dollars for a ride. If you can afford it, it is often the easiest way to end a walk. Cabbies, on the whole, are honest; be sure the meter is on, then read the official notice placed in each cab to explain how the figure on the meter is to be adjusted to the latest rise in the galloping inflation.

Unless you know the city well and have nerves of steel, don't rent a car to use within the city. Israeli drivers are notoriously impolite and also take unnecessary risks; there are few parking places downtown; in order to make a left turn on any main street you may have to drive halfway to Tel Aviv. If you still plan to get behind the wheel, all major car rental agencies maintain offices in Israel. You can even make your reservations from abroad. You will need a valid U.S. or international driver's license, and a major credit card. There are no meters at the municipal parking lots or at designated spaces on the streets: you have to buy tickets either at major ticket agencies or at the lots—where they are not always available. Buy a whole book of tickets; they are very cheap. You then tear off a sheet, punch the appropriate month, date, and hour, and put it in your side window. It is a great system, once you understand it. Don't hesitate to ask for help. If you park illegally, remember that Israeli meter maids are pretty, efficient, and cruel, and the fines are heavy. They may also fine you for jaywalking, so use the designated crossings.

Inter-city transportation includes buses and *sherut*—a cab shuttle service that leaves as soon as a cab is full. There is also a daily train from Jerusalem to Tel Aviv and Haifa, and back. The country is tourist-oriented, and many additional services are provided by special agencies (bus tours, limousines, and guides).

For taxi service, call Nesher, 223233 or 223332; Taxi Israel, 222333; or Rehavia, 224444.

Food and Drink

The quality of food in Israel has improved considerably over the past decade, and you can now get an excellent meal here and there. For years the attitude toward cooking was influenced by the early pioneers who cared only about resettling the land. They rejected the values of their middle-class upbringing, and good food became one of the victims of their anti-bourgeois stance. (In many *kibbutzim* this attitude still prevails.) During World War II and in the years following the War of Independence in 1948, foodstuffs were rationed; there were also other, pressing priorities and no time to develop the art of a fine cuisine. The country has a long way to go before acquiring a reputation for gourmet cooking, but things are getting better.

Fruits and vegetables in Israel still taste the way God meant them to, and after sampling a *baladi* tomato or eating a ripe fig you'll be spoiled for life. Bread is excellent; it comes in many varieties and is sold freshly baked. Dairy products are also very good. Don't expect steaks or juicy roast beef—good, red meat is hard to come by. But lamb is good, and at fancy restaurants veal is now available. Poultry is plentiful: Israel has become a pioneer in the industry of raising chickens, turkeys, ducks, and geese. Fresh fish comes from the sea or is grown in ponds. Seafood is rare; the eastern Mediterranean is almost devoid of shellfish. If you are a connoisseur of Jewish delicatessen, you are better off in New York: bagel, lox, and pastrami are almost unheard of in Israel. Near Eastern and North African food is often your best bet. Though hummus, pita, and shish kebab have become as American as apple pie, and couscous is now chic in New York, do try the local versions. Also try *bourekahs*, sometimes sold at food stands; they are turnovers filled with cheese or spinach. Falafel—ground chick-peas deep-fried in oil and served in pita—is part of the daily diet. Other specialties are stuffed vegetables—*mahshi* or *memulaim*—and a sort of dumpling made of ground lamb, minced onion, and cracked wheat called *qubbeh*.

The breakfasts served at Israeli hotels are often unique, and once you discard your preset ideas about what you think you like to eat early in the morning, you'll find them a challenge: herring, olives, cheeses, yogurts and *leben*, green peppers, tomatoes, fresh rolls. You can also get cereal or scrambled eggs.

Imported wine and liquor are terribly expensive, but Israel produces several decent table wines (Carmel Cabernet Sauvignon Select, Ben Ami red, Monfort red and white) and very good beer (Maccabee). Tap water is safe to drink, and in the kiosks a variety of soft and carbonated drinks are sold. Try *mitz tapuzim* or *eshkoliot*—fresh orange or grapefruit juice squeezed just for you, good even in a bottle. Drinks are often sold by the glass but if the kiosk does not look spotless, select a bottled beverage. At open-air stands and small cafés don't order meat dishes, as those places may not have proper refrigeration facilities.

If you have contracted the local version of "Mustapha's revenge," you'll need to replace the fluids and the salt that you are losing. A glass of juice with a pinch of salt and a spoonful of honey, accompanied by sips of carbonated water, will help. Rest, drink, don't eat for a couple of days, and you'll feel better.

A list of restaurants starts on page 275.

Tipping

At restaurants and hotels, a 15 percent service charge is almost always added to your bill, so check before tipping. It is customary to "round" the figure: if your bill for a meal comes to eighteen dollars, leave twenty dollars. At first-class restaurants, or if the service is unusually good, add a 10 percent tip. Porters or bellboys usually get the equivalent of a dollar. One does not have to tip cabbies, but again you may wish to "round" the fare, or add about 10 percent. A 20 percent tip is the norm at barbershops and beauty salons.

If you get invited to someone's house for dinner, you might want to bring a small gift, a token: a box of chocolates, a bottle of wine, or just some flowers.

Telephone, Telegraph, Post Offices

Telephone calls are expensive in Israel, and every minute counts, so make your conversations short. Like everywhere else, calls from a hotel cost more. You can call from public pay phones for which you will need tokens, *assimonim*, which you buy at post offices and at many hotels. Be sure you have the phone number with you, whenever possible. English phone books are somewhat outdated: Operator and Information are hard to reach. Make your calls early, before 8:00 A.M., or in the evening. Some people take a siesta, especially on Saturdays, so don't call between 2:00 and 4:00 P.M.

Overseas calls can be made from the Central Post Office, 23 Jaffa Road, open Sunday through Thursday, 7:30 A.M. to 7:00 P.M., Friday until 3:00 P.M. Cables are also sent from the Central Post Office.

Money and Banking

Bank hours are Sunday through Thursday, 8:30–12:30, Friday 8:00–12:00. Some banks are open from 4:00 to 5:00, except Wednesday, but most will not deal with foreign exchange in the afternoon. At times there are long lines at the bank, especially on Friday. When all the paperwork is finished at one window, you still have to get into another line to reach the cashier. When you cash traveler's checks at a bank, you pay a standard fee per check—the same fee for a ten-dollar or a hundred-dollar check, so don't bring too many small checks with you. Always take your passport with you to the bank. At the bazaar you often get a better deal when you pay cash—in dollars that is.

Major credit cards are honored in most restaurants but it is wise to check before you go.

There is currently a 12 percent Value Added Tax— VAT—on almost everything you buy in Israel. If you pay by foreign currency, you are exempt. This exemption does not apply uniformly for all credit cards, so ask before you pay.

Shopping

There are many good buys in Israel. Although the country now has one of the world's highest inflation rates—an honor it could do without—the dollar's buying power remains good. Leather goods, raincoats, bathing suits, knitwear, and other fashion items are well-designed and produced by skilled workmen. Furs, especially Persian lamb and broadtail, are considered a very good buy here, as are diamonds that are cut and polished in Israel. Contemporary jewelry, in my eyes, is the best buy here. Many fine artists and artisans work in the country. Fine art is a matter of personal taste; in the city's many galleries you can find everything from the sentimental to the sublime. In the Old City bazaars you'll find a wide range of embroidered dresses in an even wider range of prices. Items made of Hebron glass are certainly "native" and make good gifts. They are easily breakable, but very inexpensive. The same is true of the brittle and colorful Armenian pottery. Handwoven wool rugs are still reasonable; and, for all the work that goes into them, so are the beautiful horse and camel saddles. If you don't own a camel the saddle makes an unusual wall hanging. Items made of straw are cheap, handsome, and light, if a bit bulky. Fine antiques can be found in the city, but if you are not an expert, find someone who is. In general, for expensive items and when you want to be sure that you are getting your money's worth, look for shops that have been approved by the Ministry of Industry, Trade, and Tourism. Its seal portrays two men carrying a huge bunch of grapes.

Shopping hours vary. The day begins early: many shops open at eight, most are open by nine. Some shops close at midday from one to three or four, then stay open till six or seven. In West Jerusalem shops close around two on Friday afternoon and stay closed through Saturday. Sunday is a regular working and shopping day. In the Old City, some shops in the Christian Quarter are closed on Sunday, and most shopkeepers who are Moslem take Friday afternoon off—Friday is their day of rest. On Saturdays everything seems to be open in the bazaars of the Old City, and Israelis from all over the country fill the markets.

In large shops, especially in West Jerusalem, the prices are fixed and there is little point in bargaining. In the *suq*, try your luck. One usually pays about two-thirds of the original asking price. Start practicing with something you don't really need—perhaps a water pipe? A possible scenario follows:

"How much is this *nargila*?"

"How much do you want to pay?"

Don't fall into this trap. The merchant is testing your knowledge of the market, and you might offer too much.

"It is your *nargila*. You tell me how much!"

"For *you*, only fifteen dollars."

Always express shock.

"What? Fifteen dollars? Yesterday I saw one just like it for five dollars."

"Never. It must have had a hole in it! Look at this one. It is brand new and beautiful. Just this morning it came from India. I give it to you for fourteen dollars."

"Thank you very much, but it is too expensive. Good-bye."

"Wait, wait. Why are you in such a hurry? You tell me how much you want to pay."

Now that you have heard his price, mention a figure that is not too low. After all, the merchant has to make a living.

"I'll give you eight dollars. My final offer."

"Really, Madame, I myself paid more for it. It is excellent quality. Looks just like gold. Twelve dollars. My last price."

"It is nice, but . . . it is a bit too heavy. Still, I might pay nine dollars for it."

"I tell you what. Because you are such nice lady, I give it to you for ten dollars, and here is a toy donkey for your little boy."

At this point, you might as well buy the *nargila*.

Dress and Behavior Codes

Dressing properly in Jerusalem means more than just wearing a hat in the summer. The city is holy to three religions, and as a guest you must respect the customs of those who live and worship here. Avoid shorts and sleeveless or low-cut dresses when you visit the Old City, or if you plan to wander through some of the more Orthodox neighborhoods outside the Wall, like Mea Sha'arim. Men are expected to cover their heads when they enter synagogues; the same rule applies at the Western Wall. At el-Aqsa and the Dome of the Rock, you will be asked to remove your shoes. Often you will be lent a scarf to cover bare shoulders. Some churches object to women in pants.

Pests (Two-Legged)

Children of all sizes will pester you, especially in the Old City. They will try to sell you everything from postcards to the latest "antiques." You must firmly say

"No, thank you!" If you show the slightest interest or hesitation, they'll never let you go. If you think you can pass for an Israeli, you may try saying "*Lo, todah*" ("No, thank you"). One American friend claims he says "Ruskie, Ruskie" and is quickly left alone. Don't follow anyone who wants you to meet his "cousin," or who promises to gain entry "just for you" to forbidden places. Also, many young Arabs are only too eager to enter into political discussions; they're best avoided.

Women on their own, especially in Arab neighborhoods, may encounter a special problem. If you are anywhere between fifteen and sixty-five, and are at all friendly, many a man will feel a personal challenge to try and take you on. Most Moslem women still lead a sheltered life and do not deal freely and openly with members of the opposite sex. So if you smile or giggle, even while you bargain, you may be sending out the wrong signals. You are safe as long as you make it perfectly clear that you want to be left alone. If you let a stranger show you around or buy you a drink, he may be convinced that you wish to go to bed with him, so beware. On the other hand, Arabs are most courteous by tradition, and if you linger in a shop, the older merchant may offer you tea or Turkish coffee. If you intend to make a purchase, by all means accept the hospitality. It is part of a business transaction conducted in a civilized, traditional manner. Lest I tarnish the reputation of anyone, let me add that during hundreds of hours that I walked by myself all over Jerusalem at all hours, I encountered only two unpleasant incidents. The rest of the time, as I already mentioned, people went out of their way to help.

Despite wars and occasional political violence, Jerusalem is one of the safest cities in the world. In 1979, with a population close to 400,000, 9 people were murdered, and 4 were killed by terrorist activities. On the other hand, 28 died in traffic accidents. You are really quite safe as long as you stay on the sidewalk.

Emergencies

First Aid Stations, operated by Magen David Adom, are located near the Central Bus Station in Romema, tel. 101, and near the Dung Gate, tel. 282495.

Most hotels will refer you to a physician. After hours, you can find a doctor on call listed in the daily newspapers that print names of physicians and pharmacists on duty. You can also call 101 for information.

For emergency dental treatment after hours, call 523133/4 at Magen David Adom.

Police Headquarters are in the Russian Compound, off Jaffa Road, tel. 100.

Worth a Detour

Although *Jerusalemwalks* avoids major tourist attractions and museums, a trip to Jerusalem isn't complete without a visit to some of the following.

The Israel Museum stands on a hill overlooking the Knesset and the Hebrew University campus on Givat Ram. It is situated above the Valley of the Cross with its ancient olive trees and church. Most interesting in the museum are the archaeological exhibits and the Judaica collection, also the section of modern Israeli art. Don't miss the Shrine of the Book where the Dead Sea Scrolls are stored. The cafeteria is an extra bonus; the food is unexpectedly good. Museum hours: Sunday, Monday, Wednesday, Thursday 10:00–5:00, Tuesday 4:00–8:00, Friday 10:00–2:00. Bus nos. 9, 16.

The Rockefeller Museum was designed by Austin Harrison around an inner courtyard where water lilies grow in a reflecting pool—a rare sight in Jerusalem. On display is a wide collection of artifacts from the ancient Near East. Hours: Sunday through Thursday 10:00–5:00, Friday and Saturday 10:00–2:00.

A visit to Yad Va'shem helps explain some of the emotions within segments of Israeli society. Yad Va'shem is a memorial to the Holocaust. In one large, empty hall only the names of the camps are engraved into the stone floor, and an eternal flame burns. Light enters the windowless hall through an open space between the walls and the roof. At times birds fly in through this space; the sound of their wings fractures the silence. In another building documents and photographs bear witness to a horror that the mind still refuses to accept. A child's pair of shoes stand alone near the exit. The universal tragedy becomes personal: it could have been anyone's child.

At dawn, if you have the use of a car and are suffering from jet lag, drive up to Mount Scopus and sit on the ridge between Hebrew University and the Augusta Victoria hospital. Watch the sun appear from behind the "azure and amethyst" mountains of Moab and illuminate the Judean Desert, which has changed little since the days of Abraham. Later, turn and face the city to the west. As the streetlights go off, the Dome of the Rock begins to glitter. Soon the early morning sun is reflected in hundreds of windowpanes, and Jerusalem turns golden. Less climactic, if more sensible, is a trip to the bar of the Intercontinental Hotel. The view alone is intoxicating and the hotel serves a good lunch. At sunset try Mishkenot Haroim (p. 277).

Every Friday, between dawn and 8:00 A.M. the Sheep Market is held outside the northeastern corner of the Old City Wall, across from the Rockefeller Museum. The bargaining and confusion, the sights and the smells, have remained the same for centuries. It's worth getting up for.

For small children, the Citadel and the archaeological remains between Zion Gate and the Dung Gate are great places for climbing, exploring, and even learning. So is the Biblical Zoo, open daily from 8:00 to 7:00, Friday and Saturday 8:00 to 5:00. (Bus nos. 15, 7.) Zedekiah's Cave is located near Damascus Gate. Huge and eerie, the ancient quarry is really quite safe. Don't go there in sneakers, as the rock is wet and slippery. (Bus nos. 2, 12.) All of these places—except the archaeological park—charge a small entry fee. If you plan to go to a place that is open on Saturday, find out if you have to purchase a ticket a day in advance.

There are many parks in the city—good places for children, for a picnic lunch, or for jogging. At Independence Park there is an old Moslem cemetery and an ancient pool site. Swimming pools—usually crowded—are listed in some of the weekly events guides as are many other points of interest.

Walk Along the Wall

A walk along the top of the Old City Wall, once planned as the first walk in this book, turned out to be too long and cumbersome. Still, it is an excellent way to get an overview of the Old City, and if you wish to explore the Wall, here are some practical suggestions. First, look at a map and decide which parts you wish to see, then read the next couple of pages. Put on your nonskid walking shoes; ladies are advised to wear slacks on this walk. A hat is a must in summer, but don't venture out on this particular walk in the midday sun. The footpath on the Wall is narrow in parts but should present no problems to an able-bodied person. Bus no. 1 goes to Jaffa Gate and to the Dung Gate, and bus nos. 7 and 15 go to Damascus Gate.

The Wall as it exists today was built by Suleiman the Magnificent in the 1530s, along the remains of previous walls. It is about two and a half miles long, and has eight gates—seven open, one closed. Jaffa Gate and Damascus Gate mark the beginnings of the two major axes that divide the Old City into four quarters, a legacy from the Roman Period. At every gate there are stairs that lead to the top of the gate (the roof of a gate house in most cases) and to a footpath that was built for the Turkish guards. It is no longer possible to take one continuous walk on top of the Wall.

The Municipality has installed rails and new paving stones on the section of the Wall that begins at Jaffa Gate and continues over the New Gate to Damascus Gate (one thousand meters). This section is open between 10:00 A.M. and 4:00 P.M., and there is a small entrance fee. The walk from Damascus Gate to Herod's Gate is better done in company; single women may be bothered along this isolated section. Outside the Wall, or rather under it, is Zedekiah's Cave and across the street, behind the Central Arab Bus Station, is a large rock believed by some Christians to be the Hill of Golgotha. From Herod's Gate you can continue on top of the Wall, past fields where gypsies live. Somewhere near here Godfrey de Bouillon broke through the ramparts in 1099 and won the battle for the Crusaders.

The eastern part of the Wall, which overlooks the Mount of Olives, begins at the corner called Burj el-Laqlaq in Arabic, or "Storks' Tower." Outside the Wall is the Moslem Cemetery. The tall stone monument is a memorial to the Arabs killed in the Six Day War in 1967. The Arabs call it the War of Honor. The next gate is St. Stephen's Gate or the Lions' Gate. Here the Wall is blocked by remains of the Second Temple Period. The Moslem guards will probably not let you enter the Haram esh-Sharif, the "Noble Sanctuary" (you can enter it through other gates—see page 104 or page 235). If you are tired, you can go back to Damascus Gate by walking along the Via Dolorosa, which begins at the

Lions' Gate. Turn right when you reach El-Wad Road which continues to Damascus Gate.

If you wish to complete the walk around the Wall, go out of the Old City through the Lions' Gate. If the gate to the southern section of the Moslem Cemetery is open—it is located on the right, outside the Lions' Gate—continue the walk through the cemetery past the Golden Gate, to the southeastern corner of the Wall. If the gate is closed, or the keeper asks you to leave, walk down the hill to Jericho Road, turn right, then right again onto Derech Ha'ofl which will bring you to the impressive southeastern corner of the Wall. Here, if you wish, you can enter the cemetery and walk to the Golden Gate. If you do, note the "seam" a hundred feet from the corner, where the large Herodian ashlars meet a previous structure.

From the southeastern corner, The Pinnacle to Christians, you continue outside the Wall, parts of which were built by Herod in the first century B.C. when he enlarged the enclosure of the Temple Mount. Several of the gates, now blocked, can still be seen in the Wall. In front of it archaeological exploration and reconstruction continue. From the Dung Gate to Zion Gate it is possible to walk on the Wall, but actually the ancient remains that lie in the archaeological park outside the southern part of the Wall are more interesting. From Zion Gate you can again walk on top of the Wall all the way to the Citadel, but there is no exit there and you have to turn back. A narrow alley outside Zion Gate passes by the Armenian and Catholic cemeteries on Mount Zion and leads to the southwestern corner. Turn right at the corner to return to Jaffa Gate. This section of the Wall is described in the beginning of Walk 2.

Chronology

First Temple Period, ca. 1000 B.C.–586 B.C.

ca. 1000 B.C.	King David captures Jerusalem from the Jebusites; the City of David becomes the nation's capital.
964	King Solomon begins to construct the First Temple.
928	The Kingdom is divided in two: Israel in the north and Judea in the south.

722   Israel, the Northern Kingdom, falls to the Assyrians.

701   Sennacherib besieges Jerusalem in the reign of Hezekiah.

586   Nebuchadnezzar destroys the city and the Temple, and exiles the inhabitants to Babylon.

Second Temple Period, 538 B.C.–70 A.D.

538 B.C.   Jews receive permission from Cyrus to return and rebuild the Temple in Jerusalem.

445   Nehemiah goes to Jerusalem, following Ezra.

332   Alexander the Great conquers the country.

313   Ptolemy captures Jerusalem.

169   Antiochus of Syria desecrates the Temple, leading to the Hasmonean revolt.

63   Pompey and his Roman legions conquer the city.

37   Herod the Great rules until 4 B.C.

4 B.C.   Jerusalem is governed by Roman procurators from Caesarea.

66 A.D.   The Jews revolt against the Romans.

70   Jerusalem is demolished by Titus; the survivors are exiled or sold into slavery.

Roman Period, 135–324 A.D.

132   Bar Kochba leads a doomed revolt against Rome.

135   Emperor Hadrian rebuilds Jerusalem, renames the city Aelia Capitolina and the country Palestine.

Byzantine Period, 324–638

326   Queen Helena discovers Golgotha; her son, Emperor Constantine, builds the Church of the Holy Sepulchre.

362   Under Emperor Julian an unsuccessful attempt is made by the Jews to rebuild the Temple.

614   The Persians invade Jerusalem, aided by the Jews.

629   Emperor Heraclius recaptures the city.

Early Moslem Period, 638–1099

638   Jerusalem surrenders to the Moslems; Caliph Omar visits.

691   Abd el-Malek builds the Dome of the Rock.

715   Mosque of el-Aqsa is completed by el-Walid el-Malek.

750   Power shifts from Omayyads to Abbasids.

| 969 | Fatimid conquest is soon followed by destruction of churches and synagogues. |
| 1071 | Seljuks devastate the city. |

Crusader Period, 1099–1187

| 1099 | Crusaders conquer city, slaughter Moslems and Jews. |

Ayyubid and Mamluk Period, 1187–1517

1187	Saladin captures the city from the Crusaders.
1229	Treaty returns city to Christian rule.
1244	City is again in Moslem hands.
1260	Mamluks rule Jerusalem.
1267	Rabbi Moshe ben Nachman establishes the Ramban Synagogue.
1492	Many Jews arrive in Jerusalem after the Spanish Exile.

Ottoman Period, 1517–1917

1517	Palestine and Jerusalem become part of Ottoman Empire.
1538	Suleiman the Magnificent rebuilds Jerusalem's Wall.
1831	Mohammed Ali of Egypt rules country for nine years.
1856	After Crimean War, Turks begin to liberalize policies toward aliens.
1860	The city begins to spread beyond Old City Wall.
1892	Railroad connects city to the coast.

British Mandate, 1917–1948

1917	General Allenby accepts surrender of Jerusalem.
1920	The Mandate for Palestine is conferred on Britain.
1936	Lord Peel's Commission proposes partition of Palestine.
1947	The United Nations votes to create Jewish and Arab states in Palestine; plan is rejected by the Arabs.
1948	War breaks out; State of Israel declared on May 14.

Under Jordan and Israel, 1948–1967

| 1949 | Cease-fire finds city divided; Jerusalem is proclaimed capital of Israel. |
| 1967 | Israelis capture Old City during Six Day War; city is reunited. |

In the Christian Quarter

○

Because most good Christians willingly speak
and hear spoken about the Holy City, where
Jesus lived and died, we shall tell how it was at
the time when Saladin took it from the Christians. Many people there will be who wish to
hear of these things. Those to whom it is dis-
pleasing may pass over this place.

Anonymous pilgrim, circa 1220
(Adapted from *La Citez de Jherusalem*)

It is appropriate to begin *Jerusalemwalks* by entering the Old City through Jaffa Gate, as Western pilgrims have done for centuries past. The gate marks the end of the road that comes up to Jerusalem from the ancient port of Jaffa.

The western gateway to the city has been in this vicinity since Emperor Hadrian rebuilt Jerusalem in 135 A.D. after the Bar Kochba revolt. Modeled along the typical lines of a Roman colony, Jerusalem was renamed Aelia Capitolina by Hadrian. To this day the Old City retains the quadrilateral shape and the network of streets he determined. The original City of David, built near the spring of Gihon on a ridge south of the Temple Mount, lay outside the Roman wall.

As you face the pedestrian entry to the gate house, you can see on the left a large niche with a stone bench and two inscriptions carved into the Wall. The upper inscription is on the foundation stone of the present Old City Wall. In cursive Arabic it informs us that "In the name of Allah the Merciful, the Great Sultan, King of the Turks, Arabs, and Persians, Suleiman son of Selim Khan—may Allah make His Kingdom eternal—gave the order to build this blessed Wall" in 1538. Suleiman was the second Ottoman ruler of Jerusalem, and most of the Wall and the gates of the Old City that we see today were rebuilt by him. Remains of earlier walls dating back to the days of the Hasmonean, Herod the Great, and Hadrian were incorporated into the Ottoman Wall. The lower inscription is more modest. In both Hebrew and Arabic it commemorates another repair of the Wall completed by the Israelis in 1969. It quotes Nehemiah, who "healed" the breaches in the Wall in the fifth century B.C. after the Jews returned from the Babylonian Exile.

The gate itself has had many different names. The Byzantines called the western entry David's Gate because of its proximity to the Citadel of David. Although the Citadel had nothing to do with King David and was built long after his death, the name persists.

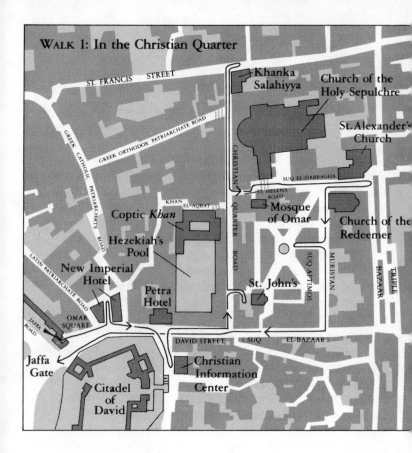

WALK 1: In the Christian Quarter

In the early Moslem era the gate was known as Bab Mihrab Daud, the "Gate of the Prayerhouse of David." The Crusaders continued to use the Byzantine name; on maps from that era the gate is marked Porta David. Now the Arabs call it Bab el-Halil, the "Gate of the Friend"; the road that goes south to Hebron begins here, and Hebron is the burial place of the Patriarch Abraham, who was the "friend" of God. The inscription over the gate reminds us that "there is no God but Allah, and Abraham is the friend of Allah."

In the last decades of the nineteenth century, as Jerusalem began to expand beyond the Wall, the area outside the gate became the commercial heart of the city. The road was lined with coffeehouses, hotels, banks, and prestigious shops. *Dilegances*—"diligent carriages"—stopped here on their way to and from the port of Jaffa. If you stand with your back to the inscriptions, on your far right and across the street you can see several damaged buildings, which are all that is left from that era. The rest of the buildings—heavily damaged in the war of 1948—were torn down in 1967 when the city was reunited.

Turn around and look at the niche again. Embedded in mid-Wall at the base of the pointed arch are the remains of two Corinthian capitals. Jerusalem was destroyed and rebuilt more times than any other major city; bits and pieces of earlier periods were always strewn around, and the Turks made good use of them. The slightly pointed arch over the entrance to the city gate and the stone roundels that protrude from the Wall on both sides of the arch are typical of Ottoman architecture. From the hollow turret over the arch, a Turkish machicolation, hot tar and oil could be poured onto the head of the enemy below.

The interior of the gate is L-shaped and is protected by heavy iron doors. These features, designed to keep out invaders, were common to the old gates of the city, which were locked at sunset. Those who arrived at dusk had to identify themselves by candlelight; late travelers had to spend the night outside the gate; early risers were lowered over the Wall by ropes. The gates were also closed around noontime on Fridays, to make sure that no infidel overtook the Holy City while the Moslems were at prayer. Note the small door in the right half of the iron gate, which allowed single entry in an emergency.

When the Crusaders surrendered Jerusalem to Saladin in 1187, Christians who could ransom themselves paid their money at Jaffa Gate and were allowed to depart. Then this became the only gate through which Western pilgrims could enter the city, enabling the Moslems to check their movements and collect entrance fees. Often the pilgrims had to send a messenger to ask permission to enter. In the seventeenth century all "Franks"—Western Christians—had to dismount, deliver their arms, and go into the city on foot. At times a Jewish *shamash*, a beadle, could be found standing outside this gate; he was in charge of *keri'ah*, a customary tearing of the garment in time of mourning. Every Jew who saw Jerusalem "in her destruction" for the first time was obliged to rend his clothes.

When you enter the L-shaped gate house, try to picture the Turkish soldier who used to stand guard here—a *tarboosh*, or fez, covering his head, a wide sash holding up his pantaloons, a minié rifle and sword bayonet in his hands. Today, inside the gate on your left, you can see some photographs of what Jaffa Gate looked like in earlier times. One photo, taken from outside the Wall, shows the moat as it looked in the 1890s, before it was partially filled in. Another shows a clock tower, forty feet tall, which was erected on top of the gate house in 1906–7 in honor of the thirtieth anniversary of Sultan Abdul Hamid. The clock—whose style was "Turkish Baroque"—had four faces, two showing Eastern time, two showing European time. As most citizens did not possess clocks or watches, it was a great convenience. In the early 1920s the British removed the clock tower, claiming that it did not "fit in with the ancient character" of this historic spot. Some Arabs are still convinced that the British really wanted the clock for themselves, and claim that they took it to their parliament in London. Those who doubt this most unlikely story are told that the clock can still be heard today on the radio, and it's called Big Ben!

When you emerge from the gate house, note the flight of steps to the left that leads to the "Promenade on the Old City Wall." It isn't part of this walk but you may wish to take it another time. The promenade is open from 10:00 to 4:00, and is about a thousand meters long. It ends at Damascus Gate.

Across the road is the Citadel of David; it forms the southern edge of Omar ibn el-Khattab Square. Omar was the first Moslem ruler who came to Jerusalem after the Arab conquest, around 638 A.D. By all accounts he was a decent man. In 1967 the Israelis thought of renaming the area Citadel Square, but fortunately good sense prevailed, as you can see from the numerous street signs around the square. The name el-Khattab Square, in Hebrew, was added to the preexisting Arabic and English versions. The Armenian-made tiles match almost perfectly.

On the left side, several nineteenth-century buildings form the northern border of this square. Until 1898 the gate house and the Citadel were connected by a crenellated wall. If you face the Citadel and look to the right, you will see a wide gap through which the paved road now passes. It used to be part of the moat of the Citadel, and a low wall went across it. Part of the moat was filled in and about thirty-five feet of the ramparts were removed to accommodate the carriages in the entourage of Kaiser Wilhelm II and his wife, Kaiserin Augusta Victoria, who came to Jerusalem to dedicate the Lutheran Church of the Redeemer. The details of this visit and contemporary reaction to the "breach in the Wall" make for a good story and it's included at the end of this walk. You can read it on your way home.

The Gate is the first shop inside the Wall. It is an example of a store that panders to the tourist trade. On the first floor you might just find the right *padarke* for Aunt Ethel (*padarke* being a Yiddish word of Russian origins used to describe all useless gifts). On the second floor there is a rather good selection of Israeli-made necklaces, rings, and earrings.

Until the 1880s a dilapidated shack stood here; later it was replaced by the present building, which was badly damaged in the War of Independence. After 1948 Jaffa Gate was blocked, tourist trade diminished, and the house was used for storage. In 1967 the gate was reopened, and—according to the owners—this shop began to function as the first Jewish store in the Old City since 1948. In photographs from the turn of the century both this building and the one next door had balconies on their second stories; on street level there were several stores. One was owned by Shmuel Raphaeli, a money changer and numismatist who used to get annoyed at customers for interrupting him at his "true calling"—writing articles for local publications. Next to him was a stationery shop where the Jewish intelligentsia used to gather.

The Gate and the adjacent building are joined at the base, where two grand cypresses tower over an ancient fig tree. Under the trees, almost hidden, lie two Moslem graves. No one really knows who is buried here. Some say that Suleiman's architects, two brothers who rebuilt the Wall and the gates, for some reason did not include the traditional site of the tomb of King David on Mount Zion within the reconstructed city Wall; for this oversight they lost their heads, but since they were such great architects they were buried here, in a place of honor. If you are the romantic type you may choose to believe that two unknown lovers lie here: in Moslem tradition the fig tree represents the fertile female, the cypress the strong male.

On the other side of the tiny graveyard is the Tourist Information Office. Here you can pick up various weekly guides such as *Hello Israel* or *Events in the Jerusalem Region* and a free map of the city—when available. The staff here is most helpful.

Between the Information Office and the street corner on the right is a small yard with an exterior flight of steps. In the late nineteenth century here stood a tiny inn where one could buy an alcoholic beverage from the Arab owner—no small feat in a city ruled by Moslems whose religion prohibits the consumption of spirits. Before World War I the Turkish Police Station was in the building that you can see in back of the courtyard. A shoe-shine man with an elegant brass polishing box can usually be found sitting here.

Cross Latin Patriarchate Road. At the corner is the New Imperial Hotel, which was known as the Grand New Hotel when it first opened in 1889 and offered European travelers such modern accommodations as rooms with baths. The building was two stories high then and had a strange-looking platform on the roof almost like a widow's walk. By 1905 a third floor was added. The balconies still have the original grillwork; a more modest pattern can be seen on the rooms facing the side street. According to an 1898 *Baedeker*, here one could buy *wein und bier*. If your *tarboosh* needed pressing, this was the place to come. In the first corner store photographs were sold by Frederick Vester of the American Colony. (The colony was founded in 1881 by the Spafford family, who came to Jerusalem from Chicago after four of their daughters drowned in a tragic incident. Together with American and Swedish friends who joined them, they spent the rest of their lives in the Holy City helping the poor. Their daughter, Bertha, married Frederick Vester.) In April 1917, as the Turkish armies were retreating and the city was filling with wounded soldiers, Jamal Pasha granted Bertha Spafford Vester permission to turn the hotel into a hospital. "The hotel was soon ready to receive the wounded," she writes in *Our Jerusalem* (Beirut, 1950). "It was neither Grand nor New, but filthy and full of vermin, and elbow grease had to fill in where soap and disinfectant were lacking."

Note the *Taphos* Φ over each doorway, the insignia

of the Greek Orthodox Church, which built the shops and the hotel. Enter the hotel's arcade between the signs advertising St. Michel Souvenirs and Patisserie Joseph, and look up at the elaborately decorated ceiling. After you pass a café filled with slot machines and an old-fashioned barbershop, you will see a street lamp standing on a stone base. The stone was uncovered when the foundation for the hotel was dug. If you look closely you will see a Roman inscription on it, from the days when the Tenth Legion was stationed here to guard the ruins of the city it helped demolish in 70 A.D. In case your Latin is a bit rusty, here is the translation: "To Marcus Janius Maximus Legate of the Emperors in command of the Tenth Legion Frentensis Antoniana by Caius Domitius Seriganus and Julius Honoratus his equerries." On the fourth line from the top you can see the "LEG X," the Tenth Legion.

Some nineteenth-century writers mention a small body of water that existed where the hotel now stands; it was covered and used as a cistern when the hotel was finished. It may have been part of King Herod's water system, which brought rainwater, gathered in the Mamilla Pool, to a reservoir nearby that we'll be seeing later in this walk. This body of water was sometimes called the Pool of Bathsheba, for David "walked upon the roof of the king's house; and from the roof he saw a woman bathing and the woman was very beautiful to look upon." (2 Samuel 11:2.) Since the Citadel across the road was mistaken for David's palace, this is "obviously" where Bathsheba bathed. Over the years two other pools within sight of the Citadel—Hezekiah's and the Sultan's—were also referred to by the same name.

Before you leave the arcade note the sign with the phone on the far left end where you can buy *assimonim*, the tokens that operate the Israeli public telephones—when they work, that is.

I hope you read the section on "Food and Drink" (page 10) before embarking on this walk. If not, do so as you return to Omar Square. Don't miss the fresh orange juice—thick with pulp and an occasional pit—which is squeezed before your eyes. The local version of the bagel is another must: a soft bun with a hole in the middle, covered with sesame seeds, often sold while still warm. The Arabs call it *ka'ak* and you can

gain a lot of face by asking for *za'atar* to go with it. You will be handed a cumin seed-and-salt mixture, wrapped in yesterday's newspaper; you dip your bagel in it. A *ka'ak* costs about a quarter; the *za'atar* is free. Add a hard-boiled egg, fresh from the farm with bits of straw still clinging to the shell, and you have a cheap breakfast!

Turn left when you leave the arcade and you'll see a building with a sign that reads Greek Catholic Patriarchate Road. In a century-old photograph by Bonfils—a Frenchman who had a photographic studio in Beirut—there is another placard on this spot: "F. Nicodeme. Photographs by Bonfils. Curiousities of the East. Other articles for the use of travellers." In the days before the camera had become a standard part of every tourist's gear, commercial photographs were sold as souvenirs. Many of the earliest photographs came from the exotic Levant, especially from the Holy City. The golden-brown albumin prints by Bonfils are most interesting, as he recorded some everyday street scenes in addition to vistas and Holy Places. Félix Bonfils died in 1885, but his wife and son kept his studio going.

On the impressive double-arched façade, the Franciscan insignia can be seen in between the two shops. The building begins to appear in drawings and photographs of the 1870s, minus the second story, which was added at some later date. In the early 1890s André Teris and Sons owned a shop here where they sold "Oriental Curiosities and Old Rugs." Later in the decade a Mr. F. Marroum advertised *objets de piété* as well as olivewood articles and, of course, photographs.

Today, inside the building is the shop of Boulos Meo. It has been owned by the same family for four generations and the present young Mr. Meo will be glad to show you the solemn ancestral portraits that hang in the store and tell you about the family, which, he claims, came to Jerusalem from Italy with the Crusaders. The stock in the store is limited, but ask to see some of the old drawings, prints, and postcards.

Cross the square to the corner of the moat in front of the Citadel. You'll be walking over hundreds of bottle caps (from nearby kiosks) embedded in the road. If

Roman inscription, Greek priest

you look down into the moat you will see the slant formed by the lower tiers of the glacis of the quadrangular tower. The large ashlars, the hewn blocks of masonry, fit together without a binder. They were cut by Herod's fine masons during the Second Temple Period and form the base of Phasael, one of the three towers that guarded Herod's palace (see page 75).

When the Roman armies destroyed the city in 70 A.D., Titus ordered that the three towers near the palace be spared "to show later generations what a proud and mighty city had been humbled by the gallant sons of Rome." Only the base of the tower named after Herod's brother, Phasael, has survived to this day.

Find a place to sit on the wide banister of the supportive wall of the moat, as we leap from the first to the nineteenth century. Until the 1860s there were hardly any buildings between Jaffa Gate and the northwestern corner of the Wall. In the area where you now find the Imperial Hotel and beyond it, there were fields where wheat grew in winter. In summer the empty fields became the dumping ground for carcasses of donkeys, camels, and horses. The smelly spot was a meeting place for packs of stray dogs, and a health hazard when the bodies began to rot under the hot rays of the sun. Foreign residents, with the help of their consuls, finally persuaded the Turkish authorities to move this "cemetery" outside the Wall. The road was not paved then, and during the rainy season deep puddles formed on both sides of Jaffa Gate. Pedestrians had to step gingerly across the slippery stones, which had been thoughtfully provided by the Municipality. The moat was much wider then, its northern retaining wall closer to the New Imperial. In the moat the *falaheen* from nearby villages sold fresh fruits and vegetables. They "parked" their camels along the eastern edge of the moat, where you now see the cars opposite the Citadel Bar and Restaurant. The camels did not contribute much to the cleanliness of the square; in 1890 those great organic polluters were banned from entering the city gates.

Take a minute to observe the square as it looks today—an ever-changing mosaic of people, images, colors, and sounds. Graceful Arab women in embroidered dresses carrying large baskets on their heads; Hassidic Jews in eighteenth-century Polish garb, side locks dangling beneath their *streimels*, the fur hats of the ghetto; bareheaded Franciscan friars in sandals and brown cassocks; elderly Arabs on their way to the coffeehouses wearing the traditional *tarboosh* or *kaffiyeh*; a few remaining monks from Ethiopia, silent shadows gliding by, cut off from their homeland; Border Patrolmen in green berets, carrying guns, reminders of conflicts as yet unresolved. And, of course, the tourists, in groups, in pairs, by themselves; schoolchildren with their teachers; a kibbutznik in shorts, a blue *kova tembel*, "dunce cap," on his head; retired British schoolteachers in straw hats and heavy stockings; an occasional Japanese with the inevitable camera. Two Swedish *Valkyrien* in brief gym outfits create a sensation on the square: storekeepers stop bargaining, street-sweepers rest on their brooms. The Orthodox Jew averts his eyes and mumbles an appropriate prayer to save him from temptation. Five times a day comes the prayer call of the *muezzin* from the mosques. On Friday afternoons a hush falls over the Old City. Shops close early. Jews from all over the city, freshly bathed and in their Sabbath clothes, stream down to the Jewish Quarter to pray at the Western Wall. On Sunday mornings the sound of a hundred church bells echoes through this "City of Many Days."

Early in the morning you might see a Berman Bakery van on the square unloading hundreds of loaves of bread onto the ledge above the moat. Perched precariously, the loaves remain there until they get distributed throughout the Old City by pushcarts painted blue, to ward off the evil eye. Over a century ago a woman called Kreshe Berman used to stand near here and sell black bread to Russian Orthodox pilgrims on their way to the Church of the Holy Sepulchre. Her husband, as one book described him, was "a God-fearing man, learned in the Torah, who had devoted himself to study and to the service of the Lord." But unfortunately, he was only "an average merchant." So while he prayed and studied, thus assuring his family a place in Heaven, earthly matters such as feeding four children were left to his wife, who discovered the secret of making black bread by using the honey of the local carob tree, and laid the foundations for the family business. (She was my great-grandmother.)

And now for a close look at the three buildings that

form the eastern edge of Omar Square. With the Citadel behind you, on the left, closest to the Meo shop, is a small building with a pointed, red-tiled roof and a large Seiko sign. Here were the late-nineteenth-century offices of the Thomas Cook and Son travel agency, until they moved to the larger building next door, where today we find the Citadel Bar and Restaurant. From about 1880 to 1914 the American Consulate was in this building on the second floor. Photos from the time show Old Glory fluttering in the wind and the American Eagle displayed on a plaque in the second window from the left.

The photography shop in the building is owned by the Nazaretians, an Armenian father-and-son team. Armenians, Christians native to the area, have traditionally been the photographers of the Middle East. Orthodox Jews and Moslems both opposed the reproduction of the human form—the Second Commandment forbids the making of graven images. The shop carries a good selection of individual slides of the city. Remember that the price of film and of developing in Israel is much higher than in the United States.

The low stools and tables outside the Citadel Bar are typical of Arab coffeehouses. Here you can get a cup of good Turkish coffee—strong, sweet, thick, and flavored with *hal*, the aromatic cardamom. The coffee must be sipped slowly, so as not to disturb the dregs at the bottom of the cup. Admittedly, this is an acquired taste. A glass of cold water is customarily served with Turkish coffee to cleanse the palate before drinking. Here coffee costs almost a dollar; you pay for the choice location.

The Christian Information Center is in the handsome building just beyond, on the right. Unlike the rest of the buildings on the square—which a Greek friend describes as "nineteenth-century French mode via Turkey"—the façade here is unmarred by makeshift signs with poor graphics or awnings.

Professor Ben-Arieh says that in the 1840s this may have been the house of Menachem Mendel of Kaminitz, who ran an almost-free hostelry for Jewish newcomers. Maps and books from that period indicate that the Protestant Bishop to Jerusalem lived here until at least 1864. Christ Church, the first Protestant Church in the Turkish Empire, is next door; it's part of Walk 2.

From 1858 to 1914 the Austrian Post Office was located in this building, as you can see from the memorial placard over the last set of ground-floor windows on the right. The letters *K.K.* in front of *Postexpedition* stand for *Kaiserliche und Königliche*, "Imperial and Royal." The Turkish postal services were most unreliable and several European countries opened their own offices. The Austrian Post Office closed at the onset of World War I. Later a branch of the Banco di Roma opened here.

Look at the middle window on the second floor, formerly a door that led to a balcony, now gone. On the plaque is the Latin Cross, also known as the Jerusalem Cross. It is displayed on all Franciscan properties. (After the defeat of the Crusaders, the Franciscans were recognized by the pope as the Custodians of the Holy Places in *Terra Sancta*.) Inside the building today the Franciscans provide a free information service. Although the emphasis is on events of special interest to Christians—there are over twenty sects of Christians in Jerusalem today—general tourist services and information are offered too. The center is open daily from 8:30 to 12:30 and from 3:30 to 6:00 except Sunday. Ask for permission to look inside. Of special interest is the inner courtyard.

Recross the square back to the Petra Hotel building, to the right of the Boulos Meo shop, which was probably built in the mid-1870s. It was then that travelers began to write of the "new" hotel with grand facilities "inside Jaffa Gate" called the Mediterranean when first open. The three-story building has a charming façade. The round arched windows are articulated with dentils beneath an archivolt. The balcony grilles are red; the sewer pipes are sky blue—a later addition. High on pedestals on the roof's railing sit six—sometimes five—"Grecian urns." The building is built of a light red variation of Jerusalem stone.

Walk past the five shops on the ground floor to the small entrance marked by Petra Hotel and Money Changer signs, and go into the lobby, where you can buy a ticket (for about a quarter) that allows you to go up to the roof. On the second floor you pass through a large, once-gracious room that looks like a set out of *Arsenic and Old Lace*. Some seventy years ago, in one of its many incarnations, the hotel was owned by a

Jewish family called Amdorsky and was known as the Central Hotel. At that time this was the most elegant ballroom in Jerusalem and many a wedding was held here—with music and dancing, which upset the ultra-Orthodox. Such sinful frivolity in the Holy City!

Continue to walk up the stairs, past a woman who might ask you where you are going and the young people who share rooms and baths that are cheap and of equivocal cleanliness. When you reach the fourth floor—the last flight of stairs is wooden—step onto the hotel's roof and turn right to look at the view. On the horizon Mount Scopus is to the left and the Mount of Olives to the right; they form the watershed that separates the city from the Judean Desert. The three tallest towers, from left to right, were built by, respectively, Hebrew University in the 1970s, the Germans just before World War I, and the Russians in the 1880s. All three are discussed in detail at another stop on this walk: the top of the bell tower of the Church of the Redeemer, which you can see behind the large TV antenna. The prominent golden dome straight ahead is the Dome of the Rock. To the left of the Church of the Redeemer is the square minaret of the Mosque of Omar, which stands like a guard over the two domes and tower of the Church of the Holy Sepulchre. To the left of the Holy Sepulchre is another minaret, Khanka Salahiyya.

The Old City is divided into four quarters of unequal sizes. You are now on the southern edge of the Christian Quarter. David Street, which begins at Jaffa Gate and goes through Omar Square and the bazaars to the Temple Mount in the east, separates the Christian Quarter, on your left, from the Armenian Quarter, on the right. The Dome of the Rock is on the Temple Mount, where the First and Second Temples stood. Beyond the bell tower of the Church of the Redeemer, the Moslem Quarter sprawls to the northeast—ancient cupolas under a forest of TV antennae. The Jewish Quarter lies west of the Temple Mount, and cannot be clearly seen from here.

The reason for coming up to this rooftop is to see Hezekiah's Pool. It lies below, surrounded by old buildings. It used to be a water reservoir that received its water from the Mamilla Pool (in today's Independence Park) and was originally built in the Second

Temple Period. The pool was outside the city walls then and it offered additional protection to this strategically important area. It was originally called Amygdalon, the Pool of the Tower. In the Byzantine Period (324–638 A.D.) this pool was called Birkat Hammam el-Batrak, the Pool of the Bath of the Patriarch, because the Patriarch of Jerusalem lived next to the Church of the Holy Sepulchre and his bathhouse nearby drew its water from here. In 985 the Arab geographer Mukaddasi refers to this as Birkat Iyad ibn Ghanem, named for a companion of the Prophet Mohammed, who came to Jerusalem with Omar in 638 and built, or most probably rebuilt, a bathhouse for which this pool provided water. Today the Arabs again call it Birkat Hammam el-Batrak.

At present the reservoir, which rarely contains any water, resembles a garbage dump. Old etchings and photographs of it give the impression of a serene body of water, with water-carriers straight out of the Bible filling their goatskins. By the nineteenth century the water was in fact unsafe to drink; in the summer the pool smelled and became a breeding ground for disease-carrying mosquitoes. If you happen to come here after a heavy rainfall, there may be water in the pool, a fleeting return to the past.

Hezekiah's Pool is the common English name of this place, a classic "recent" mistake: in *The Holy City* (London, 1849) George Williams attributes the misnaming to a "Frank"—European—monk who lived in the beginning of the seventeenth century. When Dr. Edward Robinson, an American scholar, came to Jerusalem in 1838 to try to identify the sites mentioned in the Bible, he measured this reservoir and he too thought that it "entirely corresponds" to the Biblical description of the pool dug by King Hezekiah in 701 B.C. when Hezekiah saw

> that Sennacherib was come and that he purposed to fight against Jerusalem. He took council with his princes and mighty men to stop the waters of the fountains which were without the city. . . . Why should the kings of Assyria come and find much water? . . . Hezekiah also stopped the upper spring of the waters of Gihon and brought them straight down to the west side of the city of David. (2 Chronicles 32:2–3, 30.)

This is the only pool in what was thought to have

Remains of Hezekiah's Pool

been "the west side of the city of David," and the name, Hezekiah's Pool, remains. The real tunnel of Hezekiah that connects the spring of Gihon with the Pool of Siloam—or *Shiloah* in Hebrew—was rediscovered and correctly identified later in the nineteenth century. In 1880 an inscription was found within the tunnel, left by Hezekiah's two teams of hewers at the place where, digging from both ends, they met: "lift-

ing the axe towards the other." Today, you can walk the six hundred yards of the tunnel, if you do not mind getting wet.

If you look to the left, at the north edge of the pool you can see the Coptic *khan*, or caravanserai, built in 1838. The pool was about fifty feet longer until that time. Across from where you are standing the pool is bordered by a row of houses whose entrances face

Christian Quarter Road, or the Street of the Christians. The roofs are covered with small stone cupolas, as is the roof of the Petra Hotel just behind you. The cupolas are crisscrossed with black lines where tar has been applied to make them waterproof. The reason for this type of construction was the lack of large wooden beams required to support flat roofs; there were never forests around Jerusalem to provide timber for major buildings. Solomon had to import cedars from Lebanon for his Temple. Titus, a thousand years later, and the Crusaders, yet another millennium after Titus, had to search and send away for wood for their war machines. The Turks further depleted the countryside by imposing heavy taxes on newly planted trees. So native builders used stone, always plentiful, to construct beamless, domed roofs. In 1869 the road from Jaffa to Jerusalem was widened, and carriages could bring up to the city large beams imported from Europe. Tiles, also from Europe, soon made it possible to build the red roofs that you can see from here. All roofs in the city were built at a slight angle, to help collect rainwater. The stone-covered roofs, flat in part, provided a terracelike space for the inhabitants.

When you walk around the roof of the Petra Hotel you can see several small cupolas, each on top of one room. In contrast to this nineteenth-century legacy stands a solar heating system that provides hot water for the use of the hotel guests. From behind the tanks you can look over the railing for a good view of Omar Square and the Citadel. To the left of the large TV antenna on the south is the Cathedral of St. James in the Armenian Quarter, a small silver dome with a cross on top. The bell tower and the conical roof behind the red tiles belong to the Dormition Abbey on Mount Zion.

A few words must be said about the location of the old Mediterranean Hotel if only in memory of the distinguished guests who had stayed there. The earliest description of a hotel by that name that I could find is by the English artist and writer William Bartlett in *Jerusalem Revisited*, written in the summer of 1853. "Stylish and expensive," it was located in a "handsome building" on the Street of the Patriarch, another name for the Street of the Christians, and it was new to the city since Bartlett's 1844 visit. In 1857 the famous

Roof of Petra Hotel

American author Herman Melville stayed at the Mediterranean on the advice of his Jewish *dragoman*—interpreter, guide, bodyguard, and storyteller: "Dere Arab no know how to keep hotel." Melville writes in his diary that the hotel was run by a converted German Jew named Hauser. The hotel balconies overlooked the Pool of Hezekiah, and from a platform in front of his chamber Melville commanded a view of the battered dome of the Church of the Holy Sepulchre and the Mount of Olives. Opposite the hotel he could see the ruins of an old Latin convent, destroyed by some enemy centuries ago and never rebuilt. He was referring to the ruins that are now incorporated into the Church of the Redeemer. Melville, I am sorry to report, did not like Jerusalem.

Another celebrated American writer who liked the city even less was Mark Twain, who "loafed" at the Mediterranean during his brief stay in Jerusalem in 1867. He complains at great length in *The Innocents Abroad* about poverty, dirt, and dreariness though he neglected to give the exact location of his hotel.

One of the first modern guidebooks to Jerusalem, *Handbook for Travellers*, published by John Murray in 1858, lists a Hauser Hotel on Christian Street, without much question the same as the Mediterranean, which was managed by Mr. Hauser. An 1875 map in the third edition of Murray's guidebook shows the Mediterranean Hotel almost at the corner of David Street and Christian Quarter Road. By then it was run by a Mr. Horenstein. A year later a Franciscan friar, Liéven de Hamme, lists two hotels in his guidebook: the Mediterranean near Jaffa Gate run by M. Horenstein *aîné* and the Damascus Hotel, near the gate by the same name, run by M. Horenstein *jeune*. It seems that the hotel moved to this building "near Jaffa Gate" in 1876. Other travelers in the early 1880s wrote of the "new" Mediterranean.

Now that you know all you ever wanted to know about it, leave the Petra Hotel and turn left onto David Street, which follows the east-west axis of the city, the Roman Decumanus, which was laid down by Hadrian in 135 A.D., and which terminates at the Temple Mount. The markets have been in this location for a long time, and have been often described:

> "The markets are clean. . . . All year long the city is full of foreigners. . . . No where are bath houses dirtier than in the Holy City, scholars are scarce, goods are expensive, in the inns the taxes are high . . . ," wrote Mukaddasi in 985.

> "She [Jerusalem] has tall and well built markets. The streets are paved with stone tiles," reports a Persian traveler in 1047.

> "And here too Jerusalem has greatness. Men and women walk the length and breadth of the markets . . . and there are many Jewish shops . . . ," notes a Jewish pilgrim in 1481.

By the nineteenth century things got worse. In open ditches, rotten fruits, dead cats, and camel dung often floated together. At times garbage blocked the streets. The gates then would be left open at night for the hyenas to come and scavenge. One assumes the garbage was biodegradable in those days.

The markets are cleaner today, but usually very crowded. Be sure to watch out for the donkeys and pushcarts that distribute goods where the alleys are too narrow for cars, and avoid the smooth, slippery wedges at each riser that facilitate the progress of pushcarts on the steps but menace pedestrians. Before you plunge into a serious shopping spree, look around a bit. Prices are rarely fixed in the *suq*; a rule of thumb is to pay somewhere around two-thirds of the initial asking price. Bargaining is slow and requires patience and finesse. Mingle with the crowds and feast your eyes on the riches of the bazaar, its riot of colors, textures, and shapes. Under the current commercial—if not yet political—ecumenical umbrella, gift shops have made peace between Moslem, Christian, and Jew. Olivewood beads from Bethlehem, silver Stars of David, inlaid Damascus boxes, plastic replicas of the Dome of the Rock, mother-of-pearl crosses, and an occasional brass *menorah* all coexist peacefully in the shop windows of the bazaars.

In the first group of shops on the left is a place where you can buy magnificent, if expensive, fresh fruit. Other merchandise is displayed in boxes, sacks, and barrels: rice, flour, rock candy, dried figs, Jordan almonds, pistachios, and freshly roasted *poppeetes*— melon, sunflower, watermelon, or pumpkin seeds, all delicately salted. You can buy a small bag—a hundred grams will do—of roasted seeds and pretend you are a native, although it takes a while to master the art of walking, cracking, eating the inside, spitting out the shell, and talking all at the same time.

In this block of buildings, in the second half of the nineteenth century, stood the Turkish Post Office, the Greek Consulate, and the first bank in Jerusalem— flanked by two vegetable shops—founded by Yaakov Valero. After you walk down twenty-eight broad stairs, you can see an arch spanning David Street, with two sets of windows in it and a profusion of signs guiding tourists to various hostels and public toilets. Here and there a caper shrub appears among the graphics. Just before the arch, on the right, is the Arches Café. It is the only restaurant on this walk where you can have breakfast, lunch, or dinner, and you will pass by it again in about an hour, at the end of this walk. The place is owned by two cousins, the Kurdiehs, who serve good hummus, tahini, and eggplant salads. The prices are reasonable considering the location, service is pleasant, the bathroom—note the urinal next to the sink—is clean. No beer or any alcoholic beverage is served though—the Kurdiehs are observant Moslems.

Turn left where Christian Quarter Road, or Street of the Christians, begins opposite the Arches Café. The street is exceptionally straight; its first half was built over the edge of the dam that formed the eastern side of Hezekiah's Pool. Many of the shops here belong to Armenians. Some sell shoes but they no longer specialize in ones that are made to order, for which the street was famous. Long dresses, *à la* Arabia, abound here, as they do on every other street in the market. You can find some old embroidered dresses, beautiful and terribly expensive. The designs and color of the embroidery vary, and an expert can identify the village of the wearer by the patterns on her dress. Here and there a small "error" may appear among the otherwise perfect stitches, to avert the evil eye. This type of needlework is a dying art, probably because today's fair maidens would rather watch television than engage in this ancient craft.

Currently, so many of the shops carry identical items—mostly souvenirs—that it is hard to tell them apart. I will try to direct you toward a few special ones. The names of the stores and even the street signs are often hidden by displays of merchandise, though, and the street numbers are on tiny green discs haphazardly placed on the shop signs, almost always impossible to see.

No. 117, Christian Quarter Road is the sixth store on the right, after the corner of David Street. In the window are watches and ceramics. Here one can find Mr. Ohannes Markarian, who is also the curator of the extraordinary collection of clocks and watches in the Islamic Art Museum. If you are interested in old watches, he is your man.

Two doorways down the street, at no. 113, is St. John's Convent. Over the small gate is the sign for *Taphos*, or "grave" in Greek. The grave is the Holy Sepulchre nearby, and this mark is found on all properties of the Greek Orthodox Church. The Greeks call this the Church of the Prodromos, the Forerunner, after John who baptized Jesus. Enter the courtyard and you find yourself under massive, low stone vaults, facing the church. On the left, under the vaults, is a water cistern. Lemon trees and bits of archaeological relics grace the courtyard.

Under the church is a crypt that dates back to the Byzantine Period, to about 475 A.D., making it one of the earliest in Jerusalem. The present church was built in the eleventh century by the Merchants of Amalfi and rebuilt in the twelfth century, probably by Byzantine Emperor Manuel I Comnenus. During recent excavations here a small box was found containing a fragment of the True Cross and a crystal miter. In the church the Greek Orthodox preserve a bone they believe to be part of the skull of John the Baptist. It is usually impossible to enter the church. Look at its façade: to the right of the modern glass and metal door, three rows of ashlars above the bench, is a cross carved into a stone in the wall. Projecting from the wall to the left of the bell are three capitals in secondary use; another is above the entry arch—pure ornaments in an unclassical manner. To the right of the entrance to the church is another cistern with a faded Greek inscription. Over the cistern is a tripod, from England, part of a hand pump from the second half of the nineteenth century.

Around the corner, beyond the cistern and to the left, a flight of steps leads down to the old crypt; if you look through the door you can see some of the vaults. The crypt is about 25 feet below street level, contains a large apse, and covers an area of approximately 250 square feet. All around the courtyard are verandas—with wash hanging out to dry against the background of the dome with the cross and the small bell tower. The convent area can accommodate about five hundred people and many Greek Orthodox families live here now. On your way out note the enormous lock and the small door in the iron gate, which may remind you of a similar one in Jaffa Gate. It allows only one person to enter at a time, a precautionary measure. Just across the street from St. John's is an iron door with an inner flight of steps leading to a second floor. It is a relatively new building, and, based on material already quoted, this may have been the location of the first Mediterranean Hotel.

Turn right when you leave the churchyard. After two more shops there is a road to the right, Suq Afti-mos, but don't turn here. Half a dozen stores farther on the left side of the street you will see the sign Raz-zouk, where you can get yourself electrically tattooed. In centuries past, Christian pilgrims sometimes had themselves marked by special "Jerusalem tattoos" to prove that they had actually visited the Holy City. The custom seems to have originated among the Copts. A more recent pilgrim who succumbed to the tempta-tion was Prince Albert (later Edward VII) who re-turned to England from the Holy Land in 1862 bearing his first tattoo, a small butterfly.

Two doors down and across the street from Raz-zouk is the Chicorel Exhibition at no. 93, and next door is Abu Gharbieh's shoe store. Both stores were part of the Hammam el-Batrak, the "Bathhouse of the Patriarch," dating from Byzantine times. It is even pos-sible that an earlier, Roman bathhouse stood in this area. In 1918, it was reported in the publication of the Pro-Jerusalem Society—founded by the British—that the old stone *mastabas*, sloping sides or benches, of the chambers of the *hammam* were being removed because shops were going to replace the bathhouse. In Arabic, by the way, if you want to describe a chaotic situation you say *hammam bala moyeh*, a "bathhouse without water."

At no. 72, two shops over and across the street, is the Perfumery of Fuad Abdin, which, the owner says, carries perfumes from all over the world. The tiny 10-foot-by-7-foot shop used to be the toilet that served the *hammam*. Mr. Abdin worried that it was too em-barrassing to tell tourists about this, but he finally fell for the argument that it is interesting for people to see how a place of bad odors was converted into one that smells nice.

Next door is no. 68—again the number is so dis-creetly placed it is almost invisible—the Jamal Gift Shop, which used to be the "washing place" between the toilet and the bathhouse, whatever that may mean. I am in Mr. Jamal's debt forever: I had spent several days trying to locate the old *hammam* but no one on the street seemed to know anything about it. This did not surprise Mr. Jamal. "What do they know of our old Jerusalem? They are all from Hebron," he said as he took me to many of the places I have mentioned above. He also continued to keep an eye on me during subsequent visits and if any merchant tried to pester me, he would be told by Mr. Jamal: "Leave her alone! She is a *bint balad*." That means a "daughter of the city," a Jerusalemite. A beautiful Arabic expression.

On the second floor above the gift shop is the Peace Restaurant, which in the good old days used to be a hashish den. In the shop on the other side of the entry one could buy water pipes and other paraphernalia.

Pass by two more shops along Christian Quarter Road. On the right is a nameless alley between two shoe stores, Mujahead and Original Shoes. On both sides of the arch, on the second floor, is the St. John Hotel, built by the Greek Orthodox Church at the turn of the century. The two-story building has some beautiful stonework: the arch is framed by two engaged pilasters, and there are fine moldings above the windows. The emblem *Taphos* can be seen above the flat-headed arch.

On the street pavement just in front of Original Shoes there is an inscription on what looks like a square manhole cover. It explains that when a sewer was replaced here some years ago, a third- or fourth-century road was uncovered. The ancient pavement stones, in excellent condition, were then raised to present-day street level. In a straight line due south, on Mount Zion, archaeologist Magen Broshi has unearthed the continuation of this street. The old pavement ends at the steps on the left, called Aqabat Khan el-Aqbat, the "Ascent of the Coptic Khan," at the northern edge of Hezekiah's Pool. A few shops down Christian Quarter Road, on the right, begins St. Helena Road, to which we shall soon return. The street sign is often bedecked with dresses, so take note of this location. Continue along Christian Quarter Road, which now becomes a covered market with occasional apertures in the tops of the vaults to let in light. Monks and priests from nearby convents can walk on top of the roofs to the Church of the Holy Sepulchre without having to mingle with the hoi polloi.

At no. 49, a few doors on the right past St. Helena

Road, is Angel Souvenir and Candles. The latter come in all different shapes, lengths, and colors. Farther on the right, one entry after Ohm's Store, at no. 45, is a green door with an Arabic inscription. It is the site of a small mosque that, some say, offers protection from snakebites: anyone bitten by a snake within the Wall who remains in the city for 360 days, is guaranteed not to die. Others claim that it is the Mosque of Omar that possesses this power.

Walk on until you leave the covered section of the street, and stop when you see on your left Greek Orthodox Patriarchate Road, a relatively wide-stepped street leading to an arch that spans the street and has a large *Taphos* on it. On this street is the residency of the Greek Orthodox Patriarch. The first one to move to Jerusalem was Cyril II, in 1845; before that the Patriarchs lived in the Phanar in cosmopolitan Constantinople. The move to the Holy City occurred only after the Protestants were allowed to have a Bishop in Jerusalem—the other churches began to worry about the competition.

Opposite the Greek Orthodox Patriarchate Road, on the right-hand side of Christian Quarter Road, is a segment of a strong Crusader wall with projecting piers and half a Gothic arch. The arch is hidden behind a modern grille on which—of course—hang desert robes and rugs. This was the western entrance to the Church of the Holy Sepulchre, sometimes called Mary's Gate. It was blocked by the Moslems after Saladin's victory in 1187 to facilitate the collection of fees. Over the centuries the Moslems destroyed relatively few churches, but they turned Christian devotion into a lucrative business: pilgrims paid to enter—and sometimes to exit—the churches.

Another arch, almost above your head, connects the buildings on both sides of the street. It was part of the Melita Hotel, one of the first commercial hotels to open in Jerusalem, in the 1850s. Bartlett immortalized it in one of his drawings after staying here in 1853 on his last visit to Jerusalem. It was then run by the "honest Antonio Zamit" of Malta.

The street ends after you pass half a dozen more shops. Turn right; just around the corner is a mosque

Former entry to Church
of the Holy Sepulchre

that non-Moslems cannot enter, Khanka Salahiyya. *Khanka* means "convent" or "monastery"; *salah* means "a righteous man," part of Salah ed-Din's name, otherwise known as Saladin. *Din* in Arabic means "faith." Saladin built the Khanaka in 1192 over Crusader structures, where the house of the Patriarch may have stood in the Byzantine Period. The minaret—which we saw from the roof of Petra—was added in 1417 by Sheikh Barhan ed-Din ibn Ghanem. According to Moslem tradition the Christians offered him money so that he would not erect a mosque taller than the Church of the Holy Sepulchre, but he refused the bribe and soon thereafter he was told by Mohammed, via a dream, that he would be rewarded on Judgment Day. The stone parapets, or seats, at the base of the entrance to the mosque, a mark of hospitality offered to the weary, are now covered by very forbidding nails.

The Seventh and Eighth Stations of the Cross are farther down this street, which is named after St. Francis. The name changes to Via Dolorosa as the street continues eastward.

Turn around and go back to Christian Quarter Road. You may wish to make a note of the third shop on the right after the Greek Orthodox Patriarchate Road. Follow the whiff of garlic and you will spot the sign, Gino's Speciality—black and red graphics on bright yellow. The restaurant serves good Italian food at reasonable prices.

At the end of the long vaulted section of the market turn left onto St. Helena Road, known in Arabic as Suq esh-Shamma, the Candlemakers Bazaar, for obvious reasons. Walk down the stairs of St. Helena and just before they veer to the left, stop in front of the redstone Ottoman arch with the most beautiful moldings, which is the entrance to the real Mosque of Omar. (The Dome of the Rock is often—erroneously—called the Mosque of Omar.)

One version of the story of the surrender of Byzantine Jerusalem to the Moslems has it that Patriarch Sophronius offered to hand over the city without a fight if Caliph Omar would come and personally promise that the Christian Holy Places would be spared. Omar agreed. When he came to visit the Church of the Holy Sepulchre, Sophronius asked if he wanted to pray there. "No," answered Omar. "If I pray here my men will turn your church into a Moslem shrine." Omar spread his prayer rug—according to tradition—just about where you are standing, kneeled, and prayed. Whether the story is true or not, the fact is that few churches were destroyed by the Moslems, and this is a pleasant anecdote about tolerance—a rare commodity in the Holy City.

We have few records of the early years of Islam in Jerusalem. The city did not become the capital of the country, or even a district capital, at any time under Moslem rule. We know that Omar did come to Jerusalem and found a Christian city, full of churches and other public buildings. He also found the Temple Mount desolate, covered with trash—Christians wished to perpetuate the prophecy of Jesus that not one Temple stone shall be left upon another—and had the site cleaned. By the beginning of the eighth century the Dome of the Rock and the Mosque of el-Aqsa had been built by the Moslems, perhaps to counterbalance the magnificent Church of the Holy Sepulchre. The Mosque of Omar, built only around 935, was rebuilt in 1216 by one of Saladin's sons. The square minaret was added about two hundred years later; other restoration work was ordered in 1858 by Sultan Abdul Mejid.

Look through the green iron gate, which has bunches of grapes hanging over it in the summertime. In the courtyard are prayer rugs and the shoes of the True Believers. The minaret rises from the wall to an octagonal balcony just beneath the crowning element. As live *muezzin* have been replaced by recordings, the call to prayer now comes through the loudspeaker you can see on the balcony. The minaret is decorated by fine arches, which surround the narrow slits that allow the light to enter the tower.

It is interesting to note that only after the conquest of Saladin do we find a major mosque on either side of the holiest Christian shrine in the heart of Christian Jerusalem, where few Moslems live. Perhaps this was a reaction to the slaughter and destruction brought on by the Crusaders a century earlier.

To continue the walk, follow the steps that turn abruptly to the right and down to the courtyard in front of the Church of the Holy Sepulchre. Many a volume has been written about the church in the past sixteen centuries and there is little I can add. Since it is not part of our walk, the following passage is only a brief description of the outside of the building, which has been destoyed several times by wars and natural disasters.

According to Christian tradition this is the place where Jesus was crucified and buried, on Skull Hill or Golgotha, which was outside the city until Agrippa I built the Third Wall. After 135 A.D. Hadrian erected a temple to Aphrodite on this site but this did not prevent Queen Helena, mother of Emperor Constantine, from discovering the remains of the True Cross under the pagan temple. A grand Martyrium and Basilica were erected here by Constantine in 335 and destroyed in the Persian invasion of 614. Abbot Modestus restored the buildings on a more modest scale. The church was destroyed again in 1009 by the Egyptian Caliph Hakim, and partially restored again in 1048. The Crusaders built one large structure over the different sanctuaries; the Romanesque façade and the bell tower—originally two stories higher—are Crusader in origin. In 1808 the Great Fire damaged the building, and in the rebuilding of the Basilica, done by the Greek Orthodox, the tombs of the Crusader kings disappeared, giving rise to Latin accusations against the Orthodox Church.

This has been the site of bitter disputes among the Christian sects that share the privilege of holding services here: Greek Orthodox, Armenian Orthodox, Roman Catholics, Copts, Ethiopians, and Syrians. The first three control the major part of the space. The Protestants, newcomers to the area, have no part in this church; they do not believe in worship of holy sites, and many find its Eastern traditions and imagery alien. Outside Damascus Gate is the Garden Tomb, discovered by General Gordon in the late nineteenth century. Like the Holy Sepulchre, the Garden Tomb was sealed by a rolling stone and is located near a hill that looks like a skull. Some believe it to be the Holy Sepulchre.

Since the days of Saladin two Moslem families have held the keys to the church. The Arab word for the Resurrection is *el-Kiama*. To express contempt, it was purposely mispronounced and the site of the church was called *el-Kamama*, or "the dunghill." Jews were not allowed in the Church of the Holy Sepulchre until 1967.

Leave the courtyard through the eastern gate, opposite the stairway that brought you down here, and enter a clean, spacious area known as the Muristan. The Persian word for hospital is *bimeristan*, and the name goes back to the days of Saladin and to the Christians who ministered to the pilgrims in this area even before the arrival of the Crusaders. Earlier, in the second century A.D., the Roman Forum was located here. The last two stops on this walk are within this block, the Russian Church (St. Alexander's Church) and the German Lutheran Church (the Church of the Redeemer).

The street that continues eastward, straight ahead as you leave the Holy Sepulchre, is Suq el-Dabbagha, named in honor of a smelly tannery that stood here for centuries and made life unpleasant for Christian worshipers. The visit to the Russian Church is optional. If you decide to skip it, walk past a few shops on the left, cross the street to the large, closed gate of the church with the tall bell tower, and turn to the next page. To get to the Russian Church continue past another few shops—more souvenirs. The bell tower of the Church of the Redeemer should be on your right. The last door at the end of the block on the left is the entrance to St. Alexander's Chapel and Church. The most recent sign on the left doorjamb gives the visiting hours as 9:00 to 3:00, Monday through Thursday. This does not mean that the door is always open, but if you ring the bell during these hours, someone will eventually open the door and either show you around, or, more likely, give you a pamphlet with information about the church and let you wander around. If you wish, you can come to pray here for the departed soul of Tsar Alexander III every Thursday at 7:30 A.M. The chapel, which was dedicated in 1896, was named after the tsar's patron, Saint Alexander Nevsky, who had saved Mother Russia from a Swedish invasion. The building belongs to the White Russian Church, which has its headquarters in New York. Above the front door, within the segmented crown pediment, is the emblem of the Russian Orthodox Church.

In 1859, with the help of a Coptic monk, the Russian consul acquired this piece of real estate, valuable property because of its proximity to the Holy Sepulchre.

While digging for the foundations the Russians uncovered some important ruins under the rubble, but all activity ceased in 1860 when the Russians began to build hospices and a cathedral in what became known as the Russian Compound—an enormous undertaking and one of the first building projects outside the Old City Wall. In 1883 excavations resumed here, and as you walk into the church and down the first set of stairs at the end of the entry hall and to the right, you pass under an arch that was uncovered then. Supported by a pillar and resting on two capitals, it is part of a triumphal gate built by Emperor Hadrian around 135 A.D. at the entrance to the Forum.

Turn left, and at the far end of the pink marble steps you will see the remains of what some archaeologists believe to be the Second Wall, built either in the Late Hasmonean Period (143–37 B.C.) or shortly thereafter by Herod the Great. The location of the Second Wall is of great importance to Christianity: Queen Helena discovered Golgotha three centuries after the death of Jesus, and, as the city was destroyed completely by the Romans in 70 A.D., most landmarks had disappeared by the time she came to Jerusalem. The site of the execution and burial of Jesus had to be outside the walls, as Jewish law permitted no graves within the city. If these are the remains of the Second Wall, then the Sepulchre—which is on the other side of it—was outside the walls of Jerusalem in the time of Jesus.

To the right of the wall, under the protection of a glass cabinet, is a threshold that some believe to be part of Judgment Gate through which Jesus passed on his way to Golgotha. The fourth-century Basilica, which Emperor Constantine built, utilized the Second Wall as the façade of its atrium.

At the top of the pink marble steps, behind a 1960 fresco depicting Jesus carrying the cross amidst Roman soldiers, you can see the Russian chapel, which is not always open to the public. It is decorated with many icons and large paintings of various saints. The entrance to the chapel is through the main entry hall, to the right of the portraits of the last of the Romanovs, Nicholas II and Alexandra Petrovna. On the upper floor, which is closed to the public, there is a pilgrim hospice and the living quarters of the nuns and others who work here.

Turn right when you leave the Russian church and go past three shops. Across the street you will then see the northern gate to the Church of the Redeemer, the German Lutheran Erlöser Kirche. Sections of the gate date back to the Crusaders' Church of St. Mary la Latine. If you strain your eyes you can see, in the middle of the outer façade of the grand portal arch, a circle—the sun—and to the right of it, a half moon. Framing the arch and beneath the cornice above are corbels and carved heads surrounding ornamental medallions and animal shapes. On the arch itself, now ravaged by time, were the Latin names and symbols for the months of the year: a reaper for June, a grape harvester for September. Above the inner doors of this unused entrance, on both sides of the quatrefoil oculi, are the letters alpha and omega for God is "the beginning and the ending." This is a recent addition, as are the German eagle and the shield in the spandrels. You have a nice view of the Mosque of Omar from here, and to the right, the Church of the Holy Sepulchre.

Walk a few steps in the direction of the Church of the Holy Sepulchre and turn left on Muristan Road to the western, open doors of the Church of the Redeemer. Sit in one of the pews, listen to the organ music—usually a recording—and read here about the Order of the Hospitallers, the fabulous Knights of St. John.

According to medieval legend, the origins of the Order of the Hospital of St. John in Jerusalem go back to the days of the Hasmonean: King Antiochus was its founder and Zacharias was one of its first members. While this is rather unlikely, it is possible that an early Christian hospital stood in this area. In the beginning of the ninth century, a Latin hospice was established here by Charlemagne on land that was presented to him—together with the key to Jerusalem—by Caliph Harun el-Rashid. The hospice was later destroyed by the Egyptians. By the middle of the eleventh century, besides the Church of St. John the Baptist (which you visited) and the Church of St. Mary la Latine (which stood where you are now sitting), the Church of St. Mary la Grande was also situated in the Muristan area, as was a hospice that administered to the sick. When the Crusaders entered Jerusalem in 1099, the hospital was headed by Gerard, a pious knight who took care of not only Christians of all sects but also infidels. Pilgrims writing about Jerusalem during the Crusader Period tell of a hospital that could accommodate two thousand sick people; it stood south of the Church of the Holy Sepulchre—near the Church of St. John the Baptist—on the western edge of this area, parallel to Christian Quarter Road. Next to David Street were the living quarters of the many young noblemen who, inspired by Gerard, stayed in Jerusalem and became part of the newly independent Order of the Hospitallers.

Godfrey de Bouillon granted the Hospitallers land, and many other rulers in Europe and the Holy Land followed his example. The secular character of the order changed during the Crusader Period and its members took vows of poverty, chastity, and obedience. They wore plain black robes with an eight-point cross of white linen next to their hearts. Hostile Moslems were endangering the lives of pilgrims en route to Jerusalem and the Knights of St. John soon found themselves defending travelers on their way to and from the Holy City. Raymond de Puy, who succeeded Gerard, divided the order into three classes: the first, those of noble birth, performed military service; priests formed the second class; in the third class, those "who had no pretensions to nobility of origin, assumed the function of 'Frères Servans' or assistants." So wrote Mandeville, circa 1322. At first even the most gallant knights returned after battle to administer to the sick and the poor. But gradually the desire for fame, and the riches that poured into their coffers from all over Christendom, combined to make the vows of poverty and chastity meaningless; their purity was tarnished by gold. The knights left the Holy Land in 1291 after the final defeat of the Crusaders in Acre, and settled in Cyprus and in Rhodes, where their wealth became legendary. They were expelled from there by the Turks in 1521 and moved on to Malta, where they later surrendered to Bonaparte. The order still exists and issues stamps in the Vatican. For further details consult your local *TV Guide* for a rerun of *The Maltese Falcon*. Sydney Greenstreet, Peter Lorre, and the immortal Bogart will explain the rest of the story.

Jerusalem fell into the hands of Saladin in 1187. Five years later, during peace negotiations between Saladin and Richard Coeur de Lion, el-Malek ez-Zaher, Prince of Aleppo and Saladin's favorite son, came to Jerusalem to visit his father and stayed in the former quarters of the Hospitallers.

Over time, especially during the Ottoman Period, the whole area fell into disrepair. In the first half of the nineteenth century one of the ruined buildings here was almost filled with dung; in another, bodies of dead animals were left for the dogs and the vultures. The Arabs tended to express contempt for places holy to others by locating some offensive industry next to them. As we know, a tannery stood here and a slaughterhouse was on the edge of the Jewish Quarter, both creating an unbearable stench. The Muristan was used as a garbage dump and it was considered dangerous to walk here for "the fear of catching some infectious disorder."

In 1869 the Prussian Crown Prince Friedrich Wilhelm arrived in Jerusalem during his trip to the opening of the Suez Canal. The Turks presented him with the eastern half of the Muristan. The western part, closer to the Christian Quarter Road, belonged to the Greek Orthodox Church. The Germans soon began to clear the area of the accumulated trash and debris, and decided to build an Evangelical Church here. Until then the German and British Protestants worshiped together at Christ Church. Professor Adler of Berlin designed the church; Kaiser Wilhelm II planned the bell tower. Wilhelm later came to Jerusalem, in 1898, to consecrate the church. The Germans wisely chose to incorporate the remains of the older building into the new complex, which was built along the lines of St. Mary la Latine, retaining the Gothic style. The old refectory was turned into a chapel, and the cloisters are now part of a modern German hospice. They are the only example of that type of cloister in Jerusalem and it is too bad the general public cannot enter the hospice to see them. (An English-language service is held in the small chapel next to the cloisters every Sunday at 9:00 A.M. At that time you can catch a glimpse of a beautiful courtyard with arches bedecked with green plants. Don't linger by the old cloisters or you will be asked to leave, rather firmly.)

The bell tower, 149 feet tall, is open from 9:00 to 12:30 and from 2:00 to 4:30 daily, except Sundays, Friday afternoons, and when the guardian takes a break. There is a minimal fee. To reach the top of the bell tower you have to mount a turreted stairwell of 177 steps (there is no elevator). The view is superb, in my opinion the finest within the city. You can always come back here another time; Walk 2 passes near here. When you emerge from the winding staircase, you are facing east. On the right is the Mount of Olives; filled with associations for Christians, it is covered on its southern slope with Jewish gravestones of the last three millennia. Between the mountain and the city lies the Valley of Jehoshaphat; the name contains the component *shaphat*, which means "to judge" in Hebrew. "For, behold in those days and in that time, When I shall bring back the captivity of Judah and Jerusalem, I will gather all nations, And will bring them down into the valley of Jehoshaphat; and I will enter into judgment with them there For My people and for My heritage Israel, whom they have scattered among the nations, And divided My land." (Joel 4:1–2.) The valley is also known as Kidron.

The tallest bell tower on the far right of the mountain is part of the Russian Convent and Church of Ascension, built in 1880. Arab workmen refused to haul the Christian bell when it arrived from Russia, so a group of Russian pilgrims rolled the bell, crated in a wooden barrel, all the way from Jaffa to Jerusalem. The arched colonnade at the summit of the mountain is the Intercontinental Hotel, built during the Jordanian occupation. The shimmering silver olive trees of Gethsemane are below it, near the gilded cupolas of the Church of Maria Magdalene. Farther left, in the middle of the mountain range sits Augusta Victoria, the hospital named after the kaiserin who went up to the site in 1898 to look at the city from the east, as Jesus had done. The building is a replica of a Rhineland castle.

Left of Augusta Victoria, amidst large cranes, sits the tower of Hebrew University, on top of Mount Scopus. The university was founded in 1925 and remained on Mount Scopus until 1948, when the area was surrounded by Arabs; even though the University and the Hadassah Hospital stayed in Jewish hands, access to them, except for a few policemen, was not permitted. After years of temporary shelters, the university opened another campus on Givat Ram. Now Givat Ram is devoted strictly to the sciences; the humanities

have returned to the enlarged campus of Mount Scopus (nicknamed "the white elephant"). Hadassah also
built a new facility, near Ein Karem. In the foreground
is the anodized Dome of the Rock; to its right is the
smaller, silvery dome of the Mosque of el-Aqsa.

Turn to the right now to look at the Jewish Quarter
with all its new and reconstructed houses. Between
the Temple Mount, where the Moslem shrines are, and
the Jewish Quarter on the "Western Hill" runs the *gai*,
the "valley" known by its Greek name, Tyropoeon. It
joins two other valleys, Kidron and Hinnom, south of
the Temple Mount. The three ravines form a spur on
which the City of David once stood. Building activity
still goes on in the Jewish Quarter, which was partially
destroyed in 1948. To the right of the Jewish Quarter,
farther west up the hill, lies the Armenian Quarter. On
Mount Zion, behind it, you can probably recognize
the Dormition Abbey.

Turn right again, and you will see the Citadel of David and the red wall of the Petra Hotel. Beyond is western, modern Jerusalem. The very tall building on the
left, which mars the skyline, is an apartment house.
Next is the King David Hotel, built of soft red Jerusalem stone, which takes on different colors as the day
progresses. Beyond the King David Hotel the tower of
the YMCA can just barely be seen from this angle. Just
below you is the shopping arcade of the Muristan; to
the right are the domes of Church of the Holy Sepulchre and the two minarets of the mosques we passed
on our walk. The clock steeple with the pyramidal
crown, erected in 1895, is part of the Church of St. Saviour built by the Franciscans on a site purchased from
the Georgians in the sixteenth century.

Last is north Jerusalem, the only side of the Old City
not naturally protected by a ravine. Many a conquer-
or—Titus, Godfrey de Bouillon, Saladin—broke
through the ramparts and entered Jerusalem from the
north. To the right of the tower of St. Saviour you can
catch a glimpse of the bright green, onion-shaped
domes of the Russian Cathedral. On the horizon is the
almost black dome of the Ethiopian Church. The crenellated tower is the Italian Hospital, now part of the
Ministry of Education. Closer is the northern part of
the Old City Wall, bits of which you can see. In the
middle is the top of the Damascus Gate, the most

beautifully decorated gate in the city, built by Suleiman the Magnificent on foundations laid during the
Herodian era. Behind the gate is another massive German landmark, Schmidt College. The fabric of old versus new city is best seen from here: cupolas and TV
antennae in the Moslem Quarter within the Wall; red-
tiled roofs outside the Wall, often the location of late-
nineteenth-century Jewish neighborhoods; church
domes, modern office buildings, cypress and pine
trees. On the horizon, to the right, are Ramat Eshkol
and French Hill covered by new Israeli housing, next
to Hebrew University.

When you leave the church, go a few steps to the
left and the entry to a square with several shopping arcades will be on your right. The area is named Suq Aftimos for the bishop who built it. The arcades occupy
the Greek Orthodox section of the Muristan, which is
most fitting since the area was part of the Forum in Roman times. In the middle of the square, after you pass
a few shops, you can see what is now a round, waterless fountain, built in 1901 to commemorate the twenty-fifth anniversary of the rule of Sultan Abdul Hamid.
It was a wondrous landmark when it first began to
spew water out of the mouths of the masklike faces,
and Aftimos used to come and watch it on moonlit
nights. The fountain was built by artisans from Bethlehem. The arcade was called the New Market when it
first opened. Sunny and airy, away from the crowded
alleys of the *suq*, it was a most desirable location.
Many of the merchants here were Jewish, and they
sold fabrics—which lay in rolls on tables outside the
stores—to customers who came from the churches
and monasteries of the Christian Quarter. At times a
small orchestra was hired to play outside one of the
shops—an early form of advertising. After the riots of
1929, as relations between Arabs and Jews continued
to deteriorate, acts of sabotage forced the Jewish merchants away. Many were replaced by Arab merchants
from Hebron. There are several leather shops in the
market where you will be assured that "for you, it is
only seven dollars!" Some of the leather cushions sold
here—without stuffing—make good gifts, easily
packed. As Arabic does not have a "*p*" the cushions
are known as "buffs."

Walk back toward the Church of the Redeemer. To

the right of the church there are several structures: an archaeological studies center, a hospice, and the Martin Luther *Schule*. The 1898 church was dedicated on October 31 to commemorate the day in 1517 when Martin Luther nailed his reforms to the door of the church in Wittenberg. *Ecclesia semper reformanda*, he believed: "The Church always needs reformation." This whole area is so clean, that if it weren't for the Greek *suq* and the climate, you wouldn't know that you are in Jerusalem.

To the right of the school is a memorial tablet, complete with flag. It recounts the history of the hospitals of the Knights of St. John from medieval times to the present. The eight-point white cross belongs to the Order of the Knights; it is sometimes called the Maltese Cross.

Across the street from the tablet are Armenian jewelry and antique stores, and on the right is a shop that provides Turkish coffee to the merchants in the area. If you are ready to collapse, do it here. You can get juice, or try the excellent Israeli beer, Maccabee. Or "Tea with ment [!]" as the sign advertises—highly recommended, as is the Turkish coffee.

To leave, face south (the flag and tablet on your left, the coffee shop on your right). Straight ahead, under a massive medieval vault decorated with a nineteenth-century German eagle is an iron gate. Note Barakat Antiques across from the vault. Turn right and continue all the way up David Street past Christian Quarter Road to where the road passes between Jaffa Gate and the Citadel. A low crenellated wall used to connect the two, and the moat continued on both sides of this wall. When the Church of the Redeemer was being built, the rubble and dirt removed from the Muristan area were dumped into the outer part of the moat. When Kaiser Wilhelm II came to consecrate the church in 1898, the inner moat was partially filled and the low wall removed. You can read about the royal visit while you wait for the bus outside the Wall.

The kaiser wanted to enter Jerusalem mounted on a white charger, in the manner of a latter-day Crusader. Kaiserin Augusta Victoria and her ladies expected to arrive in their open carriages, probably unaware of the fact that the Old City gates could not accommodate such modern means of transportation. Another ticklish

Interior view, Jaffa Gate

problem was the Moslem tradition that only a conqueror of the city had the right to ride a horse through the gates, and even he might run into trouble! As you may recall, when Emperor Heraclius rode into the city in 629 A.D., through the Golden Gate, a stone fell and blocked his way, even though he was carrying the True Cross, which he had just rescued from the Persians. When the Turks removed part of the wall to create "an unrecognized breach," it was considered that the kaiser never "entered" the city at all. Blissfully ignorant of all this, the kaiser arrived, draped "in the panoply of the Middle Ages," a sun helmet on his head from which a long white silk burnoose, or mantle, emerged to cover the hindquarters of the white horse. Behind him were his men, bedecked in buff-colored uniforms that the kaiser had designed for the occasion.

Reactions to the visit-*cum*-breach varied. Arab *fala-heen* were reportedly delighted by all the excitement and paid, without complaining, the extra taxes, which were used to pave the road to Jerusalem. The Jews also

enjoyed the diversion, but did not like to see the "ax waving at the stones" even though the sixteenth-century Wall was "not ancient" and no longer had any strategic value. The British residents of Jerusalem were the most vocal. They disliked the kaiser and the new friendship between Turkey and Germany. They also worried about the possibility that Western influence might adversely alter the nature of the Old City. Not only were vehicles coming within the Wall, lamented archaeologist R. A. S. Macalister a few years later, but other evils were soon to follow—like the huckster at a stall in Jaffa Gate who was selling an Arabic translation of *Tarzan of the Apes.*

In 1917, toward the end of World War I, General Allenby entered the Old City through Jaffa Gate to accept the Turkish surrender on the steps of the Citadel. He rode his horse through the new neighborhoods of Jerusalem, but dismounted when he reached the gate. He then came into the Old City on foot, not as a conqueror, but as a humble pilgrim.

Walk

2

East of
the Citadel

○

A fast walker could go outside the walls of Jerusalem and walk entirely around the city in
one hour. I do not know how else to make
one understand how small it is.
  Mark Twain, *The Innocents Abroad*, 1869

The Citadel, popularly known as the Tower of David, is an ancient fortress that stands by the western entrance to the Old City. Because it is so well known, it has often been used as the symbol of Jerusalem in art and in literature. Despite its name, the Citadel has nothing to do with King David, who died many centuries before it was built and whose city lay south of the Temple Mount, outside the present Wall. For two millennia the Citadel has been continuously occupied by different rulers and armies, strengthened, defended, destroyed, and rebuilt. It was the last stronghold in time of war; when the Citadel fell, Jerusalem fell.

Our walk begins southwest of the Citadel, outside the Old City Wall, where recent archaeological excavations between Jaffa Gate and Mount Zion have added to our knowledge of the city's development and of her defense systems, which were closely connected to the Citadel nearby.

The starting point is about two hundred yards below Jaffa Gate, down Hativat Yerushalayim (the Jerusalem Brigade Road) and across from Hutzot Hayotzer. Behind the bus station is the fosse of the Citadel, a dry moat. From it rises a glacis that was built by the Crusaders, as was the outer wall of the fosse at the southern edge of the Citadel. On the east, within the Citadel, looms the minaret that is a "recent" Ottoman addition from 1655—"recent" because, as a nineteenth-century Englishman wrote, here in the "East" even the "Crusading period is considered horribly modern."

Enter the archaeological garden through the low black wrought-iron gate. To the left of the paved walk are several olive trees and a Jerusalem Foundation marker: "National Park, Jerusalem Garden. Gift of the Jewish National Fund, Canada." Since 1967 a new green belt has been created around the Old City Wall, and it incorporates many of the archaeological remains that have been uncovered since the Six Day War. Walk along the paved lane to the first tower that projects from the Wall; it was built by the Turks in the six-

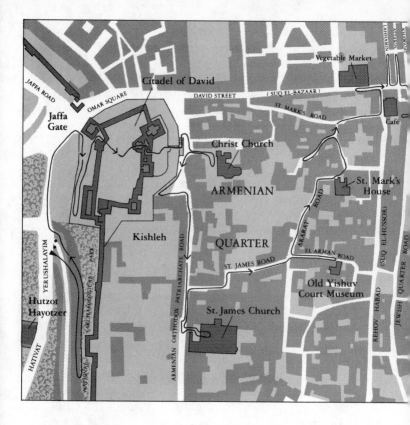

teenth century on Herodian foundations. In the tower is one loophole and two decorative flat discs. The section of the Wall between the Citadel and the southwestern corner has four projecting towers. The second one, with the wider lower section, is most interesting. A freestanding brass plaque in front of the tower gives the dates of the excavations, 1973 to 1978, and indicates the various building periods. Archaeologist Magen Broshi, who directed the excavations, has described many of the finds along the Wall in *Biblical Archeologist* (vol. 40, no. 1, 1977).

The foundation of the tower is Herodian, seven rows of ashlars that rest between two large rocks. Above the rocks the structure is probably Moslem. Note the moss and caper bushes that grow on the sloping "shelf" commonly seen on many old walls. Above the shelf is the Turkish addition, built by order of Suleiman the Magnificent when the Wall was reconstructed in 1540. The façade of the tower is well balanced: three loopholes between five decorative discs.

To the left of the tower the present Ottoman Wall, which is 2.5 meters (about 6 feet) in width, rises out

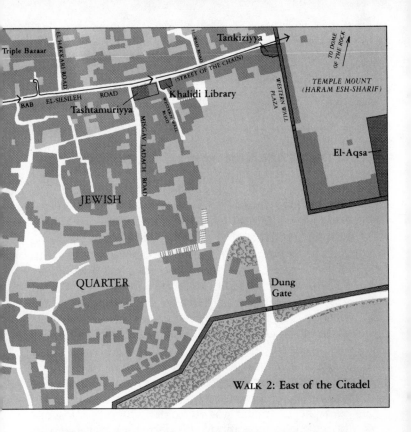

WALK 2: East of the Citadel

of the remains of an older and wider Hasmonean wall, circa 100 B.C. The Hasmonean, of Hanukkah fame, rebelled against the Syrians in 167 B.C. They were led by Judah Maccabee. This early wall was 5.4 meters wide and was built along the natural crest of the Western Hill, where the sharp drop toward the Valley of Hinnom begins. In front of the Hasmonean remains, Herodian ashlars can be seen, with their wide margins. Here the foundation of the wall was broadened until it was 8 meters—more than 26 feet—wide. As only two ashlars of the wall above the foundation have remained *in situ*, the height of the Herodian wall is not known; if you look closely at the corner where the tower and the foremost wall meet, you might be able to find one of these stones: it sits on top of a square stone where the mortar has remained intact. The stone has wide margins, typical of Herodian masonry. The wall may have reached the height of the Hasmonean wall, or else it is possible that only the foundations were strengthened here. (Herod's palace stood within the city on the other side of the Wall, and a strong retaining wall was needed to support the weight of the

71

fill used to create the platform on which the king's grand palace was built.)

About twenty-five feet south of the tower, to the right, a pile of gray soil clings to the Wall; a lone tree grows on top. The soil and the tree were left to show the level of the ground before the excavations began. All along the Wall the upper ashlars are dark and gray, having been exposed to the elements, while the lower ones, protected by layers of debris, have retained their original hue.

Farther south, just left of the third projecting tower, is an ancient lane, about ten feet wide with low stone walls on either side and three broad stairs. It leads to two other stairs built on top of a rock and attached to the Wall where a gate from the Second Temple Period stood. Immediately to the left of the two stairs, six short rows of Hasmonean ashlars can be seen in front of the Ottoman Wall. With your back to the Old City Wall, walk down the lane with the three wide stairs, and on the ground on the right you can see the outline of six large rooms that may have served as a house of industry in the seventh century B.C.

Another dramatic story unfolded when two inscriptions were found among the debris. One, broken in three and dated 1212 A.D., was near the remains of an Ayyubid gate in the southern section of the Wall, below Zion Gate; this isn't part of our walk. An earlier inscription, from 1202, was found near here. The inscriptions, one in bas-relief and the other incised in stone with traces of red in the background of the Arabic script, looked almost new as they had not been exposed long to the sun and the rain. They bore the name of el-Malek el-Mu'azzam, nephew of Saladin and governor of Damascus. From other sources we know that el-Mu'azzam tore down the walls of Jerusalem in 1219, fearing that the Crusaders might regain control of the city. Not wishing them to find a fortified town, the nephew of the man who rescued Jerusalem from the infidels in 1187 destroyed the towers and the walls and left only the Citadel untouched. Until the present Wall was built by Suleiman (1538–1540), Jerusalem remained an unwalled city. El-Mu'azzam's fears were well founded: ten years later, in 1229, Frederick II, the Holy Roman Emperor, obtained possession of the Holy City in a treaty with el-Malek el-Kamil of Egypt, and Jerusalem remained in the hands of the Crusaders for another decade.

Walk back along the Wall and return to the entrance of the archaeological park, then turn right to walk up the road toward Jaffa Gate. As you climb the hill, with the Citadel on your right, note the small parking lot that taxis share today with two huge gray dumpsters. Walk past the underground public toilet with its three ventilating glass hoods. The toilet occupies an old cistern that used to collect rainwater from the roofs of the courtyard of the Citadel. In the nineteenth century the water was sprinkled on the city's unpaved roads in a futile attempt to keep down the clouds of dust created by passing carriages, horses, and camels. (The first car arrived in Jerusalem in 1908, driven, of course, by an American.) Just past the public toilet and before the wide, paved road enters the Old City, you will see an opening on the right with palms on either side in front of a quadrangular tower in the Citadel. Walk up seven steps to a landscaped terrace where a mosaic-covered rock left of the steps says David Garden and on a board there is a sign for the Jerusalem City Museum. From the far end of the terrace, which overlooks the Valley of Hinnom, you get a sweeping panoramic view of the new city. On the far left, where the Wall and the footpath seem to end, you can see the western slope of Mount Zion. Across the valley is a gleaming white building, the Ariel Hotel. On its right is the Scottish Church of St. Andrew, with two small domes and a tower. The road south to Bethlehem and Hebron, which begins at Jaffa Gate, winds its way across a dam in the valley, an ancient route. To the right of the dam is the Sultan's Pool; repaired by Suleiman, it no longer holds water. A concert stage has recently been built on the site. On the slope left of the former pool is Mishkenot Sha'ananim (a long row of apartments) and the Montefiore Windmill; to the right is Yemin Moshe with its red-tile roofs (see Walk 4). Against the skyline is a gathering of hotels: the massive, almost windowless one is the new Sheraton–King Solomon. On its right are the yellow-arched windows of the Moriah Hotel. Better proportioned, in amber hues, is the King David, and, in similar tones, the French Consulate with triple arches beneath three large windows. Beyond it is the enormous white Plaza Hotel, and farther right are the office buildings and apartment houses of downtown Jerusalem. On the other end of the half circle, on the far right, is the northwestern corner of the Wall; within the Old City the clock tower of St. Saviour can be seen as well as the red roof of Casa Nova, the seat of the Latin Patriarch.

Before you return to the entrance to the terrace garden, in a medieval tower within the Citadel you will find one of the best buys in town. For a small fee, Sunday through Friday, at 9:00 and 11:00 A.M. and at 1:00 and 3:00 P.M. (no 3:00 P.M. showing on Fridays), you can see a multiscreen audiovisual program with an English sound track. The program, which lasts about a half hour, covers the history of the city, her meaning to the three monotheistic religions, the faces of the citizenry, the many moods and colors of Jerusalem—hundreds of exquisite slides interwoven into a fast-moving epic. At times the sound track is too loud, echoing off the stone walls of the cavelike hall.

If you do not wish to see the slide show, you can, for the same small fee, enter the inner court of the Citadel through the same entrance. (If the map of the Citadel is available, buy it, too.) The visit to the Citadel is also optional. The walk resumes at Christ Church, across from the main entrance to the Citadel on Omar Square; see page 78.

Inside the Citadel, in the hexagonal hall across from where you entered the court, there are maps, charts, and detailed descriptions of the Citadel over the last two millennia. You can explore the area within the Citadel's court on your own; most of the remains are well marked and clearly identified. Here are some tales from the different eras during which this fortress has protected the city, a reflection of the history of Jerusalem:

> Jerusalem was defended by three walls except where it was shut in by impassable ravines; so that a single rampart was enough. It was built on two hills facing each other and separated by a central ravine [the Tyropaeon], at which the terraces of houses ended. Of these two hills the one occupied by the Upper City [this western hill] was much the higher and straighter along in length; being so strong it was called the Stronghold by King David. . . .

So wrote Flavius Josephus in the first century A.D. after Jerusalem was destroyed by the Romans and the Second Temple Period ended. Much of our knowledge of that era comes from the extensive writings of a man who was born Yosef Ben Mattityahu, and who was governor of Galilee when the Great Rebellion against Rome broke out in 66 A.D. Soon he switched sides and betrayed his people. In his books, without apology, he describes his own duplicity and the atrocities committed by his new masters, the conquering Romans. Unpalatable as his character was, history would be the poorer without his record. The original Aramaic text is lost, but the extant Greek version was translated by Josephus.

In the late 1960s archaeologists Ruth Amiran and Avraham Eitan found evidence that this western hill was already settled in the First Temple Period (which ended in 586 B.C.). There is no evidence, however, that the area was enclosed by a protective wall. Remains of a Hasmonean wall and tower, from the second and first centuries B.C., can also be seen in the Citadel's courtyard. In the northeastern corner, to the left of the hexagonal hall, is a quadrangular tower with a Herodian base. The lower tiers consist of large, double-margined, finely bossed ashlars cut by Herod's masons. The tower, usually referred to as Phasael, was one of three towers that Herod built to protect his palace, which stood south of here. The ashlars, wrote Josephus, were "so perfectly united that each tower looked like a single rock, sent up by mother earth and later cut and polished by artists' hands into shapes and angles; so perfect from any viewpoint was the fitting of the joints." King Herod was disliked by the Jews who questioned his origins, called him an Idumite, and resented his cooperation with the Romans. Hoping to gain their loyalty, he began to glorify Jerusalem. He enlarged the Temple and built himself a new palace; the old one belonged to the Hasmonean, the previous dynasty, memories of which haunted his twisted mind. Eventually he killed his wife, Miriamne, the last descendant of the Hasmonean dynasty, and his two sons by her, fearing their popularity. Because of his magnificent buildings, he is known as Herod the Great.

The Lower City and the Temple were destroyed on

the 9th of Av, in 70 A.D. The Upper City and the stronghold by Herod's palace resisted for one more month, until the 8th of Elul. Titus then ordered the city demolished, except for the three towers that were left to show what a mighty city had been conquered by Rome. Only the base of the tower assumed to be Phasael, named for Herod's brother, still stands. The Tenth Roman Legion remained in the area; clay water pipes were found in the Citadel bearing their emblem, a wild boar and the letters *LXF—Legionis X Fretensis.*

As mentioned before, the Citadel was not built by David yet the myth persists. Already in 333 A.D. a pilgrim from Bordeaux was telling of a place within the Wall, near Mount Zion, where King David's palace used to be, and in 560 Antoninus Martyr, another Christian pilgrim, wrote of the Tower of David where the king used to sing the Psalms. Perhaps, as this was the only large structure left from older days, the Byzantines assumed that it must have been the royal palace from David's days. By the time of the first Arab conquest, circa 638 A.D., only the tower called Phasael seems to have survived. The Moslems added a *mihrab*, a place of prayer, and have called the site Mihrab Daud ever since.

The Citadel was well fortified when the Crusaders besieged Jerusalem: it contained several water cisterns and a storage space for grain. It was the last holdout of the Egyptian commander, and its final surrender signified the end of the 1099 battle for Jerusalem. The Crusaders enlarged the Citadel and called it Turris David. King Baldwin lived here for three years. Later, a royal palace was built south of here, where Herod's palace used to be. It was in the Citadel that Queen Melisende found refuge in her battle against her son, King Baldwin III, over the crown of Jerusalem. In the wall to the left of Phasael is a Crusader postern that led to an outer parapet. The large arch in the center of the courtyard is also Crusader in origin. When Saladin conquered Jerusalem in 1187, the Moslems tore down the large golden cross from the top of the Dome of the Rock and brought it to be melted in the courtyard of the Citadel. Ten years after the Crusaders regained control of the city, they were attacked in 1239 by Sultan el-Nāsir Daud of Kerak and they fled to the Citadel, the only fortified place left in the wall-less city. After their surrender, the Moslems destroyed much of the Citadel, so that what we see today is mostly Mamluk and Ottoman, walls rebuilt on earlier foundations. Like the rest of the city in the years after Suleiman, this area began to deteriorate. By the time the British entered Jerusalem in 1917 sections of the Citadel were filled with trash, and an open sewer flowed into the moat.

The British were shocked by the neglect they found and soon formed the Pro-Jerusalem Society to preserve and safeguard some of the historic sites in the Holy City. The list of members of the society deserves mention. Sir Ronald Storrs, the military governor, was president. Among the members were the Right Reverend the Anglican Bishop in Jerusalem, His Beatitude the Armenian Patriarch, as well as the Latin and the Orthodox Patriarchs, His Eminence the Grand Mufti, the Very Reverend Chief Rabbi I. Hacohen Kook, Eliezer Ben Yehuda, and Père Vincent. Many other dignitaries grace the long list—bankers, scholars, consuls, merchants—a virtual 1918 "Who's Who" in Jerusalem. Among the names from abroad we find Rothschild, Warburg, Schiff, Mrs. Andrew Carnegie, and the Khangi Karbari of Baroda!

In order to raise money to clean the Citadel and repair the ramparts, "name" seats were sold: for twenty pounds sterling a donor could have his name carved on a "seat in Palestine marble." Wooden or metal seats at convenient points on the "Ramparts Walk" with one's name painted on could be had for five pounds. No trace remains of those seats either in the Citadel or on the Wall.

To leave the Citadel, walk through the hexagonal tower, across the courtyard from where you first entered, where all the charts are. Outside on the right, before the footbridge, is an open-air mosque from the Ottoman Period. Many interesting inscriptions are displayed in the small courtyard. The main double-gated entrance to the Citadel, which we are approaching from the rear, was built by Suleiman the Magnificent in 1531. The covered footbridge was made of wood and was replaced when some cannons were brought to the Citadel and the supportive beams collapsed. Turn around after you leave the second, outer gate; on either side of the iron door are niches, places for the guards. In 1917 General Allenby stood on this small platform and accepted the official Turkish surrender, ending four centuries of Ottoman rule and granting the citizens of the Holy City civil and religious liberties.

Opposite the platform is a large metal gate, the entrance to another world: the first Protestant church in the Ottoman Empire, Christ Church. Walk into the courtyard where you can sit on a bench under a magnificent oleander, with plum and loquat trees behind it, planted by British ladies who were homesick for the green fields of England. The diplomats and the missionaries who lived and worked in this compound helped change the quality of life in Jerusalem to the benefit of all citizens.

By the beginning of the nineteenth century, Jerusalem was "a neglected city on the edge of the Ottoman Empire." The citizenry numbered nine thousand. High taxes, lack of commerce and industry, greedy pashas, dirt, and poverty prevailed. No new buildings, not even repairs of the Holy Places, were allowed by the Turks. All this began to change when, in December 1831, the Turkish garrison in the Citadel surrendered to the armies led by Ibrahim Pasha. Ibrahim was the son of the Egyptian ruler Mohammed Ali who had rebelled against the Turks. For nine years Jerusalem and most of Palestine remained under Egyptian administration. Living conditions improved: roads became safer, churches and synagogues were reconstructed, pilgrimages increased. England was allowed to open a consulate in Jerusalem—the first diplomatic mission to the city since the beginning of the eighteenth century. Initially British diplomats and missionaries were united in their efforts to gain a foothold in the Holy Land. The first missionary arrived in Jerusalem in 1820 but seems to have had little impact. Next, the London Society for Promoting Christianity Amongst the Jews sent the Reverend John Nicolayson to the city, and he was eventually allowed to rent living accommodations near here. In 1838 the society opened an infirmary (another stop farther on in this walk), but plans for constructing a church met many obstacles. Mohammed Ali gave permission to purchase this plot of land and have it registered in Nicolayson's name, permission being needed because foreign nationals could not normally own land in Palestine. But many objections were raised by

Moslems, who felt there was enough Christian presence in the Holy City. Rumors circulated that the Latin and Orthodox Churches were undermining the Protestants' efforts as well.

Finally, in 1845, the Sublime Porte allowed a private chapel to be built, for the use of the British consul. As the consul lived in a rented house on the other side of town, hasty preparations were made for a residency in this compound. When the foundations for the church were dug, thirty-five feet of accumulated debris had to be cleared to reach bedrock. While excavating, the builders uncovered part of an aqueduct, a vault, and other ancient ruins, causing delays. The first architect died of fever; masons had to be brought from Malta to teach local workers how to put up a large structure; a stone quarry had to be opened in Anatot to supply the white stone. The church was finally consecrated in 1849. It cost twenty thousand pounds to build.

While negotiations for construction were going on, King Friedrich Wilhelm IV of Prussia, who was hoping to recover Episcopal orders for Lutheran Germany, proposed a scheme whereby England and Prussia would alternately nominate an Anglican Bishop in Jerusalem. The offer was backed by a handsome sum of money, and for a while the joint venture worked. Michael Solomon Alexander became the first Anglican Bishop in Jerusalem. Born in Prussian Poland in 1799, he arrived in England in 1820 as a rabbi to a congregation in Plymouth, and was converted to Christianity in 1825. He arrived in Jaffa with his wife and six children aboard a Royal Navy frigate named *Devastation*. Earlier he had refused to travel on another vessel, *Infernal*, but as most Navy frigates bore militant names, and as the bishop was anxious to get to his new post, he decided to ignore the ship's name. He arrived in time to lay the first stone in the foundation of the church, but, alas, his premonitions turned out to have been well founded: he died before the church was completed and was buried on Mount Zion. The Turks, incidentally, never recognized him because they were apparently not consulted about his appointment. His successor was Bishop Gobat.

Relations between church and state soon began to deteriorate right in this compound. The British government was interested in extending its "protection"

to Jews in Jerusalem since, unlike the French or the
Russians, the British could not gain influence in the
country through long-established churches. The missionaries, on the other hand, were interested in converting the Jews, and they antagonized the Jewish
community. Moslems were prohibited by state law
from converting: thus the London Society for Promoting Christianity Amongst the Jews was formed in 1834.
It brought the first European-trained doctor to the city,
opened a clinic and a pharmacy, founded a workshop
to teach trades and crafts, and later operated schools
and orphanages. Great panic ensued, as Jews and
eventually other Christian sects worried that their coreligionists would use the services offered by the doctors
and teachers of the Protestant mission. Soon a Jewish
doctor arrived and a hospital for Jewish patients
opened. Because of the Protestant bishop, the Greek
Orthodox and the Latin patriarchs moved to Jerusalem. This competition created new building activity,
expansion, better health and education, which benefited the citizens of all religions. The missionaries were
not too successful in their efforts to convert the Jews.
When the expenses of the society were totaled later in
the century, it seemed that each "soul" saved had cost
about one thousand pounds. And of course, the con-
versions were often temporary.

The church is open to the public. It is simple, spare
Gothic inside. Originally there was no cross in sight so
as not to offend Jewish converts. Note the ceiling,
which is made of wood—unusual in Jerusalem. Outside, the stones from Anatot, cut under the supervision
of masons from Malta, have chisel marks different
from those usually seen in Jerusalem. As you face the
church, look to the left at one of the two first church
bells installed in Jerusalem in 1854. The other is in the
Church of the Holy Sepulchre. Since the days of Saladin, Christian bells had once more not been allowed
in the city, and it was only when the Turks became
indebted to the Western Powers for helping them in
the Crimean War that several restrictions were lifted,
among them the ban on bells.

One of the consuls who lived here was James Finn,
who, with his wife, Elizabeth, served from 1845 to
1862. Both wrote about life in Jerusalem, and left us
sensitive records of the period. In 1849 Finn became

Christ Church

president of the first Literary Society in Palestine, which, besides collecting some thousand volumes, used to meet weekly for lectures and discussions, and in effect was the forerunner of the Palestine Exploration Society. As you leave the compound, note the wall on the left where you see Christ Church written in yellow graphics on a bright blue board. The sign of the society used to be displayed here.

Turn left when you leave the courtyard, past the red mailbox on your left (a holdover from British Mandate days) that is built into the wall. The post office and Bank Leumi Le'Israel are in the small building that may have been the site of Bergheim's bank in the mid-nineteenth century. Later it was the location of the Anglo-Palestine Bank. In a tiny shop, perhaps 3 feet by 3 feet in size, an old lady sells cigarettes and matches. Next door you can find Bibles "in all languages."

Across the street, to the left of where the Citadel's moat ends, is the entrance to the Kishleh, or barracks, now the headquarters of the Old City police. Ask permission to enter the compound from the policeman at the gate. If he will not let you in, just look at the building from the outside. This 1838 building was the first major structure to be built in the city in almost three centuries. Ibrahim Pasha built it to house his troops, and he had to use forced labor to do the construction work. Since then it has been occupied by Ibrahim's Egyptian troops, followed by Turkish, British, and Jordanian soldiers, and now by Israeli policemen, most of whom in the Old City are Arabs. If you turn to face the large antenna by the entrance, on the left will be the stables of the mounted police. The rooms with the latticed windows were part of the Turkish prison. On the right were the winter barracks, now used as supply rooms. On the south end of the Kishleh, opposite the entrance, are the quarters of the police orchestra, where the former Turkish military band used to practice, as many nineteenth-century memoirs fondly recall. Westerners were less enthused about the Oriental "squeaks and shrieks, irrelevant beating of drums and cymbals" that passed for music in provincial Jerusalem. The playing was mostly by ear, as few of the "musicians" knew how to read notes. A Jewish friend of one Turkish conductor taught him the music for "Hatikvah," the song that was to become Israel's national anthem, and the band used to play it, though unwittingly—anything that smacked of nationalism was forbidden by the Ottoman rulers.

Behind the orchestra house, in the Armenian gardens, traces of the palace of King Herod the Great were discovered—only a few remains of a platform on which the building stood, so thorough was the destruction. No tongue could describe the magnificence of the palace, wrote Josephus, who witnessed its destruction in 70 A.D. He then proceeded to describe it in *The Jewish War*:

> There were ceilings remarkable for the length of the beams and the splendour of the ornamentation, and rooms without number, no two designed alike, and all luxuriously furnished, most of their contents being of gold and silver. . . . The open spaces between them were all green lawns, with coppices of different trees traversed by long walks, which were edged with deep canals and cisterns everywhere plentifully adorned with bronze statues through which the water poured out.

To this palace came the three Magi to inquire about the newborn King. Twelve centuries later the Crusaders built their palace in the same location, in the shadow of the Citadel.

Turn right when you leave the Kishleh. Note the lower corner of the wall of the Kishleh across from Select Restaurant, where some stones have been removed to widen the corner for vehicular traffic. Turn right onto Armenian Orthodox Patriarchate Road. It is a very narrow street, so be careful, especially in the late afternoon when Orthodox Jews in eighteenth-century garb sit behind the wheels of late twentieth-century cars, and race down this lane to pray at the Western Wall. In their fervent desire to serve the Lord, they pay little attention to minor obstacles such as pedestrians. On your right is the eastern wall of the Kishleh; on the left are residences of the Armenian Quarter, a walled city within a walled city. Walk past St. James Road, on the left, to which we shall soon return. Across from it, on the right, is a small shop with pistachio green shutters where bulgur, or cracked wheat, is sold. Behind this shop, the wheat lies in the sun and dries. Walk under the vault to where the road widens slightly. On the right is a restaurant, Ararat, done in bright red plastic. Straight ahead is another arch that spans the road with a small "building" on top of it, part of the residency of the Armenian Patriarch. Next to it is a very old pine tree on a small square. In the last century, this area used to be one of the few open and safe places within the Old City where people could take walks. A bench that stood here became a symbol of the "new" era among Jews, a place for *onkooken-ish*, or "looking over," in Yiddish. When the younger generation began to object to arranged marriages in which the couple often did not even see each other until the formal engagement, the following compromise was made: the young man would sit on the bench here, flanked by two male members of his family. As if by chance, the prospective bride would walk by, equally well chaperoned. Not a word was exchanged between the parties, but each side could exercise a veto without causing the other to lose face.

The Armenians claim to have first come to Jerusalem as soldiers who fought under Titus in 70 A.D. Christianity began to spread among the Armenians by the middle of the third century. In 303 A.D., King Tiridates was baptized by Gregory the Illuminator; the Armenian Church is also called the Gregorian Church. Not accepting the Holy Trinity doctrine, the Armenians separated from the main body of Christianity in 491 A.D. A Christian Armenian community was established in Jerusalem by the third, or early fourth, century. Today the Armenian Quarter contains a school, a seminary, a library, a museum, and the first printing press in the city, from 1833. Their collection of more than four thousand ancient manuscripts is world-famous, especially since many old documents were destroyed in Armenia itself.

If you have not been here before you may want to visit the Cathedral of St. James, which you enter on the left, immediately after the first vaulted part of the road. The sign over the door says Couvent Armenien St. Jacques. The church is open for services between 2:30 and 3:30 P.M. When you enter the hall, to the left of the fountain there is a guards' room where you can ask permission to see the courtyard when the church is closed. The fountain dates from 1901; it was built in honor of the twenty-fifth anniversary of Sultan Abdul Hamid. A small gate on the other side of the fountain leads to the courtyard in front of the church. Across from the gate, behind a latticed partition, there are two old clappers, one wooden and one made of iron, called *nakus* in Armenian. Since the days of Saladin the Armenians have used these clappers to call the faithful to prayer. The cathedral is a twelfth-century Crusader structure built over a Georgian church of 1050. It is the traditional site of the beheading of the Apostle St. James the Greater by order of Herod Agrippa I in 44 A.D. The head is believed to be entombed here, and under the altar St. James the Lesser is said to be buried. He was the cousin of Jesus, and the first Bishop of Jerusalem.

The church is shaped like a cross; inside, the dome sits on four central piers and arches and the interior is splendidly ornate. In addition to the throne of St. James the Lesser, gilded images of saints and kings are displayed. The tiles are glazed in blue and green, soft carpets cover the floors, mother-of-pearl and silver are embedded in the doors of the chapel on the left. Oil lamps cast shadows on the clergymen in their fine vestments. As they sing the liturgy, the aroma of burning incense spreads through the air.

When you leave, note the wall across the churchyard where there are stones decorated with different crosses, gifts brought by pilgrims. When you get back to the street, in a small alley past the second arch is the Edward and Helen Mardigian Museum—not part of this walk. The museum is housed in an 1843 building, the former Theological Seminary. It contains miters, vestments, staffs, books, and manuscripts, many of which were presented to the church by pilgrims. One is told that the most precious items are not on public display but are in the patriarchate.

Turn right to go back to St. James Road, across from the bulgur shop. Walk down St. James, and in the second house on the left there are two partially sealed arches, the remains of the Crusaders' Church of St. Thomas. An old church window can be seen around the corner, after the street veers to the left, and just beyond it is another window, behind metal bars and a screen. This was the location of a branch of the Austrian Post Office at the turn of the century. Once or twice a week, a boat would arrive in Jaffa carrying the mail from Austria. A carriage drawn by three horses would then bring it to Jerusalem, usually at daybreak. Here a line of hopeful persons would form to receive the mail: consulates and patriarchates would send their *kawwasses*, the Moslem "protectors" who were allowed to carry arms and were assigned by the Turks to the heads of the foreign delegations and religious sects; also in line were the representatives of various Jewish institutions hoping that financial help had arrived. There were some private citizens, too. After the more important clients were served, the clerk would call out the remaining names, such as "Rivkah the Midwife" or "David the Lame." Addresses given in those days were "below the Tower of David" or "within Jaffa Gate." As the city was small and people knew one another, most letters reached their addressees. In the stiff competition between the post offices of the different countries, special concessions were offered. One could buy stamps here on credit!

Turn left, then right with the road, which continues between two walls of Armenian compounds, and stop at the intersection where Ararat Road crosses St. James Road. Ararat is the name of the mountain where Noah's ark came to rest, a mountain holy to the Armenians. The peaked head cover of Armenian priests is said to be in the shape of the mountain.

Ararat Road formed the border between the Jewish and the Armenian quarters, and this intersection became crucial to the Jews in the War of Independence. The Jewish Quarter went on the alert on November 29, 1947, when the United Nations approved the partition plan that was reluctantly accepted by the Jews and rejected by the Arabs. The British, whose Mandate officially ended on May 15, 1948, made life difficult for the defenders of the Jewish Quarter by confiscating their arms. An old Arab flour mill stood where the grocery store is now, on your left, and two British soldiers used to sit here and observe the activities in the Jewish Quarter. Diagonally across from the mill was an Arab-owned house into which the British also moved, but on May 13, when the British were evacuating their troops from Palestine, the Jews claimed it. The lookout was called Emdat Cahanna after a rabbi who was living next door, and it remained in Jewish hands until the quarter—approximately 1,700 women, children, and old men, 185 wounded, and 35 soldiers—surrendered to the Jordanians on May 28, 1948.

On Ararat Road on the right you can see an old Armenian house and beyond it some new Jewish houses. About a third of the Jewish Quarter was destroyed after the 1948 war. Since 1967 reconstruction and restoration has been continuously changing the face of the quarter. Cross Ararat Street and continue down El Arman Road. The street sign is on the right and cannot be seen from St. James Street, but just follow the arrow for the Old Yishuv Court Museum. Enter no. 4, Maison des Arts, which offers tea, music, and Asian and African crafts and antiques, and is presided over by Mr. Yuri Miloslavsky, the spitting image of Sydney Greenstreet. He was born in Russia, grew up in France, and lived in Egypt for many years; thus he speaks half a dozen languages fluently, Hebrew not being one of them. Here you can rest, chat with a charming host, and perhaps succumb and buy a treasure off the wall. The house itself is worth seeing.

Old Yishuv Court Museum

Next door is the Old Yishuv Court Museum, which is well worth a visit. In the compound are two old synagogues: one is in the room where, according to tradition, Rabbi Yitzhak Ben Shlomo Lourie Ashkenazi was born in 1534. He was one of the early proponents of Mysticism, the Kabbalah. The other is Or Hahayim, named after a commentary on the Bible by Rabbi Haim Ben Attar, who came to Jerusalem from Morocco in 1724 and established a house of prayer on this street. In the courtyard and in the thick-walled rooms with their high-domed ceilings, the Weingarten family lived for five generations, and now Rivkah Weingarten, whose father was the head of the Jewish community until the surrender in 1948, is the founder and director of the museum. She came back in 1967 and began to collect personal items from families who had lived in the area in an attempt to reconstruct a picture of the old way of life. In the rooms and the yard, ordinary items are displayed: furniture, china, clothes, pots and pans, artisans' tools, and utensils that had belonged to the people who had inhabited the quarter for hundreds of years. The museum is small and compact and does not take long to visit.

Go back to the corner with the grocery store and take a right on Ararat. Here you see some typical, flat Old City rooftops enclosed by latticed banisters that are made of small sections of clay pipes. The banisters provide privacy for the occupants who use the rooftops as balconies; the open pipes let in the cool evening breezes. A contemporary touch is provided by solar energy panels. The barbed wire is a reminder of the 1948 battles.

In the second courtyard on the right Dr. Moshe Wallach lived for many years; he was a German Jew who worked in Bikur Cholim Hospital and later became the stern director of another hospital in the new part of the city, Sha'arei Tzedek. Dr. Wallach spoke only Hochdeutsche and needed several interpreters to deal with his patients, who spoke Yiddish, Ladino, or Arabic. A short-tempered pedantic man, he was known occasionally to slap a patient. He sounds like an ogre, but in fact he treated hundreds of patients free of charge and always offered compensation to those he had offended. (In 1934, if I may interject a personal note, he ushered me into the world.) When he moved out, Yehiel Amdorsky, an important man in the hotel industry, opened his first guest house here. The foundation for the business was laid by his mother, who lived around the corner across from the museum. She used to cook and sell cutlets in tomato sauce, and boiled calves' brains.

Continue down the wide stairs, lined with small gates of Armenian and Jewish courtyards. You are now descending "the brow of Zion"—a favorite phrase used by nineteenth-century writers, whose felicitous descriptions are often not very helpful when one tries to locate the site they're describing. After the second vault, where the stairs veer sharply to the right, note on the left the studio of Harout Haleblian, an Armenian who lives in the Armenian compound, where he was born in 1948. You can buy decorated tiles in almost every souvenir shop but few will match the quality of the ones made here. Traditional blues, greens, yellows, and browns are used to depict Biblical scenes or to create more modern intricate designs. This indigenous Armenian craft goes back to the third century.

With your back to the studio go down twenty stairs and on the right you will see the entrance to the Syrian Orthodox Convent and St. Mark's House. The Syrian Orthodox claim that the Last Supper was held here, not on the top of Mount Zion outside the present Wall as is more commonly believed. According to them, "the house of Mary the mother of John, whose surname was Mark" (Acts 12:12) stood on this site, and it was chosen by the Apostles to be the first church because both the Washing of the Feet and the Last Supper happened here. After the angel released St. Peter from prison, he came here, to the house of Mary. Peter knocked at the gate and joined the crowd of worshipers who were at prayer, and they marveled at his escape. The church, the Syrians say, was destroyed by Titus, then rebuilt and destroyed again by the Persian invasion in the seventh century. Like many other places in the city, it was restored and damaged several more times. The church bears the marks of Crusader architecture and stands on Byzantine foundations.

If the door to the church—elaborately decorated with crosses carved into the wood—is open, enter and look to the right where a sixth-century Aramaic inscription states that this is the house of Mary, proclaimed a church after the Ascension of Jesus, and rebuilt after Titus's destruction. Over the font in which Mary is supposed to have been baptized hangs a parchment painting of the Virgin and Child that is attributed to St. Luke but is probably Byzantine. The wood carvings are from the seventeenth century. Under the lectern are thrones and tombs of patriarchs and archbishops of this ancient community whose bishops have lived in this monastery since 1471. The sect is also known as the Jacobites, after their sixth-century leader. It is very small now. Only about fifty of their members live here, and they have lost most of their holdings in the city. They speak Aramaic and possess many ancient liturgical books in that language, the vernacular of the late Second Temple Period.

When the Dead Sea Scrolls were found in a cave in Qumran, they were taken to a man in Bethlehem who thought that they were written in Syriac and sent them here, in the spring of 1947. They were brought to the attention of Archbishop Athanasius Yeshue Samuel, who recognized the Hebrew script; after burning a tiny piece of the parchment, he realized the scrolls were very old and offered to buy them. The Bedouin who owned them came to Jerusalem a few days later to discuss the matter; but, unaware of what was happening, the priest who let them into the courtyard decided that both the scrolls and their bearers looked dirty and worthless and he sent them on their way, to the great distress of Samuel. How the scrolls were relocated and the grave doubts about their origin, all complicated by war, make for a fascinating and suspenseful story, and several books have been written on the subject, if you are interested. Today the scrolls are on display in the Shrine of the Book at the Israel Museum.

When you leave the monastery continue to walk on Ararat Road. Don't turn right at the bright yellow double-headed hydrant but walk instead up four broad stairs to the last gate on the left, no. 2, Ararat Road, and look into the courtyard if the gate is open. This was the location of the first hospital in the city, founded by the London Society for Promoting Christianity Amongst the Jews. As we mentioned before, most missionary activities met with little success. But the clinic, which was opened in 1838 by a medical missionary named Gertsmann, a "Christian Hebrew," drew many

Jewish patients. Because there were no other medical facilities available to them, these patients ignored the rabbis' threats of excommunication (*herem*). In 1842 Dr. A. MacGowan arrived and opened a twenty-bed hospital in this courtyard. "A suitable house was soon found and fitted up. It was opened on the 12th Dec. 1844, and it has ever since been fully occupied." So wrote William Bartlett in *Jerusalem Revisited* in 1853. A steel engraving by Bartlett depicts the archway, windows, and balcony that are still in the yard. As the missionary society was often called the London Jews' Society—a somewhat misleading title—Bartlett called his engraving *Jewish Hospital*. Over the years his sketch was copied frequently, and this site became confused with the "real" Jewish hospital around the corner, our next stop. There were three hospitals here, almost next to one another, all described as being located "on the brow of Zion." That phrase has been the source of much confusion.

Keeping the old hospital on your left, walk a few steps to the fork in the road where you see another yellow double hydrant and turn left. If you wish, walk to the end of the alley where a youth hostel is located, operated by the Jewish Heritage Center. This was the location of the Bikur Cholim Hospital that opened in 1857. (*Bikur cholim* means "visiting the sick" in Hebrew.) As the Jewish community became alarmed by the missionary medical activities, an appeal was sent to Sir Moses Montefiore; and in 1854 Dr. Simon Frankel, a Jew, arrived in the Holy City to dispense drugs and medical advice. In 1854 the Rothschild Hospital opened in the Jewish Quarter. The hospital here, almost on the border between the Armenian and Christian quarters, was a clear attempt to offset the influence and attraction of the missionary hospital around the corner. Bikur Cholim moved to the new city after World War I and this place became a home for people with incurable diseases. It was abandoned during the war of 1948.

Walk back down the wide stairs to the hydrant, turn left and go through the vault. You come out facing the German Lutheran Hostel and Guest House, as the large sign to the left of the door, behind a lattice, informs you. Note the other signs, all on glazed tiles. To the right of the door it says Guest House of the Propst, the "provost" of the German Protestants. Over the arch it says Watson House in Arabic. The cross belongs to the Order of the Knights of St. John, and the crowned lion stands for Britain. These signs tell the history of the house that was built by Dr. MacGowan and later, according to Wilson's 1866 map, was the "English Pharmacy." The pharmacy was operated by the London Society for Promoting Christianity Amongst the Jews. Sir Charles Watson worked here at the end of the nineteenth century. He was a Knight of Grace of the Order of the Hospital of St. John and he took part in the activities of the Palestine Exploration Fund. Later the house became property of the German Lutheran Church.

Stand with your back to the door of the German hostel and face the archway where Ararat Road begins; there is no street sign, only an arrow pointing to the Youth Hostel. If you look at the lower left side of the vaulted archway, just above the threshold, you can see a bench mark on the second stone, about twelve inches above the street pavement, that looks like a broad arrowhead: ⵣ. It was engraved in the stone in 1864 by the British Ordnance Survey Mission, which came to Jerusalem to explore the water supply system. A Miss Burdett Coutts made funds available for the survey in the hope of finding additional sources of water for the city. The population doubled between 1800 and 1860, bringing the number of people up to eighteen thousand, and the old cisterns could no longer supply enough water; fevers and plagues often broke out in autumn, before new rainfall refilled the cisterns. Charles Wilson led the mission. He was a Royal Engineer in the British Army, and his were the first scientific measurements ever taken in Jerusalem. (I am grateful to Dr. Zev Vilnay's four-volume work on Jerusalem for pointing out Wilson's bench mark, an interesting but almost obscure landmark.) On the right side of the archway there is a pillar embedded in the wall with a Corinthian capital next to it, under a window with a green grille. Because remnants of an ancient wall were found under this street, there are those who believe that the pillar may have been part of the Iron Gate mentioned in the New Testament.

With the archway on your right, and the German hostel on the left, walk down the street. At the bottom

of the stairs, across the alley and to the left of the Ha-
bad Road sign, you can see the remains of the top of
an arch buried beneath the street. Only the keystone
and a few other stones appear above ground level. In
Herod's time the city's First Wall stretched between the
Citadel and the western wall of the Temple. This has
led some people to speculate that the arch is part of
Gennath Gate, whose exact location is not known. Archaeological excavations are not possible in this
crowded, populated section of the city.

You will be turning left here to enter the geographi-
cal heart of the Old City, usually so full of people that
one can barely walk through it, let alone read a guidebook. You might take a minute at this quiet corner to
read the next few pages. We will be seeing a café built
over the crossroads of Roman Jerusalem, a Crusaders'
market, and the Three Covered Markets, also called the
Triple Bazaar.

After you turn left at the end of the steps, behind the
third door on the right, painted green and with no
sign, you will see el-Bashoura Café. It is filled with pin-
ball machines, pool tables, and the latest and loudest
hit tunes. The café is patronized by Arab teenagers, all
males. It is worth stopping in here for coffee or a cold
drink, despite the din. During the Crusader Period the
Latin Exchange was located in this building, which
stands at the crossroads of the main streets, the Qua-
drivium. It is built over the remains of the Roman Te-
trapylon, the four gateways where the Cardo (the
street running north-south) met the Decumanus (the
east-west axis). The four pillars supporting the vaults
in this café are most likely ones that lined the elegant
Cardo in the Roman or Byzantine eras.

Early in the twentieth century this café was fur-
nished with the traditional stools and low tables of
Arab coffeehouses. The music was Oriental, the pa-
trons, both Arabs and Jews, enjoyed a quiet board
game of *damkah* or *shesh-besh*, or relaxed while puff-
ing on a nargila. Leave the café through the same door
through which you entered it. Turn right, walk by
piles of straw baskets, and after two more wide stairs
you will reach the corner of David Street, or Suq el-Bazaar. Stop for a minute before you plunge into the bazaars; chances are that you will get lost but don't
worry about it. Enjoy the sights and the smells. But be-

Crusader market

fore turning left on Suq el-Bazaar, look to the right, all
the way down to the end of the street and pick some
landmark there because the walk will continue from
the end of Suq el-Bazaar after a tour of the markets.

Turn left now, on Suq el-Bazaar, or David Street,

and walk up past half a dozen shops. On the right you will see the Vegetable Market, which is in two parts inside enormous vaults. In the days of the Crusaders the poultry market was located here. When the British conquered Jerusalem in 1917 the place was filled with debris. It was cleared and since then the market has been alive with wheeling and dealing. The noise is deafening, and bargaining goes on in half a dozen languages. A tough old Arab woman who brought her grapes by bus from Hebron is shouting *la, la* at the Copt monk who is trying to purchase for a pittance some of the elongated pale green fruits of the vine for his brethren at the monastery. A Polish Jew in *kaftan* and side locks is telling a *falah* from Siloam that his tomatoes are no good and too expensive, but they both know that he will buy some in the end. A gaunt *tregger*, a carrier, with a pad on his head over which lies a rope that goes down to his back and shoulders, hauls a load of vegetables that is twice his size for a fat matron. The display is a feast for the eye: shiny black eggplants, red *baladi* tomatoes unmatched in flavor, large bunches of fresh dill and mint, tiny cucumbers that bear no resemblance in taste or appearance to their American relatives. Also on display are apples, pears, sugar cane, plums ranging from golden yellow to dark purple, and large sweet figs with the dew still on them. The colorful costumes of the buyers and sellers mingle with the fruits and vegetables to create a shimmering Oriental tapestry. Only here and there a somber note appears: the black robes of an Armenian priest, the drab khaki uniform of an Israeli soldier. When you leave note the magnificent spice shop across the street, Ramadan Toury & Sons.

The Three Covered Markets, also called the Triple Bazaar, begin down the street on the left. They run perpendicular to Suq el-Bazaar and parallel to one another. As you explore them, just remember to return to Suq el-Bazaar. Turn left when you leave the Vegetable Market. The first street, about 50 feet down and on the left, is called Suq el-Lahhamin, the "Butchers' Market." Here you are most likely to run into the hindquarter of a sheep, the carcass of a lamb dangling enticingly on a meat hook, brains, kidneys, intestines, or—if you prefer—a cow's head. There are also several old craftsmen on this street; the tinsmiths are fascinating to watch. In the Crusader era this was the herb and vegetable market where fresh food was sold.

The central bazaar is Suq el-Attarin, the "spice market." It was called *malquisinat* or "bad cookery" by the Crusaders, a comment on the quality of the meat that was roasted and sold to pilgrims here. This market was built by Queen Melisende in the middle of the twelfth century. The income from some of the shops went to the Church of St. Anne and the letters *SCA ANNA*, though difficult to locate behind the merchandise, still remain carved into several vaults. Other shops belonged to the Order of the Templars and bore the letter *T*.

The last and most easterly market, Suq el-Khawajat, also called the Street of the Goldsmiths, was the Covered Market of the Crusaders. Light enters the bazaar through square openings at the top of the vaults. Originally the street was even narrower; in front of each store was a stone bench about two feet high and three feet wide, on which the merchant sat and displayed his wares. By now the three markets have lost their distinct individual flavor, and a variety of goods can be found in each. In winter, the stone pavements are slippery; merchants burn wood in tin cans and huddle over them to keep warm.

If you have not gotten lost, you should now be where Suq el-Bazaar, or David Street, seems to end as it meets Suq el-Khawajat. With Suq el-Bazaar behind you, and el-Khawajat on your left, turn right, pass the W.C. Men, and note the tiny cigarette shop on the right. (We shall return to it shortly.) Turn right again among sheepskin coats and rugs to get a better look at the ancient vaulted crossroads where the Cardo and Decumanus met, in front of el-Bashoura Café. On the left the street is lined with cobblers. Return to the tiny cigarette shop and stand with your back to it. On the left is Suq el-Khawajat and on the right is the Jewish Quarter Road, Rehov Hayehudim in Hebrew. Straight across is Bab el-Silsileh Road—it means the Street of the Gate of the Chain—where the walk continues. As you enter the street there is a souvenir shop on the left, and a shop with sheepskin products on the right. Count six shops on the left, follow your nose, and turn left into the lane where the W.C. Ladies is located. Ignore the smells and the filth, and walk through the medieval, roofed passage, which is lined with balconies supported by broken corbels. A capital lies in the rubble, a reminder of a more gracious past. In the middle of the passage there is a tall gate through which camels laden with goods could enter the spacious inner courtyard of the *Wakala*, the urban caravanserai called Khan es-Sultan. (*Caravanserai* comes from the Persian, via French; *kāruān* means "caravan" and *sarāi* is a "palace" or "inn.") Once inside, the camels were tied up in the center of the yard, the goods were locked in the storerooms on the ground floor, and the merchants relaxed and spent the night on the second floor. The inn was built in 1386. The income from it was dedicated to the "Noble Sanctuary"—the Haram esh-Sharif, where the Dome of the Rock and el-Aqsa stand.

Return to the Street of the Gate of the Chain, which was named for the gate that leads into the Haram at the end of this road. The stench is soon replaced by the exotic smells of the spice shops: burlap bags filled with dried peppercorns from the Moluccas, cinnamon sticks from Chinese cassia trees, cardamom seeds from Ceylon. The precious yellow stigma of the *Crocus sativus*, also known as saffron, is kept in special glass jars. The aromas of the condiments and herbs conjure up images of camel caravans on the trade routes of central Asia, of sailing ships east of Java awaiting a favorable wind. Spices from distant lands have been used here since pre-Biblical days. Walk past El Hakkari Road, and another W.C. Men on the left, then through two more covered sections of the market, and you will pass Misgav Ladach Road on the right. Misgav Ladach was an old hospital that used to be in the Jewish Quarter. Street of the Chain is a continuation of David Street and is built along the line of the old Roman Decumanus, which began at Jaffa Gate. The Jewish Quarter lies south of it, the Moslem Quarter north.

On Street of the Chain are several important Mamluk buildings. The first is Tashtamuriyya, which begins just after you pass Misgav Ladach Road, on the right, and continues to the corner of Western Wall Road. Although the Mamluks enter Jerusalem's history only in 1260, the Mamluk Period (1187–1517 A.D.) is often used as the collective name of the era that began when Saladin defeated the Crusaders and ended with the Turkish conquest. The city changed hands several times in that period: the Crusaders were back for a decade, Tartars invaded during the thirteenth century. But it was the Mamluks who left a lasting imprint on Jerusalem. They repaired the waterworks, the Citadel,

Spice vendor

and the Haram esh-Sharif area. And they built charitable institutions, many of them *madrasas*, "religious schools," which turned Jerusalem into a center of learning. *Mamlūk* means "slave" or "captive" in Arabic, and the dynasty of sultans known as the Mamluks began when the bodyguard of Turkish slaves, formed by Saladin, usurped power in Egypt in 1250.

The fourteenth-century Mamluk buildings on this street have many architectural details in common. The entryway, as you can see in Tashtamuriyya, is the most outstanding feature of the façade: the vault of the door recess, often more than thirty feet above ground, is a stalactite-decorated niche. In this building the niche has been painted over. Interlocking voussoirs in different colors are also common to most Mamluk façades. Here, to the right of the door, many of the pink and gray stones are missing. Over the two windows on the right is an Arabic inscription, both decorative and informative. It tells that "this blessed place" was built by order of the "most honorable nobleman Saif ed-Din Tashtamur el-'Ala'i" in 1384. Tashtamur was the chief

secretary, or *dawādār*, of Sultan el-Malek el-Ashraf. He
served as viceroy of Egypt in 1370 and viceroy of Syria
in 1377. With a change in ruler—a frequent event under the Mamluks—he was exiled to Jerusalem. Like
many exiles, he built a building that has perpetuated
his name.

Inside the building, which is not open to the public,
is a large hall with a *mihrab*, a prayer niche, which indicates the *qiblah*. The *qiblah* is the compass point
that denotes the direction of Mecca, the holy city that
all Moslems face when they pray. In a smaller room on
the right of the entrance is the tomb of Ibrahim Tashtamur, the son of the viceroy. Note the second-story projecting window, built of stone over four corbels, and
the drinking fountain trough in the small half-shell to
the right of the doorway. This once-magnificent building is now very run down. Crudely installed electric
wires further mar the façade, as do the embroidered
dresses on display. Several families live in the house,
which belongs to the Imam family, who say they arrived here with Omar in the seventh century and were
members of the prominent Husseini family. Theirs is a
sad, typical story of a Palestinian family; their sons are
all studying and working in the Gulf countries now.
Mr. Imam works as a guide; he can be found near the
Church of the Holy Sepulchre.

Just past Tashtamuriyya on the right is an alley
called Aqbat Abu Madyan in Arabic, Rehov Hakotel in
Hebrew, Western Wall Road. It ends with a flight of
stairs that lead down to the Wall. You may wish to return here at the end of the walk. On the left across
from the alley is another Mamluk doorway with a stalactite-decorated half-dome. The lintel and the sides of
the iron gates are brightly painted, indicating that a
resident of the building has recently been on pilgrimage to Mecca. This is the Kilaniyya Mausoleum, built in
1352 and used for many years as a school. The Archaeological Islamic Department, which is part of the Waqf
Department in Jerusalem, has recently surveyed the
building as the first step in a plan to repair and restore
it, a most welcome development. Similar attempts are
being made in other historical Islamic buildings in the
city.

The two blocked windows to the right of the door
belong to Kilaniyya; the third window is in the façade

of another building, Tajjiyya. The inscription over this (third) window says: "In the name of Allah the Compassionate and the Merciful, this is the mausoleum of the servant yearning for Allah the Exalted, His Most Noble Excellency Saif ed-Din Taj who died—may Allah have mercy on him—in the year 763." Moslems use a lunar calendar and their year is shorter than ours. All Moslem dates are counted from 622 A.D., the date of the Hegira, the flight of Mohammed from Mecca. 763 was the year 1362 A.D. Taj el-Nāsiri held various offices under Mohammed ibn Qalāūn, including the governorship of Aleppo. On either side of the inscription is a goblet, the coat of arms of Taj, indicating that he was a court officer, a cupbearer. The use of blazons in Mamluk and Ayyubid societies was the privilege of the emirs, the military commanders.

Across Western Wall Road, beginning at the corner, is the house where members of the Khalidi family lived for many years. The Khalidis are said to have come to Jerusalem with the first Moslem conquerors in the seventh century. Since the days of Saladin various members of this illustrious family have held high positions under the different rulers of the city. This building contains a library that was assembled by Haj Ra'ab el-Khalidi and established in 1900. It contains many old Arab manuscripts. If you look through the window under the arch you can see part of the library. The Romanesque arch that has several fine moldings over it was probably the original entry to the large room where the library is currently located.

The building has undergone many changes. If you look to the left, above the large window with the grille, and at the door with the sign Khalidi Library, you can see the outlines of two large relieving arches. The door is a bit off-center, within the left arch, and the space between it and the arch is filled with a different type of stone. The small niche to the right of the door, behind a newly installed grille, is a drinking trough. At the roofline above the door four stone corbels can be seen, meant to support a projecting window, as in Tashtamuriyya.

The large window with the grille opens onto a courtyard in which three gravestones can be seen. The two inscriptions over the window tell us about the origins of the building. Over the window's lintel is a row of tricolored interlocking voussoirs. In the center, now hardly visible, is the word *Allah*. Above the voussoirs is an inscription in memory of Hasam ed-Din Barakat Khan, who died in 1246 and was buried here. Barakat Khan was a Tartar ruler of a Crimean kingdom whose daughter married Sultan Rukn ed-Din Baybars I. Another two-line inscription just above the grille is from 1390. It lists the repairs and additions to this building: a new portal, the trough, the window, and some shops that may have been located in the courtyard. On both sides of the inscription are circles with a U shape in the center, and a tear inside the U. This was the emblem of Mohammed ibn Ahmad, who was responsible for the repairs. The Khalidi Library is called el-Maktaba el-Khalidiyya in Arabic, and the building is also known as Turbat Barakat Khan, the Tomb of Barakat Khan.

On the other side of the street, past Antiquities Jericho, Jerusalem Laundry, and a small gate decorated in blue, there is a large window with iron bars and a latticed wooden screen. The language of the inscription above the window is most elegant: "In the name of Allah the Merciful, this is the mausoleum of the most magnificent and great emir, the vanquisher, the defender of the faith, the warrior at the frontiers in the path of Allah the Exalted, Rukn ed-Din Baybars el-Jaliq es-Salihi. Passed into the mercy of Allah the Exalted the 10th of Jumada I of the year 707. May Allah forgive him and who so ever asks mercy for him." El-Jaliq, whose name means "strong and frolicsome horse," died on November 7, 1307. His blazon was a fleur-de-lys with double leaves, which you can see at the upper corners of the inscription. In his younger days he was the *jamdar*, master of the robes, under el-Malek es-Salih Ayyub. Under the Turks, the chief secretary of the city lived here, the *Bash Katab*. Most of the information about the inscriptions and blazons comes from two works: Max van Berchem, *Matériaux pour un Corpus Inscriptionum Arabicarum* (Jerusalem, 1923) and L. A. Mayer, *Saracenic Heraldry* (Oxford, 1933).

On the upper left side of the arched entrance to El-Wad Road, just above the street sign, is another inscription, partially erased. It was installed in 1469 by Mohammed Nashashibi in honor of Sultan Ashraf abu el-Nāsir Kait Bey, who brought water to Jerusalem. He became sultan in 1468, after a palace revolution, and spent much of his time struggling to protect his lands from the clutches of the expanding Ottoman Empire.

The valley, *el-wad* in Arabic, runs from Damascus Gate south to the Dung Gate and beyond. Known by its Greek name, the Tyropoeon, the valley was much deeper before it became partially filled with rubble, and it separated the Upper City from the Temple Mount. A causeway was built across the valley to facilitate entering the Temple courts directly from the Upper City. Josephus describes the causeway over whose remains this street is built. Some of the supportive arches of the causeway can still be seen (Wilson's Arch, page 239). On the other side of the entrance to El-Wad Road there is a strange-looking façade that may have been part of a water fountain.

About halfway down the vaulted part of Bab el-Silsileh Road on the right is a small doorway with a Star of David on the grille in the arch, and two stone benches in front. The southern exposure of this house overlooks the Western Wall plaza. It was purchased in 1926 by an American Jew, Nathan Straus, in the hope that a direct passage could be made from here to the Wall enabling Jews to approach it without having to pass the houses of the Mugrabi Quarter, where they were often abused. The shortcut did not come to pass, but for many years this place served as a soup kitchen for poor Jews.

Just as you emerge from under the first vault, on the left, is the beautifully decorated façade of Turbat Turkan Khatun. *Turba* means "tomb" in Arabic, *khatun* is "lady" or "princess." Turkan was the daughter of an emir from Uzbak who died in 1353. The decorations carved in the stone above the two windows blend in well with Arabic script on the pillar that separates the windows. Islam, like Judaism, forbids the creation of "graven images"; there are few human figures reproduced in Islamic art. Oft-repeated geometric figures or interlaced patterns of flowers and leaves are frequently used in decorating, and this wall is a fine example of those intricate ornamentations that gave birth to the term *arabesque*.

After you pass through another vault, the street ends in a small square in front of the gate to the Haram. The water fountain, *sabil*, across from the gate, consists of remains in secondary use: the basin is a fourth-century sarcophagus; the flowerlike pattern under the arch is a Crusader rose window. These relics fit in well with the inscription, which recounts that the fountain was built by Suleiman the Magnificent, "our Master, the Mighty King, the Exalted Ruler, King of the Nations, Sultan of the Turks, Arabs, and Persians, the Strength of Islam, the Defender of the Shrines . . ." The fountain stands in front of the lateral façade of another Mamluk building, Sa'adiyya, named after Emir Sa'ad ed-Din, who is buried in it. The building with the camera shop that encloses the square on its northern side is Baladiyya. Built in 1382 and used as a *madrasa*, it contains the tomb of Mankligugha, the Chief of Police under Sultan Shaikh.

A gate to the Temple Mount stood here at the end of the causeway. The early Moslems believed that the vaults that supported the causeway were a secret passage through which King David used to come to the Temple from the Citadel, where he presumably lived, and called the gate Bab Daud. In 1047 a traveler, Nāsir-i-Khusrau, described it as "a beautiful gateway . . . two wings . . . adorned with coloured mosaics . . . cut into patterns so beautiful that the eye becomes dazzled in contemplating them." That magnificent gate was destroyed, almost certainly by the Crusaders. The present gate was built in 1492 and it has twin, twisted columns on either side that are probably Crusader in origin. It is the only double gateway to the Haram esh-Sharif. The gate, now called Bab el-Silsileh, may be named after a dome in the Haram, Qubbet es-Silsileh, where, according to Moslem tradition, in the days of Solomon, a chain reached down from heaven. Another fable tells of an Austrian king who was hanged from a chain here. At times half the gate was called Bab es-Salam, "Gate of Peace"; another name was Bab es-Sakinah, from the Hebrew *Shechinah*, "Divine Presence," which has hovered over the Western Wall since the Temple was destroyed.

The most important building on the street is Tankiziyya, on the left when you stand with your back to the gate. It was built in 1328 by Saif ed-Din Tankiz who, in the service of Mohammed ibn Qalāun, became governor of Damascus in 1312. After a change in government he was arrested in 1340 and he died in

צבא הגנה לישראל

מצפה הכותל

Fourteenth-century Mamluk doorway

prison shortly thereafter. The two stone benches in front of the doorway are typical of Mamluk portals. The vault is an elongated half-shell formed by three layers of stones carved like stalactites. The rows of black and white joggling ashlars here are a crude twentieth-century replacement. The long inscription, situated between two rows of ashlars, has goblets in the middle, the coat of arms of Tankiz. The inscription reads: "Founded this blessed building in the hope of Allah's reward and forgiveness, His Honorable Excellency Saif ed-Din Tankiz, Officer of el-Malek el-Nāsir [same as Mohammed ibn Qalāūn] may Allah forgive him and give him a reward. The year 729 [1329 A.D.]." The latest addition to the portal is a Hebrew sign: Israel Defense Forces. Western Wall Observation Point.

The building's history is a microcosm of the city's history. The Herodian foundations can be seen today next to the Western Wall, at Wilson's Arch. According to Jewish tradition, late in the Second Temple Period the Chamber of the Hewn Stone stood here, the original seat of the Supreme Council, the Sanhedrin. Tankiz made use of the existing foundations when he built the *madrasa*, the religious school that was famous for its scholars. Later it became the seat of the Moslem Court of Law, the Mahkama Shar'iyya, which remained here until the end of the Ottoman Period. In the 1830s Ibrahim Pasha made some changes in the building, and during the British Mandate the Mufti Haj Amin el-Husseini lived here for a while. The highest religious leader of all the Moslems in Palestine, he was responsible for instigating many of the riots against the Jews in the 1920s and 1930s. When Jordan ruled the city, the Moslem Committee for Jersualem sat here. The building was empty in 1967, but, fearing that the Jews would occupy it, the Arabs moved a high school in here. The Jews took over the building anyway, claiming that this strategic location had to be in Israeli hands to ensure the safety of those who prayed at the Western Wall, which Tankiziyya adjoins.

The guided part of the walk ends here, and now you have several choices. If you wish to return to the Citadel, walk back along Bab el-Silsileh Road, turn right where it seems to end at the tiny cigarette shop, then turn left immediately onto Suq el-Bazaar, which will take you to Jaffa Gate and the Citadel. Another exit to the nearest bus stop is through the Dung Gate. To get there, start to walk on Bab el-Silsileh Road and take the first left, just past the Khalidi Library, down the steps of Western Wall Road. You will pass an inspection post; then, with the Western Wall on your left, continue through the plaza to another inspection point from which you will see the Dung Gate straight ahead. Bus no. 1 stops outside the Wall on the right. (Walk 6 begins there.)

If you have not yet visited the Haram esh-Sharif, you can walk in through Bab el-Silsileh. Beyond it lies one of the most magnificent buildings anywhere, the Dome of the Rock, which, together with el-Aqsa, merits a visit. Non-Moslems cannot enter the area on Fridays. (Ancient Jewish law forbade taking a shortcut here or entering the area carrying a staff or with dust on one's feet.)

The enclosure on top of the Temple Mount where the First and Second Temples once stood is called the Noble Sanctuary by the Arabs. After the Bar Kochba revolt in the second century A.D. the Romans built a pagan temple to Jupiter here. In the Byzantine Period the area lay in ruins, because Christians believed it to be cursed. According to later traditions, when Omar came to Jerusalem around 638 A.D. he found the site filled with garbage. Omar had the area cleaned, then a temporary, "rudely constructed" place for prayer was built near the southern edge of the enclosure.

In 691 the Dome of the Rock was completed, a perfectly balanced marble octagon covered with glazed blue tiles and crowned by a golden dome. It is built over the rock that the Jews believe to be the Foundation Stone, where according to tradition Abraham brought Isaac to be sacrificed. The Arabic name for the shrine is Qubbet es-Sakhra, "Dome of the Rock." It is often mistakenly called the Mosque of Omar.

The mosque of el-Aqsa, unlike the Dome of the Rock, has undergone many changes and repairs since it was built in 715, as it has been damaged several times, mostly by earthquakes. The name comes from the Koran (sura 17, verse 1), which describes the Night Journey of the Prophet Mohammed from Mecca to the "distant shrine" or "outer edge" where he as-

Dome of the Rock

cended to the Seven Heavens. Moslems believe that Mohammed departed for Heaven from the Temple Mount, although the Koran does not identify either the Mount or Jerusalem by name.

West of el-Aqsa, to the right, where you see ancient
capitals strewn around the courtyard, is a gate through
which you can leave the area. Turn left at the bottom
of the ramp. Bus no. 1 stops outside the Dung Gate.

Walk

3

Around the Russian Compound

●

Jerusalem is one of the few places of which the
first impression is not the best.
Arthur Penrhyn Stanley,
Dean of Westminster 1853

> In the spacious area in front of the Russian Hospice,
> which since time immemorial has sheltered camels, don-
> keys, garbage, and dung, we now have a lovely garden.
> Its gates are open to all and twice a week the Turkish mili-
> tary band plays here, to the delight of those who come to
> repose in the garden after the day's labor is done.

So wrote Avraham Moshe Luntz, the blind Jewish
historian and publicist, in 1891 when the small garden,
now called Gan Daniel Auster, first opened. It was a
revolutionary concept then, a planned public garden
with an open-air café amidst flowers and shrubs. The
Arabs called it *baladiyya*, here meaning the "municipality's garden," and it came into being in the days of
Mayor Salim Husseini, under whose reign the streets in
the Old City were paved with cobblestones, and street
lanterns, night watchmen, and sweepers were intro-
duced to Jerusalem. Daniel Auster, for whom the garden is now named, was the first Jewish mayor of
Jerusalem after the city was divided by war, in 1948.
Under Ottoman and British rule the mayor was always
Moslem, even after 1870, when the Jews became the
majority in the city.

When you face the eight steps that lead up to the
garden, the sign under the stone lamp post will be on
your right; it says Gan Auster in Hebrew. As you walk
up the stairs you see, also on the right, a chart with
population statistics. Straight ahead is a mosaic map of
the city; on the far left is the southern wall of the Russian Compound, built in the early 1860s. Turn around
and look at the section of Jaffa Road in front of the garden, the main commercial artery of the city at the end
of the nineteenth century. Although the sidewalks
were already built in 1886, the road itself was not
properly paved until 1898, and water had to be sprinkled over its surface several times a day to keep down
the dust. The two long blocks of buildings on the other side of the street were built by the Armenian Church

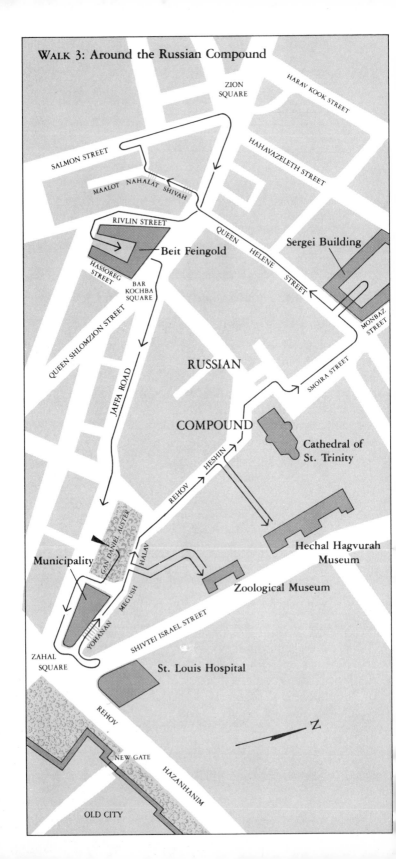

WALK 3: Around the Russian Compound

ZION SQUARE

HARAV KOOK STREET

SALMON STREET

HAHAVAZELETH STREET

MAALOT NAHALAT SHIVAH

RIVLIN STREET

QUEEN HELENE STREET

Sergei Building

Beit Feingold

HASSOREG STREET

BAR KOCHBA SQUARE

MONBAZ STREET

QUEEN SHLOMZION STREET

JAFFA ROAD

RUSSIAN

SMOIRA STREET

COMPOUND

Cathedral of St. Trinity

REHOV HESHIN

GAN DANIEL AUSTER

Hechal Hagvurah Museum

Municipality

HALAV

Zoological Museum

MEGUSH

SHIVTEI ISRAEL STREET

YOHANAN

ZAHAL SQUARE

St. Louis Hospital

Z

REHOV

NEW GATE

HAZANHANIM

OLD CITY

between 1895 and 1899. To this day, over the doorways, you can see the emblem of the church, which looks like a U with a backward, open-ended B in it. On street level, the shops were elegant and spacious; on the floors above, offices and apartments were rented to generate income for the church. At no. 19, on the right, you will find the administrative offices of the Courts of Justice. At the turn of the century the Greek Consulate was located on the second story. On ground level was the Russian Post Office, in the days when many countries did not rely on the Turkish mail and operated their own services. The building is nicely balanced: the projecting frontispiece has three sets of arched doors on each floor. Both this building and no. 17 have recently been cleaned of the accumulated soot that traffic and air pollution have produced, and the Jerusalem stone has been restored to its original beauty.

No. 17, Jaffa Road, on the left, the older of the two buildings, is slightly more modest. Before World War I the Hughes Hotel, owned by a German of that name, was located in the building. After the war the offices of the Zionist Commission to Palestine were here until they moved to Rehavia, where the Jewish Agency is still located. A most elegant store of made-to-order shoes, Gabardian, was in this building until the 1940s. Today we find the Hachoma Press at no. 17 as well as the Bible Society, a drafting and art supplies shop, and a good Moroccan restaurant, Au Sahara.

Turn left while still in the garden, and walk down four steps. (The buildings in back of the garden will be discussed later in the walk.) Cross the street to the white building with the bronze menorah on top and the Lion of Judea over the portal. It's no. 22, Jaffa Road, the Municipality, where the famed Mayor Teddy Kollek spends much of his time. The sign to the right of the entrance provides us with a lot of information about the building, which was designed by the British architect A. Clifford Holliday. The cornerstone was laid in 1930 during the administration of Mayor Ragheb Bey el-Nashashibi. When the doors are closed you can see the eight gates of the Old City sculpted in bronze. Note the Municipality of Jerusalem plaques in Arabic and English on the left, and in Hebrew and French on the right. The Lion of Judea is the emblem of the city.

You are actually looking at the back of a very important public building. Walk to the right of the Municipality entry and turn left along Jaffa Road to get the full impact of the building, which stands by the northwestern corner of the Old City like a bridge leading to the new Jerusalem. The strong arched convex of the double-story façade gives a prominent edge to the street. The style is "Mandatory Modern" with an Eastern gloss. Well integrated with the design of the window bars are the letters *BB,* for Barclays Bank, which used to be here. To the right of the large door, on the wall between the second and third windows of the ground floor and on the tenth ashlar above the pavement, there is a bench mark, ⊼, identical to the ones left by Charles Wilson of the British Ordnance Survey Mission in 1864 (page 92). Perhaps it replaces an older bench mark that was carved in the rocks before this building went up. The walls are full of bullet holes, a reminder of the fierce battles fought here in 1948.

You are now on Zahal Square, one of the busiest intersections in the city, where fumes from buses and diesel trucks hasten to turn black the Jerusalem-stone houses. If you sit on a bench in the minigarden with your back to the Municipality building, across the street, east of Jaffa Road, you see the Old City Wall behind the grassy embankment bedecked with palm trees. The Wall is overshadowed by the French Christian Brothers College and the bell tower of the Franciscans. At the northwestern corner of the Wall, there used to be a Crusader tower over which the present Ottoman Wall was built in the late 1530s. This corner, explored by archaeologists Dan Bahat and Menashe Ben Ari in the early 1970s, is called Goliath's Castle, perhaps because of its proximity to David's Citadel. It is also known as Tancred's Tower, after the Crusader who breached the Wall here in 1099.

Between this intersection and Jaffa Gate, both sides of Jaffa Road were lined with elegant shops, hotels, cafés, and banks at the end of the nineteenth century. The area began to decline after the riots of the 1930s; most Jewish shopkeepers left. This whole neighborhood suffered great destruction in the war of 1948 and the precarious ruins were razed in 1967. There are now plans for an underground traffic thruway that will bypass Jaffa Gate, as well as plans to redevelop the Ma-

milla district west of Jaffa Road, to your right. Controversy has surrounded this massive project, which was
designed by Moshe Safdie.

A crucial battle was fought at this important junction
on May 8, 1948, when the tanks of the Arab Legion,
which were advancing from Damascus Gate, were
halted here. After the cease-fire the border line between the two halves of the divided city split this
square. Arab snipers, sitting on the battlement, were
too close for comfort, so the Israelis erected a tall concrete wall on their half of the square. The wall was removed in 1967 when the city was reunited. The street
on the left, which runs parallel to the northern section
of the Old City Wall and meets Jaffa Road at this junction, was called Suleiman Street. After 1967 a sugges-
tion was made to change it to Rehov Hazanhanim,
"Street of the Paratroopers," after Parachute Brigade
55, which played a vital role in the Six Day War. Not-
ing that Suleiman the Magnificent also did his share for
Jerusalem (rebuilding the City's Wall, for instance), a
compromise was reached: the road is called Suleiman
Street from the northeastern corner of the Wall to Damascus Gate, and from there it continues to this
corner as Rehov Hazanhanim. To complicate matters,
the street's name changes again beyond this intersection; the road goes downhill bearing the name Rehov
Hamelech Shlomo, after King Solomon.

The square itself was renamed Zahal Square in 1948,
for the Israel Defense Forces. Until then it was called
Allenby Square in honor of the British general who
had "rescued the Holy City from the Mohomotan [*sic*]
yoke" in 1917. Some Arabs claimed then that from the
moment Allenby entered the battle they knew he
would conquer Jerusalem, for his name, el-Nabi,
means "the Prophet."

Turn your back to the Old City Wall. To the right of
the Municipality is the Marcus Birunfeld Bakery. The
sign is in Hebrew only but samples of the hard version
of local bagels hang outside the door, making the written word superfluous. The two-story building is very
old; traditional twin-arched windows can be seen to
the left of the bakery's door. Inside, the owner will be
only too happy to tell you his stories of the last three
decades in this location. When you leave walk a few

steps to the corner of the street called Shivtei Israel, the "Tribes of Israel." On the other side of the street— not part of this walk—is the enormous complex of St. Louis Hospital, built in 1887, with the hospice of Notre Dame de France just behind it. While building, the French made sure that the head of the Madonna's stat- ue atop Notre Dame (not seen from here) was taller than the domes of the Russian Cathedral nearby. The two buildings are a fine example of the French neo- classical style, transcribed to the Orient. Note the great articulations at the corners and the ornate, paired col- umns, all in marked contrast to the humble building on our side of the street. Soon after these buildings were completed, the New Gate was opened in the Wall to allow for a more convenient approach to the Holy Places.

Turn left at the corner and walk up the ten steps of no. 1, Shivtei Israel Street, into the courtyard of one of the oldest buildings in the city outside the Wall. Part of it appears on Wilson's 1864 map, and an 1876 revised edition of the map shows a large building here with an inner courtyard. By 1881 a Hotel Feil was here, prob- ably the first hotel outside the Old City, according to Professor Yehoshua Ben-Arieh. Today the yard and the building are terribly decrepit. They smell of old dirt; paint and plaster are falling off the stone walls. But the staircase is still picturesque, and the exterior of the building is a fine example of mid-nineteenth-century Jerusalem vernacular.

Turn right when you leave and immediately right again at the corner, and walk past the bagel bakery to the end of the old building. On the right is a short flight of stairs alongside the narrow alley. Walk up the ten steps to a group of arcaded shops, defined by large white stone quoins that stand out against the rusticat- ed reddish stones. Several old workshops are still func- tioning here including a bindery and a curtain maker. The printer's shop marks the beginning of the oldest part of the building.

Continue to walk along the lane, which widens as it passes behind Gan Auster. It is called Yohanan Me- gush Halav after a Galilean leader of the Jewish rebel- lion against Rome, a revolt that ended in destruction in 70 A.D. Under the British Mandate another hero lent his name to this lane, Tancred the Crusader.

No. 9, Yohanan Megush Halav is now occupied by the Zoology Department of Hebrew University, as are the rest of the buildings along this short street. No. 9 is known as Connaught House, after the Duke who became governor-general of Canada, and was designed by Holliday in 1926. The foundation stone was laid by High Commissioner Field Marshal Lord Plumer. The building was the headquarters of the British and Foreign Bible Society, and, as the plaque to the left of the door indicates, it was dedicated "to the Glory of God and in the Faith of Jesus Christ." Holliday tried to incorporate local vocabulary into his designs, like the pierced triangles that you can see just below the roofline above the large arched door. In the Old City, where the roof of one house often serves as the balcony of another, the holes provide ventilation without compromising privacy. An ugly asbestos shed, a later addition to the roof, fortunately cannot be seen from this angle.

No. 7 was built in the late 1860s or early 1870s, and it was one of the most elegant private residences in the city. It had seven bedrooms, several living rooms, a stable, and a shop that must have been where the large window on the left is now, under the arch with the air conditioner. A red-tiled addition, which you have to step far back to see, may have served as an attic or a laundry room. The three balconies on the fine façade still bear the original grillwork; only the ground-level windows have bars across them. The traditional small stone benches on either side of the front stairs are purely decorative here, too far above the ground to be functional. The land on which the house stood reached down to Jaffa Road. The owner of this establishment was Melville Peter Bergheim, a German Jew who converted and came to Jerusalem in the 1830s with the London Society for Promoting Christianity Amongst the Jews. He soon forsook his missionary work and by 1858 was listed in Murray's guidebook as one of the city's first bankers. Among other things he owned a shop in the Christian Quarter that sold photographs, wine, and spirits; an early windmill where flour was ground; and a lot of land, including the site of the Biblical town of Gezer. Bergheim was also an excellent photographer in the early days of the medium, and some of the finest images of the city and especially of the Western Wall were captured by him in the 1860s.

There were several Bergheim children. One daughter married the German consul, von Tischendorf. Three sons, Sam, Christopher, and Timothy, helped run the business. Troubles began in the 1880s. The bank lost money; Sam was murdered in 1885 by some *falaheen* on his way to Gezer; and a few years later both the father and Christopher died. The business went bankrupt and the property was divided among the bank's creditors. The land between the house and Jaffa Road was taken over by the Municipality for the park. Marquis de Bute, a Scotsman, became the owner of the house. Later, during the British Mandate, part of Government Hospital was located in the building.

Try to enter this complex of zoological buildings at no. 5 (the two small green discs, no. 44 and no. 46, are a British heritage). If the guard stops you—and he will if you look like you don't belong here—say that you want to see the Zoological Museum. If this doesn't help, find a place nearby and read the next few pages. Don't be too disappointed because you will see other former Russian buildings along this walk which are open to the public.

Inside no. 5, the inner courtyard is filled with shacks. Turn left, then right under the asbestos-covered walkway with the purple posts, and left again through a building that used to be the French Consulate. Follow the Zoological Museum sign, which sits amidst a multitude of other signs indicating many scientific activities. Turn left and cross a small alley that is blocked off by a gate on the left, and go into the empty stone guardroom built into the wall of the Russian Compound. When you emerge from this maze of interior corridors, go around the shack in front of you and across one more alley and you will find yourself inside the neglected garden of the old Russian Consulate. On the right is a mess of structures, temporary and permanent, stucco, aluminum, stone, and iron. In back of the more damaged marble bench is a strange-looking fountain through which water used to flow into a small pond. Judging by the remains of the well-laid flower beds, this must have been a beautiful garden.

Although the first Russian consul came to Jerusalem

in 1858, the consulate was completed only in 1864. Walk down to the bottom of the garden to look at the former consulate, barely visible for the trees. At the end of the path there is a door with a brown shutter and a small Zoological Museum sign. Above it, close to roofline and slightly to the right, there is a stone circle with a crown over it and the letters **HII** inside it. The Cyrillic **H** is like the English *N*; this stands for Nicholas II, the last Tsar of All the Russias. As he came to power in 1896, we may assume that the second story was added on after that year. Above the **HII** there is a large metal loop on the roof that used to hold the consular flagpole. There are old photographs of various dignitaries inside the consulate, men with large mustaches and small goatees, their chests covered with decorations; ladies in gowns and upswept hair, wearing long chains with crosses. The walls were draped with brocade, the floors were hidden under Oriental rugs. Little remains of that elegant era: the building is now subdivided into cubicles and only here and there a few marble tiles survive. Some pickled fish and a turtle mounted on a wall are the only evidence that this is a Zoological Museum—most samples are behind locked doors.

You are now looking at the rear of the building. Walk to the right, then go around to the front of the building, today an amalgamation of electric circuitry, pipes, and makeshift and unsightly additions. The once-elegant pointed-arch entry, flanked by stone buttresses, is now partially blocked by a tin shed, a toilet. Above it is another stone circle, with an **H** for Nicholas. Two orange trees still flourish in the garden.

The history of the Russian Compound begins in the next paragraph. You might wish to sit on one of the marble benches in the neglected garden, which is still a peaceful oasis, and read there. In case of inclement weather, turn to page 125, where this walk continues, and find shelter in Hechal Hagvurah, or you may save this historical description to read at home.

Pilgrims have been "going up" to Jerusalem for the last three millennia. Since the days of Solomon's Temple, three times a year Jews from all over the country came to offer sacrifices to God. After the destruction of the Second Temple in 70 A.D., the Jews, though no longer dancing or playing the lute, still arrived in Jerusalem to pray for the coming of the Messiah. Since the first century A.D. the city has also been holy to Christianity. After Queen Helena of Byzantine visited the city in the first half of the fourth century the Church of the Holy Sepulchre and many other churches were built on sites traditionally associated with the events of the New Testament; increasing numbers of Christians from all over the world came on pilgrimages to Jerusalem. In the seventh century, after the Moslem conquest, the Omayyad caliphs tried to turn the city into a center of worship for political reasons: they wanted to divert their subjects from going to Mecca and Medina. Jerusalem never replaced the other two cities, but over the years, and especially after Saladin's victory over the Crusaders, many Moslems tried to stop in Jerusalem on their way to or from Mecca.

By the beginning of the nineteenth century, about one to three thousand Christian pilgrims were arriving in the city every year, mostly Armenians and Greek Orthodox. As steam power replaced the sail and travel on the high seas became safer, the number of pilgrims increased. By mid-century some five to ten thousand were coming, almost doubling the Christian population of the city. The numbers fluctuated, reflecting rumors of war, actual fighting, and recurring epidemic outbreaks en route to or in the Holy Land.

Among the Russians, one of the earliest well-known pilgrims was Abbot Daniel, who, in 1106 A.D., walked all the way from Kiev to Jerusalem carrying a large silver lamp for the Church of the Holy Sepulchre. Eight centuries later, in 1911, the pilgrimage was made by a somewhat less savory religious figure and one of the last Russian pilgrims, the infamous Rasputin. Most of the Russian pilgrims were simple peasants whose devotion and piety left a deep impression on those who saw them. From the shores of the Baltic, from Siberia, from the banks of the Danube and the Dnieper they came, leaning on their wooden staffs; most traveled by boat from Odessa to Jaffa. They were very poor and they carried their food supplies with them, rusks and dried meat. Often a whole village collected money to send one old man or woman to the Holy Land. They would arrive before winter made travel on the Mediterranean even more hazardous, celebrate Christmas in Bethlehem, then stay in Jerusalem until after Easter. On their route they kissed every holy site. They wore heavy boots, fur hats and coats, and warm undergarments, which they neither took off nor changed, even in the warm spring. They bought many objects to bring back, often to sell, to their villages: little cakes with the image of the Savior stamped on them, thorn crowns and palm branches, candles, and skullcaps for the dead. As they had little money to spend they were hard bargainers. A new phrase was coined in the city: "stingy as a *bogomolka*"—a Russian woman pilgrim.

The lot of the pilgrims was not an easy one. After all the perils of the journey by sea they had to navigate the narrow, almost nonexistent, road to Jerusalem, on foot or on the back of a donkey, a mule, or a horse. Only briefly were they well treated, when their feet were washed upon their arrival at the hospice or monastery where they stayed. A highly symbolic gesture, and of course, most practical. Next they were urged to make a list of all their relatives, dead, or alive, so that the proper prayers could be said for the well-being of the living or for the souls of the departed. The fee was exorbitant, regardless of the state of the body. Poor people were relegated to distant monasteries where they were charged little for their stay, but were expected to "volunteer" to sweep, clean, and mend clothes. As their stay coincided with Lent, it did not cost much to feed them. On the Thursday before Easter their feet were washed again.

For centuries the Russians stayed in Greek Orthodox hospices, but as their numbers increased, especially after the Crimean War ended in 1856, many complained about the poor facilities and the lack of protection. Although free education had been offered in Jerusalem by the Russian Imperial Palestine Society since 1837, and a Russian Archimandrite was sent to the city in 1844, there was no consul, no official representative of the government. Lengthy negotiations began because the tsar was interested in increasing his influence in the area. Thirty-two acres of choice real estate—the compound we are about to see—were then acquired by the Russians after the Crimean War. They paid for most of the land; the sultan made a gift to the tsar of one part. Construction began in 1860. It is hard to imagine today that, except for the compound on Mount Zion, there were no other buildings outside the Old City Wall until that time.

This plateau, which dominated the northern, unprotected approach to the city, has served as the camping ground of many an invader. From here the "Assyrians came down like the wolf on the fold" when Sennacherib besieged Jerusalem in 701 B.C. Later Titus and his Tenth Legion stayed here as, for four years, the Romans fought until they conquered the city in 70 A.D. The Crusaders also avoided the ravines that surround the walled city on the other three sides, and Tancred's soldiers' attack in 1099 came from these grounds. The Arabs called this area el-Meidan, a place for horse racing, and the Turkish militia and cavalry held maneuvers and contests here. In the hot summer months the pasha often camped on this plateau to escape the crowded Old City. On September 19, 1853, a Turkish battalion left from here to enter the Crimean War.

By 1864 three large hospices, a hospital, a consulate, a cathedral, and several water cisterns were built by the Russians and the area was surrounded by a protective wall. Rumors put the total cost at one million pounds sterling. For years the compound dominated the city's skyline. The Arabs dubbed it el-Moscoobiyya, the Russians called it Novy Ierusalim. The pilgrims flourished in their new facilities, but the estimated twelve thousand who came in 1914 turned out to be the last. Russia fought along with the British in World War I against Turkey and Germany: after the war and the Russian Revolution, religion was looked down upon as the "opium of the people" and pilgrimages ceased. About two hundred priests, nuns, and monks were stranded in Palestine during World War I. Their plight did not improve when the war ended, as funds no longer arrived from the motherland; nor was there any income from pilgrims. Some nuns were so poor that they were reduced to work as gravel-crushers. During the Civil War in Russia the Church declared that each district should obey its highest clergyman in an attempt to save the Church-in-Exile by severing its relations with Bolshevik Russia. Splits occurred among the White and the Red priests here, and the battles and intrigues that followed in the years between the two

World Wars were worthy of the courts of Byzantium. When the Patriarch of all the Russians came from Moscow to Jerusalem in 1945, he was not allowed into the churches that were under the domination of the Church-in-Exile.

After World War I Jerusalem became the administrative center of the British Mandate, and in the under-used Russian facilities civil servants soon replaced the departed pilgrims. Attempts by the Soviet Union during the Mandate era to put control of the property into the hands of the Church in the U.S.S.R. were not successful, and it wasn't until the early 1960s that a settlement was made with the Israeli government, which purchased most of the buildings in the area from the Soviets.

To leave the garden of the former consulate, you have to wind your way back through the maze. Go back to the concrete shack, walk around it, then through the guardroom, past an old cistern on your left and into the former French Consulate, and through the purple posts to the corridor, on the right of the white shed, which leads to the entrance. Turn right where the façade of the next building, the French Consulate, is hidden behind overgrown greenery. At the end of the street you will see a gate: no. 1, Yohanan Megush Halav reads the sign on the left postern. Walk through it to the Russian Compound, past the small guardhouse where the street sign says Rehov S. Z. Heshin, named for Heshin, a Supreme Court Judge.

The first building in the compound, on the left, is no. 8, S. Z. Heshin Street. It began as a spacious hospital, with a doctor, nurses, and a pharmacy—all rare commodities in mid-nineteenth-century Jerusalem. It was taken over by the British in 1917 and it too became part of Government Hospital, the location of the Office of Rabies Control. The name changed to Avi-ha'il Hospital after 1948, and in back the Hevrah Kadishah, the Jewish Burial Society, was temporarily housed. Plaques today announce a journal of medical sciences and an environmental health laboratory. Above an elegant double window, the triangular pediment is broken to reveal the oval emblem of the Russian Orthodox Church, which can be found on all the buildings in the compound. Later we shall take a closer look at it. A green sign pointing right directs you to Hechal Hagvurah Museum, the Hall of Heroism, a museum dedicated to the history of the struggle of the Jewish underground against the British. There is a modest entrance fee, and the visit is optional. If you decide to skip it, resume the walk on page 129.

On the iron gate, white letters on a blue background announce in three languages: Central Prison Jerusalem. The building we are about to see is now in its third incarnation. It was the Russian women's hospice, completed in 1864. The British used it as a prison, and added the old-fashioned toilet, on the left, for the benefit of visiting families. The tombstones you pass were the work of the prisoners, an attempt to keep them occupied. *PP* stands for Palestine Prison. The small house opposite the entrance to the main building served as guards' quarters. A royal crown is above the door.

Inside, the exhibits are almost self-explanatory as the record of the battle between the Jewish underground and the British authorities. There were actually three undergrounds. Lehi, for Lohamei Herut Yisrael, the "Fighters for the Freedom of Israel," were the most extreme. They were also known as the Stern Gang, after one of their slain leaders. The second, Etzel, was Menachim Begin's underground; Etzel is an acronym for Irgun Tzvai Leumi, which means "National Military Organization." The third was the Haganah, "Defense," a semiofficial organ of the Labor Party, which concentrated on self-defense. In the post–World War II days the Haganah helped refugees from the Holocaust enter the country illegally after the British, under Arab pressure, limited their number to fifteen hundred per month. Etzel and Lehi were more violent, believing that their actions would hasten the departure of the British. To this day bitter disagreement exists among Israelis about the validity of the tactics used by the three factions.

Inside the entry hall are enlarged photographs of members of the underground who were executed. Turn right into the long corridor. In the first cell across on the left is the documented history of the struggle, which begins with the riots of April 4–7, 1920, when Arabs protested against British promises of a National Home for the Jews in Palestine. An Arab mob gathered

Execution room, Hechal Hagvurah

to celebrate the feast of Nebi Musa, honoring the same
Moses who brought the Jews out of Egypt back to the
Land of Israel. The mob turned against the Jews: six
were killed, women were violated, and property was
destroyed. Arab police actually helped the attackers
and British police managed to arrive three hours late.
After this event Jews began to organize in small
groups, an attempt at self-defense. One cell, according
to a list posted on the wall, consisted of five people,
six pistols, three bayonets, one gun, no bullets. Ze'ev
Jabotinsky, who gathered some six hundred defenders, was arrested and sentenced to fifteen years of hard
labor. The press in England cried out against the harsh
sentence of the Military Government and Jabotinsky
was offered a pardon, which he refused to accept,
claiming he was not a criminal. Finally the Supreme

Military Court in London acquitted him. There is a lot of material in this room, reproductions of newspaper reports and documents of the period, which lasted until 1948.

Examine some of the other cells down the hall on the other side of the main entrance. Walk up the five steps inside the first door to the right. In the cell just off the steps, with the two mattresses and the holes in the wall, Meir Feinstein and Moshe Barazani blew themselves up with a hand grenade that was smuggled to them. They meant to take their executioners along with them, but when they heard that a rabbi planned to stay with them to the end, they committed suicide early in the day, depriving the British of killing them. (Suicide is forbidden by Jewish law and those who commit it receive a "donkey's burial" outside the cemetery. The exception is *Kiddush Hashem*, when a person takes his own life rather than convert or transgress against the Lord. The act here was considered *Kiddush Hashem*, "Sanctifying the Name.")

From this cell you can see the gallows unused—as the British decided to hang prisoners in Acre, because they feared riots in predominantly Jewish Jerusalem. The poem on the wall is by Jabotinsky. Here is a rough translation:

> Overcome, all obstacles and straits.
> Don't falter through the depth and the heights
> Of the rebellion.
> Carry a torch to burn, to ignite.
> Since quietude is like mire
> Risk your blood and your soul
> For the glory that is unseen.
> To conquer the mountain or die.
> Yodephet. Masada. Beitar.

The last line of the poem consists of the names of three towns that fought heroically against Rome. In the end they all fell. You have probably heard of Masada, where more than nine hundred defenders committed suicide, preferring it to surrender. The expression "Masada complex," sometimes used to criticize Israel's current policies, refers to this event in the first century A.D.

At the far end of the corridor is a list of the operations of the three undergrounds.

When you leave the museum, look to the right after you pass the gravestones. There, among stately Jerusalem pines beyond the barbed-wire fence, are concrete cones known as Rommel's Teeth, left behind from the days when it seemed possible that the German general's tanks would sweep through North Africa to Palestine. Later the British used them to stop the vehicles of the underground organizations.

Turn right at the gate. When there were fewer cars in the city in the 1950s, this parking lot was covered by tall grass in winter, pine needles in summer. It was a quiet, deserted spot, Jerusalem's version of a lovers' lane at a time when one didn't wander to the outskirts of Jewish Jerusalem out of fear of snipers.

Across the parking lot from Hechal Hagvurah, on the left when you face the cathedral with the pistachio green domes, is no. 6, Heshin Street, a former hospice for wealthier pilgrims, built around an inner courtyard with a chapel and a library. Today the Supreme Court meets here, as it did under the British. Most sessions are open to the public, as are those of several other, less august judicial bodies; court is held from 8:30 to noon. You have to explain your intention to the security guard. The contemporary signs on the building are in Hebrew and Arabic; over the lintel is an older Russian inscription.

Walk toward the cathedral and you will see a large cistern surrounded by a metal fence to the right of the oleanders. It is one of several in the compound, essential to the large number of pilgrims who stayed here every year. The snow-white Cathedral of St. Trinity is built in the manner of sixteenth-century Moscow Baroque, with ten green domes topped by gilded crosses mounted on arched hemispheres, ornately framed windows, and arched doorways. Unlike the low, functional hospices around it, the cathedral stands out against the skyline alien to the landscape: its smooth white façade has not been softened by age, nor have the bright green domes been touched by the mellowing hand of patina. Built outside the cramped quarters of the Old City, this was the first monumental structure in Jerusalem in many centuries that was not squeezed between existing buildings, and it could be seen from a great distance. The money for the construction of the church came from donations in Russia. Look through the glass panes of the modest front doors and you can see pictures of Jesus and of saints hanging in the narthex, and the decorated wooden doors that lead to the sanctuary. Services are held here at irregular intervals.

Stand with your back to the main entrance to the cathedral. About thirty feet ahead, in a pit below street level and surrounded by a low iron fence, lies a forty-foot monolithic column still attached to the bedrock. Archaeologists date it back to the time of Herod the Great, and it was probably destined for the Royal Portico in the courtyard of the Second Temple, but cracked during the quarrying. Children call it "the finger of Og, King of Bashan"—a giant king whom the Twelve Tribes had defeated. The large building beyond the cracked column is the Jerusalem Police Headquarters.

With the north side of the cathedral on your right, and the column and the police station behind you, walk along the low building on the left, no. 1, Dr. M. Smoira Street and turn left at the corner. Smoira, too, was a Supreme Court judge. The building, now used for laboratories and storage by the Ministry of Health, was another Russian male hospice. It could hold up to a thousand pilgrims in third-class, no-frills accommodations. Here they cooked, ate, and slept in tiny, crowded cells. Stop at the main door and look at the Cyrillic insignia above it, an oval relief in a triangular pediment: the large *P*—our *R*—is intertwined with the *X*; they stand for Christ. The small alpha and omega come from the New Testament: "I am Alpha and Omega, the beginning and the ending, saith the Lord." (Revelation 1:8.) The words on the rim of the eclipse are from Isaiah: "For Zion's sake I will not hold my peace, and for Jerusalem's I will not rest." (62:1.) As mentioned before, this emblem can be seen on all Russian Orthodox Church properties.

The small guardhouse projecting from the far end of the building marks the northern edge of the enclosed compound. Across the street is a late-nineteenth-century hospice, named after Prince Sergei Romanov, who visited Jerusalem in 1889. It was built for the more aristocratic pilgrims; the rooms are large with high ceilings, and in the spacious courtyard there were stables for those who could afford horses. The two-story Sergei Building is fairly simple in its design, with two exceptions. One is the very prominent three-story circular turret at the angle where the two wings meet; the pink and white stones, its elongated arch-framed windows, and the crenellated parapet are all purely decorative. The other exception is the main entry on Monbaz Street—not part of the walk—a classical frontispiece, triple-arched, with Ionic pilasters on the second story.

To the left of the tower, at no. 13, Queen Helene Street, or Rehov Helene Hamalka, is the side entrance to the present offices of the Ministry of Agriculture. The guard is a most suspicious fellow. Tell him that you are going to the Society for the Protection of Nature in Israel, Haganat Hateva in Hebrew. It is located on the far right-hand corner of the inner courtyard (the stables used to be beyond it, on the right). The hours are 9:00 to noon, tel. 222357. It offers a great many walks and tours, and while most are conducted in Hebrew, some English-speaking guides are available. On Wednesday afternoons at 2:30 they usually have a tour of the excavations at the Temple Mount, which at present are still closed to the general public. They are not to be missed! The society must have sufficient requests for this tour in advance to schedule it, so do call or stop by.

If you arrive in the afternoon, when the society's office is closed, ask to see the Agricultural Museum. In the middle of the courtyard is a collection of ancient agricultural implements including an olive press. The signs are all in Hebrew, but I must confess that being able to read the names is not very enlightening, because most of the archaic terms yield no clues as to the use of the objects, so try and guess—it's a real challenge. In the tower in the yard is an "outhouse." The door that is closest to the entry is for ladies. (The signs are in Hebrew only.)

Turn right when you leave and continue down the street that is named for Queen Helene—not to be confused with Queen Helena, Mother of Emperor Constantine. The latter is reputed to have found, in 326 A.D., the True Cross in a crypt under the Temple of Aphrodite where her son later built the Church of the Holy Sepulchre. *This* Queen Helene arrived in Jerusalem around 45 A.D. from the Kingdom of Adiabene in

Mesopotamia, and built a palace in the city where she and her family lived after they had converted to Judaism. The family graves in east Jerusalem are known as the Tombs of the Kings. It is a fine example of a necropolis, having about thirty burial chambers and a rolling stone. The British named this same street after another queen, Melisende, who ruled the Kingdom of Jerusalem briefly in the days of the Crusaders.

No. 9, Queen Helene Street is Beit Tefahot, the headquarters of Israel's largest mortgage bank. The tall white-stone building, in post-statehood bureaucratic mode, is the forerunner of several other undistinguished downtown buildings erected during what may yet become known as the "Jerusalem Plaza Era."

In the last decades of the nineteenth century, the Amiel family residence stood here. This North African Jewish family was so wealthy that when they came to Jerusalem they brought their baby Avraham along in a golden crib. Their house was built into the ground so that the windows facing the street were near the ceiling and one could see only the legs of the people walking by. One day Avraham, now grown up, fell in love with a pair of legs. "She will be my wife," he said. How he discovered the body that went with the legs is not clear, but the legs belonged to a famous beauty, Tzila Kritchevsky, whom he later married, to the surprise of those who knew them. She had been educated at the University of Heidelberg and was brought up in the Western tradition; he was a conservative Sephardic Jew who felt, initially, that women belonged in the house and should not be seen in public. It turned out to be a good marriage.

Around 1890 the forerunner of the National Library found temporary shelter in part of the Amiel house. Its librarian was a man who had gone to Germany to learn a trade and returned equipped with a sock-knitting machine but could not make ends meet. As he was an educated man, he was offered the librarian's position, yet he remained known as Horowitz *der zocken-macher*, "the sock-maker" in Yiddish. On an early Mandate map from 1922, the building is marked "Orphanage, Jewish." In the 1940s the British Depart-

Courtyard and implements,
Sergei Building

ment of Migration was here. It was attacked by Etzel in retaliation for the policies of the Foreign Office, which limited Jewish immigration. The present Beit Tefahot was built in 1970.

Across the street is a group of buildings from the same era as the Amiel house, with small domes and red tiles covering the round and pitched roofs. Note Levy's "steakiah"—a little steak place—with the Hebrew version of the Coca-Cola logo. The arched twin windows have an additional relieving arch over them, typical of local construction. The sides of the windows are emphasized by alternating stones of different sizes; the thresholds are made up of longer blocks. In the 1890s these buildings belonged to the Haimoff family. Peek into the courtyard, which is filled with a generally decaying yet wonderful configuration of steps, archways, and gas tanks. A flight of steps leads to a simple blue doorway amidst newly whitened stones, the offices of architects. Down the alley on the right is Mandy Tachi, a Chinese restaurant, and Pie House (called Hatzrif in Hebrew), which serves good pies, filled with meat, chicken, vegetables, or fruits.

Continue down Queen Helene Street and five building styles will meet your eye at the next intersection. On your immediate right are two pink-stone buildings whose windows are exotically arched and framed with blue and white floral tiles. There are several other late 1920s buildings of a pseudo–Art Nouveau style that continue westward to Zion Square and constitute the heart of the downtown section. The seven-story modern building directly across Jaffa Road is Beit Yoel; to its right is a group of small individual houses with pointed red-tile roofs, part of Nahalat Shivah—where our walk will continue—a quarter established in the late 1860s. Diagonally across to the left is Beit Feingold, an 1890s house that covers a whole city block. Built around a central court, it has only a few of the original wrought-iron balconies still in place. On your left, across Queen Helene, is no. 34, Jaffa Road, whose convex façade harmonizes with the curved sidewalk; it is part of the Jerusalem Municipality and the location of the Union Bank of Israel. The circa 1930 building is very Bauhaus, and was designed by the British architect Clifford Holliday. Above the bank's portal, near the roofline of the three-story building, is the emblem of the Russian Orthodox Church, whose property this was.

You can cross Queen Helene Street and sit on the ledge of the planting beds on either side of the bank's entrance and read the background of the settlement called Nahalat Shivah, or you can turn right to Manolitos Café at no. 36, Jaffa Road. You may choose to break for lunch in any one of the restaurants along Rivlin Street—the continuation of Queen Helene—or inside Beit Feingold across at no. 27, Jaffa Road. The walking resumes on page 138.

Nahalat Shivah, the "Estate of Seven," is named after the first seven settlers who left the Jewish Quarter in 1869 and moved to this area, which was then remote and dangerous. Many books tell that this was the second Jewish attempt to escape the crowded Old City. Mishkenot Sha'ananim was first, but it was built with money from abroad, unlike Nahalat Shivah, which represents an indigenous movement, the desire of nineteenth-century Jews to help themselves. In fact, this is the third settlement, preceded also by Mahane Yisrael in 1867. So why has the story persisted that Nahalat Shivah is number two? One explanation is that its founders came from among the leaders of the Ashkenazi establishment, and they and their descendants were very vocal and wrote books and articles that perpetuated their deeds, while Mahane Yisrael was populated by poor Moroccan Jews whose deed was soon forgotten. This is not really a controversy, as the facts are all on the side of the Moroccans. Nahalat Shivah was number three. Now comes the second dispute: Whose idea was it to move out here in the first place, Yoel Salomon's or Yosef Rivlin's?

The Salomon version begins with the cholera epidemic of 1865, which raged through the Jewish Quarter. Among its many victims were the parents of Yoel Salomon; he then began to advocate a move to a place with clean air and uncontaminated cisterns—a place where trees and gardens could grow. A couple of years later, on a Jewish holiday called Lag Ba'omer, Salomon went for a walk with some friends to the site where Nahalat Shivah now stands. It was then a field of wheat, or maybe peas—sources differ. Some Arab *falaheen* got angry with the Jews, who were trampling their crops. Salomon, whether to pacify them or by divine inspiration—again the sources are of no help—offered to buy the field at an inflated price. The next day he discussed the matter with his good friend Yosef Rivlin, and with five other men, and they agreed to buy the land. Under Turkish law, aliens—which many Jews were at the time—could not own or purchase land, so the wife of one of the seven men, Esther (or Altusha) Horowitz, who was born in Hebron and spoke perfect Arabic, put on local garb, bought the land, and had it registered in her name. Last names were not required then in transfers of deeds, and she was taken for an Arab.

The Rivlins make three simple claims: one, that in 1859, long before the epidemic, Yosef Rivlin went to Russia to raise money for what later became Nahalat Shivah, and he actually collected eight hundred rubles; two, that even before the land was purchased it had been leased by Rivlin's brother and by Leib Horowitz for growing wheat for *matzah shemurah*, a super-Kosher version of unleavened bread; three, and a fact undisputed by all, that the first house in Nahalat Shivah was built and occupied by Rivlin. Salomon moved here only several years later. Rivlin was a more restless and daring man, and he moved away eventually to help found other Jewish neighborhoods. Salomon spent the rest of his life here and left his house to his children. The street that forms the southern border of the quarter is named after Rivlin, the northern one after Salomon. Beit Yoel bears Salomon's name, which is a slight injustice, as its parking lot covers the ground where Rivlin's house once stood.

When the land was acquired, the seven pioneers drew up an agreement, an ordinance book, which was the custom in new neighborhoods in Jewish Jerusalem. The agreement covered mostly practical matters: each member was to deposit twelve and a half Turkish gold pounds into a joint kitty by a certain date and later to make three additional payments. Two houses were to be built as soon as possible, and lots were to be drawn among the seven families to see who would move here first. Aside from worldly affairs, other matters are dealt with rather movingly in the agreement: "The inner desire that raged within us to build these houses became stronger in our hearts, in our souls, in our spirit. And we decided to gain strength together,

to support each other, and with God's help to success-
fully reach completion [of this project]."

In reality, lack of money and the fear of living in an
isolated place delayed construction until 1869. Finally
Rivlin built a small house here and moved into it by
himself. It was considered too dangerous for his wife
and daughter to follow him—thieves, robbers, and
beasts of prey lurked in the night. Every evening he
came to sleep here, to show others that it could be
done. His in-laws, family, and friends thought him
mad, and every morning for two and a half years they
waited for him by Jaffa Gate and prayed for his safe return. Eventually he won, and others joined him.

The dream included open space, fresh air, and trees,
but the mentality of the settlers and the model they
had—of streets and houses in the Old City—created a
cluttered neighborhood much like the environment
from which they had escaped. Unlike later neighborhoods, which were preplanned and often built by in-
vestors, these houses were put up by individuals, who,
to meet the growing needs of the households, soon
had to add lean-tos, additions often made of the ham-
mered-out cans in which petroleum came from Russia.
Already in 1877 a resident was complaining about the
shabby looks of some of the houses and about the
narrow lanes: "two fingers in width" was all the space
left for pedestrians between rows of "houses of hon-
or"—a Hebrew euphemism for toilets.

As Jaffa Road was improved, several shops were
opened in the first floors of the houses that faced the
street—just as they do today. Artisans settled on the
side streets: a locksmith, a tinsmith, a carpenter, and
practitioners of some of the same traditional crafts are
still located here. Synagogues were opened, and a *beit
midrash*, a "study house," was built in 1874. Freethink-
ers met at a local café. Although we read of a kinder-
garten *melamed* (teacher) who was killed by three
Turkish soldiers, and of similar incidents, and we hear
complaints about the authorities, who neither pursued
nor punished the culprits, conditions kept improving
and about fifty families of Ashkenazim and Sephardim
lived here by the turn of the century. Soon we find an
English teacher here who gave private lessons, and
even a ladies' millinery.

Now back to walking. To enter Nahalat Shivah, cross over to Beit Yoel at no. 33, Jaffa Road. Amidst the nineteenth-century vernacular of red-tiled pitched roofs and patined stone, the seven-story building looks enormous, with useless formal piers tapering to a ground-story loggia. When you face the building, on its right is a stairway called Maalot Nahalat Shivah; the sign is on the wall, with many other signs and arrows. Turn and walk down eight steps, past the shoe store, and peek into the first courtyard through the arched entry, where little has changed over the past century except for the gas tanks behind the mouth of the cistern. After this gate, which has a placard of a stamp above it, there is a shoe repair shop. The sign says *sapoznik*, "shoemaker" in Russian, and *matzliah*, "successful" in Hebrew. One wonders how the shoemaker makes a living—he speaks no Hebrew and the shop is the size of a closet. Over the other side of the alley looms the lateral façade of Beit Yoel with its air conditioners.

Look to the right at the first corner, where the windowpanes are painted pink, and you can see the inside of Tea and Pie—"Don't pass me by," says the sign—with cushions, rugs, and low tables. The rest of the house is occupied by a tailor. If you look into the next courtyard along Maalot Nahalat Shivah through the barred window, you can see a small, square outhouse in the far left corner, behind the stairs. There are typical lean-tos on the balcony, pots of geraniums, and bunches of drying garlic. At the next corner is house no. 6, with two portholes on the second floor, a Sephardic synagogue called Ohel Yitzhak. The main entrance is behind a modern, sculpted gate, down the tiny side alley on the right. Take a few steps along this alley, past the synagogue, and you will find yourself in a village in midtown. The courtyards are unpaved, flowers grow in pots, and laundry, hanging on lines to dry, blusters in the wind—a brief return to the nineteenth century.

Back on Maalot Nahalat Shivah, across from no. 6, is Nahalat Yaacov, which claims to be the first synagogue outside the Old City Wall. Just past no. 6, behind a pile of stones on the right, is the back of a Hassidic synagogue, where the Hebrew sign is to the right of the pink wall. Why three synagogues so close together?

Maalot Nahalat Shivah

Perhaps the only answer lies in the story of the Jew who was rescued from a desert island where he had built two synagogues. "Why two?" he was asked. "One was where I prayed," he answered. "The other was the synagogue I wouldn't be caught dead in."

Walk down eight steps, newly refinished in stone, and on the left will be no. 5, the studio of painter Herbert Bluhm. It is interesting to see the inside of this typical house, with its cool rooms, high ceilings, and thick walls. The windowsills, almost three feet wide, are a place to sit and observe the street. Mr. Bluhm's paintings and etchings are mostly of Jerusalem. When you leave, look back in the direction of Jaffa Road and then walk up two steps to the small alley on the left with the carpenter's workshop—charming old grill-work on the windows, and a sickly green plastic awning. When you get to Salmon Street (same as Salomon), turn left and look at the building, with its fine rough stonework and smooth quoins at the corners. It is no. 17, one of the oldest remaining houses in the quarter, built before 1875. At the first shop you can get your brass, copper, and nickel objects cleaned and restored. A large key hangs on the door. Farther on you pass a glazier and a small jewelry shop.

No. 21 is one of several new shops in this neighborhood, an indication of spontaneous urban revival. It is a boutique called Marionetta—the sign is in handsome graphics—run by two sisters, Tami and Tzila Hubra, whose father used to own a business in the area. These two young ladies are not only beautiful to look at but they also possess a good eye for color and design. They sell clothes, bags, pelts, pillows, dolls, all one of a kind, often made by women who have small children and therefore do their handicrafts at home. It's sort of a cottage industry. Next door is a 4-foot-wide store. Its sign bears the well-known Marlboro logo; it sells cigarettes, of course. In the small yard down the road grows a lovely old fig tree that spans the street.

Stop and look toward the far left end of the street, beyond the dug-up site and the parking lot, and you can see Independence Park, which is not part of this walk. You might wish to take note of it for future reference. Located in the park is the Mamilla Pool, a reservoir that dates back to the Second Temple Period. Some say that the name comes from *moyeh min Al-lah*, "water from God" in Arabic. Late in the nineteenth century there was water still in the pool and children used to swim in it. In the park is an old Moslem cemetery with a domed mausoleum, Zawiya Kubakiyya, which is traditionally regarded as the tomb of Juhah, a jester who was a folk hero. The park is a good place for strolling and jogging.

Walk back on Salmon Street toward Jaffa Road, away from the park. After the store with the large key you pass no. 13, Kahal Hassidim, a synagogue with a gray stucco façade, a modest building indistinguishable from an ordinary house, characteristic of small, poor congregations. At no. 3 is the Champs Pub, followed by the last courtyard on the right of Salmon Street where Video-52 Bar has replaced an older one, Disco Bar Puss Puss. On the second floor is an American Ulpan—a language school—in case you need to brush up on your English. This corner building is known as the "ship" because of its shape. Across the street on the left, on the site of the famous Zion Cinema, a twenty-two-story building is scheduled to go up.

Back on Jaffa Road you will be reaching the intersection called Zion Square, the center of modern Jerusalem. Ben Yehuda Street, with its many shops, enters it from the left. Don't cross the square, but note the five rose-stone buildings stretching south—each a block wide, with stores and office space—which have functioned as the commercial axis of the city for the past half-century. The first of those buildings, on the left across the square, is no. 44, Jaffa Road; you can see the Ron Hotel and a camera shop with a large Kodak sign. In the façade are elegant single and double windows framed in white stone. The lone eucalyptus tree at the corner may be a survivor from the early days of the British Mandate when an attempt was made to turn Jaffa Road into a tree-lined artery. It was not pollution that killed the noble attempt but the citizens who kept removing the young saplings and planting them in their own backyards. An early "greening" of Jerusalem.

Down the small alley between nos. 44 and 42 is a restaurant called Oneg, which claims to have the cheapest food in town. At no. 42 is Jordan Bookshop, personally run by Mrs. Meir, whose father established the store. The English selection, while limited, is worth a try. Next door is the Alba Pharmacy; the wife of the owner, Rina Paz, is the granddaughter of Eliezer Ben Yehuda. On the second story is Europa, a good, homey Hungarian restaurant.

Turn right on Jaffa Road and stay on the eastern edge of Nahalat Shivah, though you may wish to note some of the goods and services available on the other (left) side of Jaffa Road.

At no. 39, Jaffa Road, on your right, is Steimatzky, featuring Jerusalem's best selection of foreign-language books and newspapers. On the left is Hahavazeleth Street, named after one of the earliest Hebrew newspapers. It appeared in 1863 and was called *Habazeleth*, or "lily." Today the offices of *Haaretz*, Israel's best daily newspaper, are on this street. Also there is a bookstore called Ha'atid that will mail books to you abroad if you establish credit with them.

At no. 40 is a copying service, still not common here. Upstairs are offices of the Regional Rabbinical Court. Near the cylindrical red mailbox, a legacy of the Mandate, is no. 38. The Cahana-Ben Naim agency sells tickets to concerts, theater performances, and sports events. You can also get tickets here for municipal parking lots.

On the right are the small houses of Nahalat Shivah, with shops in every house. Pass Beit Yoel and turn right at the corner, where Yosef Rivlin Street begins with a row of restaurants, all within remodeled Nahalat Shivah quarters. The first house on the right, past the parking lot, remains much as it was in the nineteenth century: a modest two-story building with a balcony and an attic with a window. In 1976 Rasputin, a pleasant restaurant, moved here. Classical music, rustic decor, reasonable prices. David, the present owner, took the space over from a carpenter who was located here, and he has done a fine job preserving some old features of the inner space. Down the street are further examples of urban rehabilitation, small shops and more restaurants. Not every business can make it; there is a large turnover. At no. 14, Rivlin Street, are two eating places, Chocolate Soup and Tavlin. Farther down at the Tavern you can buy draught beer, hamburgers, and chips. Chips in Israel, as in Britain, are what Americans call french fries. Next is Katy, at no. 16. Through a lovely courtyard one enters a small, tastefully decorated restaurant, run by a charming woman named Katy. It is a very good French restaurant. Katy is followed by Pat Bag, another eating place.

As you were walking down Rivlin Street, on the other side of "restaurant row" you passed by the lateral façade of Beit Feingold. Its main entrance is at no. 27, Jaffa Road. If you stand with the Tavern behind you, on the left you will see a large black iron gate with the signs Carpentry Gerecht and Pinis Pub. Two balconies project from the second story. Enter through the iron gate (the back door of Beit Feingold) into a large inner court. (If the gate is closed, walk up Rivlin Street back to Jaffa Road, turn right, and enter not through the first large gate but through the smaller one, beneath the sign Iran Restaurant—Taj.)

The 1890s building is built, typically, around a central courtyard. The gates were locked at night, and the entrances to all the apartments faced the yard for security reasons. Mr. Feingold was a converted Jew who married a wealthy Englishwoman and built this whole block of shops and apartments to produce rental income. Jews who were his contemporaries did not like him: he was referred to as Feingold the *meshumad*—from the root *sh'mad*—meaning "someone who has destroyed himself," a Jew who had converted. We are told that he hired another convert to teach small children who came mostly from poor Sephardic families. Their parents did not understand the missionaries' true intentions, lamented the writer David Yellin in 1896 after he passed by here and heard the children's voices. They simply thought of the English Protestants as "Ingles," not as Christians who were after their children's souls.

Inside the yard is a mixture of old and new. Several storehouses, like Shahor's Pharmaceuticals, or the Havillio candy-making shop on the second floor, have been here for a long time. Now that nineteenth-century buildings are becoming fashionable—a most heartening trend—several eating places have opened here in the last few years, like Stekiat Ha'chaser—the "Courtyard's Steakhouse," and The Little Pub—loud American rock music amidst Alpine decor. This area is especially lively at night—most places stay open until midnight, which is late for Jerusalem. On warm evenings you can sit outside and enjoy this charming urban place—once the loud music is turned off!

The most interesting restaurant in this court is Taj, which was opened in 1978 by the Kermasha family, who came to Israel from Iran in 1948. The chef is Rachel, the sister of the owner. She explains that the cuisine is basically Middle Eastern but the herbs and spices are different, Persian. The food is interesting, and reasonably priced. The service is friendly; most of the staff is related to the owner.

Exit to Jaffa Road through the main gate, which is on the opposite side of the courtyard from the back iron gate that you entered. Across is no. 34, Jaffa Road, where at Wizo you can always find well-made handicrafts. Also in the building is a Tourist Information Office where maps and listings of daily events can be found. The staff is most helpful and will try to answer all your questions. On Saturday mornings free walking tours begin here; see your newspaper for details. At the corner with Heshin Street, at the end of the block, is the Nicolai Building, part of the Russian Compound. On the second floor you can buy maps from the Government Land Survey Bureau. The entrance is around the corner. Formerly the British C.I.D. (Criminal Investigation Department) was located in this building; in 1944 Etzel blew up part of it and destroyed many of the records of the British police.

Past Beit Feingold is no. 29, Jaffa Road, where the Israel Bank offices are located behind barred windows in a building known as Binyan Mitzpeh. Look to the right down Hassoreg Street and you will see a good pastry shop, Hauga, which means "The Cake" (naturally). In the corner building, no. 2, Queen Shlomzion Street, above Peltours is the oldest Chinese restaurant in Jerusalem, Mandarin. Chinese food in Israel is neither cheap nor distinguished, but if you cannot wait to have some, this is as good a place as any. Next door, at no. 4, is Ludwig Mayer Books—lots of books and a good mailing service.

Bar Kochba Square is named for the leader of the doomed revolt against the Romans in 132 A.D. Jaffa Road seems to split here; actually it veers left while Queen Shlomzion begins to descend to the right. The almost trapezoidal building at the fork is the Generali, built in 1931 by an Italian insurance company, Assicurazioni Generali. At the roofline, just below the winged lion that crowns the building, you can see a Roman date carved in the stone: MDCCCXXXI, or 1831. Since it does not seem probable that someone forgot a century, it is most likely the founding date of the insurance company.

Cross over to the Generali. (On its Queen Shlomzion side, in the inner court, are the offices of the Ministry of the Interior, where foreigners have to go to have their visas extended.) Our walk continues on Jaffa Road, on the left side of Generali, where you pass a bank, then a liquor store. There aren't many such shops in the city because almost every large food market carries wine, beer, and some hard liquor. Israelis are not heavy drinkers.

Toward the very end of the British Mandate, when the activities of the underground increased, the British created several "Security Zones" within the city, and surrounded themselves with barbed wire, pillboxes, and antitank blocks. The heart of the British administration was here. Generali, the Russian Compound, and all the buildings up to the northwestern corner of the Old City Wall became part of Zone C, soon dubbed Bevingrad, after the British foreign secretary whose policies prevented the bulk of Hitler's refugees from entering Palestine.

Across the street from the Generali are nos. 30 and 28, Jaffa Road. There you can see a French bookshop and lending library, and a small unpretentious Oriental restaurant, Hen. The English sign says only Restaurant in yellow graphics. Very good food, where even President Navon sometimes has lunch. Next to it is a Xeroxing shop.

After the Generali comes the Central Post Office at no. 23, the only major administrative building that the British government put up in Jerusalem. It was built in the late 1920s by the Department of Public Works. British policy held that the development of colonies had to be financed by money from within, not by investment from England. The architect in charge of the building was Austin Harrison, the man who designed the Rockefeller Museum and the residence for the high commissioner on the Hill of Evil Counsel. The post office building is simple and functional; its proportions

Billboard, Jaffa Road

are good, not too massive. If you wish to make international phone calls, enter the second large door to find assistance.

The last building on this walk is Bank Leumi Le' Israel, the former headquarters of the Anglo-Palestine Bank, built by the famous architect Erich Mendelsohn, who came to Palestine from Germany in 1934 before his final move to New York in 1941. Except for a change in the bank's name, the building has remained the same. It is International Modern in style, with an asymmetrical entrance on the left side. The use of stone was mandatory in Jerusalem but Mendelsohn chose to deemphasize it by using smooth, finely hewn ashlars. Yet even a modernist like Mendelsohn could not completely escape the influence of tradition in the Holy City: on the massive bronze front doors of the bank, twin lions are carved, perhaps for Judea and Great Britain. Above the doors on the left is a torch, an old Jewish symbol; it also appears in smaller form next to every window on the façade. Note the bronze lines that extend the height of the building, and the fine inscriptions in Hebrew, English, and Arabic. After you pass the building, turn and look at the side wall that faces Yedidya Street; the row of portholes can be seen on several of Mendelsohn's buildings.

Across Jaffa Road from the bank are three giant billboards with many listings: music, theater, cinema, plus some black-bordered funeral announcements. To the right of the billboards is Gan Auster—and many bus stops—where this walk through the center of modern Jerusalem ends.

The Slope of the Valley of Hinnom

Fair in situation, the joy of the whole earth . . .
the city of the Great King.

Psalms 48:3

The first two buildings on this walk, the YMCA and the King David Hotel, were completed in the early 1930s. Find a place to sit—the wide stone banisters of either building will do—and read the introduction to this walk.

The two buildings, which face each other, are built on the crest of a hill that overlooks the Old City: if one could not live within the Wall, the next best thing was to be where one could at least see it. On the east the Valley of Hinnom separates the hill from the Old City. West of the hill, the Valley of Rephaim begins its gentle descent toward the coastal plain. The names of both valleys evoke sinister memories from Biblical days. In Hinnom stood the Molech, the terrible god to whom live children were sacrificed. Rephaim means "shadows" or "ghosts," and indeed the ghosts of soldiers killed in the battles between King David and the Philistines may still linger in the flat valley land, an ideal battlefield. In between battles, the fertile valley provided wheat for ancient Jerusalem.

This area began to expand after the British occupation in 1917, an occupation that brought peace and stability to the war-torn land. Jerusalem became the administrative capital of Palestine and was soon to prosper. In urban development plans, the British gave prime consideration to the city's topography and to the sanctity of the Mount of Olives and Mount Zion. The network of roads that they drew spread in a half-circle north and west of the Holy City, thus preserving the visual effects of the ramparts and the mountains.

The tall tower of the YMCA can be seen from almost everywhere in Jerusalem. It appears to reach for the sky, the lesson of the Tower of Babel all but forgotten. Unlike many other monumental Christian buildings, the YMCA is not a replica of some European castle or medieval basilica. The architect, Arthur Loomis Harmon, tried to create a local style by combining elements from several traditions. The white-stone building is strictly symmetrical; on either side Byzan-

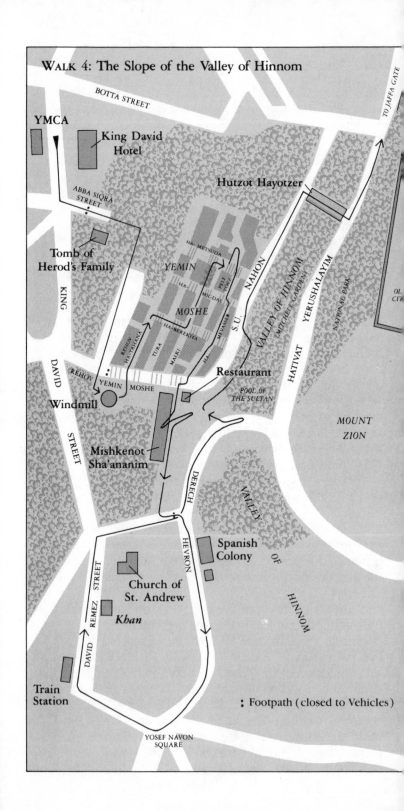

WALK 4: The Slope of the Valley of Hinnom

BOTTA STREET

YMCA

King David Hotel

ABBA SIQRA STREET

Tomb of Herod's Family

KING

DAVID

STREET

Hutzot Hayotzer

TO JAFFA GATE

HA-METSUDA

YEMIN

HA-MIGDAL

PELE YOETZ

NAHON

MOSHE

HA-BEREKHA

S.U.

REHOV HA-TZHANA

TURA

MALKI

HA-MEVASEH

Restaurant

YEMIN MOSHE

POOL OF THE SULTAN

Windmill

Mishkenot Sha'ananim

DERECH

VALLEY OF HINNOM

MITCHELL GARDEN

HATIVAT

YERUSHALAYIM

NATIONAL PARK

OL CIT

MOUNT ZION

VALLEY

HEVRON

Spanish Colony

OF

Church of St. Andrew

HINNOM

Khan

DAVID

REMEZ STREET

Train Station

: Footpath (closed to Vehicles)

YOSEF NAVON SQUARE

tine-style square halls support low domes that are connected to the main building by arched loggias of pink
and white stone. In the middle of the 120-foot tower is
a six-winged seraph, in accord with Isaiah's vision. As
this building was going up, architect Harmon's firm
was helping design another skyscraper, the Empire
State Building in New York, ten times taller than the
YMCA. But no steel frames, concrete, or Art Deco in
the Holy City! When foundations were being dug in
1928, remains of another era were uncovered. Found
was the tombstone of a Georgian bishop, Samuel,
from a sixth-century cemetery; now it is at the Rockefeller Museum. The Georgians were early converts to
Christianity. Their patron was St. George of Lydda.

The YMCA was first established in Jerusalem in
1878, in more modest quarters. This building, which
opened its doors in 1933, was made possible by a one-
million-dollar gift given by James Newbegin Jarvie of
New Jersey. Today the association no longer caters ex-
clusively to young Christian men. Male and female,
children and senior citizens, Jews and Moslems, all use
the Y's many facilities: a reading room with current
periodicals in English and Hebrew, a small archaeological collection, a concert hall. Three chapels provide spiritual comfort. The Y boasts several athletic
facilities, in addition to its hundred guest rooms.

Walk up the steps to the main entrance. Look above
the doorway and you see a grape-tendril frieze, an ancient motif. Look down at the floor and you see a
small faded copy of the Madaba map. The original, a
mosaic map of sixth-century Byzantine Jerusalem and
other parts of the Holy Land, was uncovered in 1884 in
a ruined basilica in Madaba, Jordan. It is the earliest
pictorial representation of the city. Major buildings,
gates, and roads can be clearly identified.

Our destination is the top of the tower, an excellent
viewing place. For a small fee you can buy a ticket
from the man at the front door, who will then take
you up in a slow elevator. You have to tell him when
to come to bring you down. When you get out of the
elevator, walk up the short, spiral-stepped passage to
the arched windows guarded by saints.

Standing between John and James the Elder, look
east in the direction of the Old City beyond the roof of
the King David Hotel. On the horizon are Mount Sco-

pus on the left and the Mount of Olives, described in detail on page 60. On a clear day, farther to the right of Olivet, one can see the smoky blue mountains of Moab. Within the Old City Wall, on the left is the clock tower of St. Saviour and the belfry of the Church of the Redeemer, behind the red roofs of Casa Nova. Straight ahead is the golden Dome of the Rock, and halfway between it and the smaller dome of el-Aqsa is the minaret in the Citadel. On top of Mount Zion, on the right, sits the early twentieth-century Dormition Abbey with its conical roof, built in the manner of the palace-chapel of Charlemagne at Aix-la-Chapelle.

Turn right and stand between Simon and Judas for a bird's-eye view of the rest of this walk. On the left are the red-tiled roofs of Yemin Moshe and Montefiore's 1857 windmill. South of the mill, to the right, is a compactly built white church with a small dome and a light blue flag, the Scottish Church of St. Andrew. Closer to the YMCA is the recently completed Sheraton–King Solomon Hotel, an overpowering building. Behind it and to the right you can see the train tracks of Jerusalem's only railway station, which was built in the late nineteenth century. Amidst dark green pines farther to the right and toward the horizon is Talpiot, a Jewish neighborhood founded in 1924. On the right edge of the wooded area, not easy to distinguish, is the Greek Orthodox monastery of Mar Elias, named after the Prophet Elijah, who is said to have stopped there to rest when he was escaping to the desert. Beyond the new houses of Giloh lies the town of Bethlehem. Between the YMCA building and the train tracks stretches the Valley of Rephaim where flintstone implements twenty thousand years old have been found. The Arabs call it the "Valley of the Roses," Wadi el-Vared, for the roses that grew here supplied rose water for the Holy Places.

Thomas and James the Younger will be on either side when you turn right toward west Jerusalem. Beyond the football stadium is Rehavia, a spacious "garden" neighborhood established in 1921. On the hill behind is Beit Hakerem, a more modest early 1920s development that was considered to be way out of town until the 1950s when Jewish Jerusalem could expand only westward. Now Beit Hakerem is linked to the rest of the city by a chain of public buildings: the

Israel Museum, the Knesset, the Kirya's government offices, and the campus of Hebrew University on Givat
Ram.

To complete the circle, turn right again to look
north, with Philip and Bartholomew on either side.
Below is a large open space, Independence Park. The
park is shared by the Mamilla Pool—an ancient reservoir, now waterless—Moslem tombs, and, all too obviously, the massive block of the Plaza Hotel. To the left
of the hotel is the dome of Hechal Shlomo, the seat of
the two Chief Rabbis—the Ashkenazi and the Sephardic—and the Supreme Rabbinical institutions. In the
foreground, note the white circular building, the Convent of the Sisters of the Rosary. To the right is modern, downtown Jerusalem, where tall, bureaucratic
buildings seem to mushroom. You may be able to recognize the green, onion-shaped cupolas of the Russian
Cathedral and the dark dome of the Ethiopian Church,
to the left of the Russian Compound. On the horizon
is French Hill, next to Hebrew University on Mount
Scopus, a housing complex built since 1967.

After you leave the YMCA, cross the street, Rehov
Hamelech David—King David Street—to the King Da-
vid Hotel. Built in 1930 in the tradition of grand hotels,
by Egyptian Jews who owned the famous Shepheard's
Hotel in Cairo, it was designed by two Swiss architects,
Emile Vogt and G. A. Hufschmid.

The ground floor is built of rusticated ashlars, the
upper stories of smooth ones, all in rose Jerusalem
stone called *mizzi ahmar* in Arabic. The window
frames and the shutters are painted lime green. The
building was better proportioned before two stories
were added to it. Today one can barely notice the
seam in the southwestern corner of the hotel, to the
right of the front entrance. The whole wing, which
housed British government and military offices, was
blown up by Etzel—one of the underground organizations—in 1946. Ninety-one people died in the explosion. The British apparently ignored a phone call that
forewarned them of the bombing.

Inside, the decor is an attempt by Hufschmid to de-
fine a "local" style. The motifs are supposedly Assyrian
in the lobby, Hittite in the lounge, and Phoenician in
the dining room. The early days of the hotel were
splendid indeed. Tall Sudanese waiters, each attired in

white pantaloons and a red *tarboosh*, slid silently along freshly waxed marble floors carrying precariously perched trays above their heads—trays laden with pots of teas blended in India and Ceylon, buttered toast that always stayed warm, exotic jams, starched linen napkins. Those elegant days are gone forever. Today, barefoot guests run about the main lobby in their bathing suits, and young waiters are often more interested in the anatomy of female tourists than in providing good service. But there are some high points left: the bar, decorated in a "Solomonic" manner, is mostly cool and quiet; the grill at La Regence serves some of the best steaks in Israel—not cheap, but you get what you pay for. The main dining room serves standard hotel fare. The best buy here, and one of the best in Jerusalem, is the terrace overlooking the Old City. For a couple of dollars you have a choice of beverages and pastries. In late afternoon, the piano music and the view of the domes and minarets caressed by the last rays of the sun are on the house. You can also use the swimming pool for a few dollars a day. Find a place under a tree and plan to take a dip either early or late in the day. If you want to swim laps, you are in the wrong place. Avoid the poolside café: the food and service are reasonable; the prices are not.

The King David is still a lovely hotel, my favorite in the city. Over the years many VIP's have stayed here— in the more recent past Kissinger, Sadat, and Carter. Several elegant shops inside the hotel display clothes, jewelry, and art, and there is a newspaper stand below the main lobby with foreign papers and magazines, postage stamps, and beauty aids.

When you leave the hotel turn left and walk to the end of the sidewalk. Turn left onto Abba Siqra Street, a short lane at the corner of the small parking lot of the King David Hotel. On your right is a newly constructed luxury apartment house. On the left are the gardens and swimming pool of the hotel. At the end of the lane, almost hidden by an enormous pink oleander bush, is an iron gate with a plaque on the left, Tombs of Herod's Family. Inside the gate, on the right, is a small white structure. Its shutters are usually closed. On it is the *Taphos*, the emblem of the Greek Orthodox Church, which sold the property to the city. Thirteen steps down the paved walk and on your right you will see a large rolling stone and an opening to a sepulchre.

The mausoleum of King Herod the Great is not here but in Herodion, a palace *cum* citadel that he built not far from Bethlehem. There he was buried in great splendor, in a gold casket draped in red silk linings, wearing a crown with precious stones. Herodion is now being excavated, but so far the archaeologists have yet to discover the remains of the king, which must please this wily man, wherever he is. He was not exactly loved by the people, and must have feared that his body would be desecrated after his death. He even gave orders, fortunately unexecuted, that a number of dignitaries be put to death after he departed to ensure that the population would go into mourning.

The grave on this particular site, behind the rolling stone, is generally believed to have held the remains of his wife Miriamne, of the House of the Hasmonean, whom Herod, in his madness, killed along with their two sons. He worried that the people would dispose of him in favor of the last descendants of that beloved dynasty. He is said to have regretted this murder, so perhaps he buried Miriamne here in order to gaze at her tomb from his palace behind the Wall, near the Citadel. There was a monument here, but all that is left of it is one layer of dressed square stones that you can see to the right of the opening of the tomb. (Recent archaeological discoveries may yet prove "Herod's Monuments"—as mentioned by Josephus—to be located elsewhere, north of Damascus Gate.)

Behind the rolling stone, said to be the largest of its kind in the country, the sepulchre is carved into the rock, a cruciform plan with a central chamber lined with stone slabs. If you have matches or a flashlight you can enter and see the graffiti-covered walls. Four stone gates lead to the chambers off the central one. The longest chamber, across from the entrance, contained two sarcophagi that were removed to the Greek Orthodox Patriarchate after Conrad Schick excavated the burial cave in 1891. This chamber is lit from above through a chimney that is cut into the rock.

Go back to the path and walk down to where it forms a T, and turn to the right. The several monoliths

Sepulchre of Herod's family

that you see have the *Taphos* sign carved into them. This whole area was called Nikephoriyya after the Archimandrite of the Greek Orthodox Church who purchased it in the nineteenth century; in recent years it has been covered with grass, a good place to stroll, jog, or rest under the olive trees—if the sprinklers are not on. The path continues in the direction of the windmill. On the right you pass a large cave; beyond it is a strange-looking iron trellis that will eventually be covered with jasmine, morning glory, and other vines, and will provide shade for visitors to the Bloomfield Garden. A word should be said here about Mayor Kollek and the Jerusalem Foundation to whose collaboration we owe this and many other parks. Teddy Kollek has become known as the Prince of the *Shnorrers*, or "beggars," because of his efforts to raise money all over the world and use it—among other things—to beautify Jerusalem. "How did you get Jerusalemites to stop picking flowers from public gardens?" a friend once asked him. "By planting more flowers," answered the mayor.

Where the path splits, don't walk toward the trellis but take the small branch to the left and pause at the top of the steps. This is a good place to observe some early violations of the city's skyline from the Ottoman and British eras. If you look toward the ramparts, on the east, and follow the outline of the Wall to where it ends on the left, you may be able to distinguish two crenellated turrets with a statue of the Madonna between them—the complex of Notre Dame built in the 1890s, overshadowing the Wall. Both the aforementioned Dormition Abbey on top of Mount Zion and even the YMCA were built on high ridges; the Dormition to this day dominates the sacred mount. In contrast, close to the windmill are the red rooftops of Yemin Moshe, modest, clinging to the slope, in the tradition of local construction. To the left is the *haqura*, "empty lot" in Arabic, now filled with fruit trees, a favorite meeting place of young lovers from Yemin Moshe in the early days of the neighborhood.

The steps will take you down to the parking area. Walk to the windmill, where you will see a green board on the left with a map of Yemin Moshe. Just past it, down fourteen steps, is the windmill platform. The view is breathtaking; the landmarks should be familiar—you have just seen them from the top of the YMCA.

The windmill, built in 1857, was another futile attempt by Sir Moses Montefiore to bring industry to the city. Take a look to the right of the mill, at his carriage, brought here from England long after his death. In his day the road to Jerusalem could not accommodate anything as grand as a four-horse carriage, and he—a rather large man—had to be carried up to Jerusalem by a number of mules, or else borne on the shoulders of several men. On his personal coat of arms, flanking "Thynk and Thank" are the British Lion and a hart, as the Holy Land is sometimes called the Land of the Hart in the Bible. Queen Victoria gave Montefiore special permission to add the word *Jerusalem* to his heraldry (it is written on the banners in Hebrew) following his successful negotiations for the release of some innocent Jews accused in a blood libel in Damascus in 1840. In the upper-left corner of the emblem are two Stars of David and the palm of a hand, the *hamsikeh*, which prevents those who possess an evil eye from doing harm.

To the left of the carriage is a mosaic placard by sculptress Leah Majaro Mintz. Commissioned by the Builders Union, it depicts many of the projects that Montefiore had started and is "dedicated to Moses Montefiore who did so much for the Land of Israel. Father of the neighborhoods outside the Wall; supporter of industry and agriculture; fighter for Jewish rights in the Diaspora."

Amidst the many flower beds find a ledge where you can sit and read about this remarkable man whose kindly face appears on the one-shekel notes. The eldest son of a successful Sephardic merchant in England, he was elected sheriff, then knighted by Queen Victoria in 1837. Well known for his charitable contributions to many civic causes, he was also a devoted Jew concerned with the fate of his coreligionists, especially those living in the Holy Land. Seven times he came to Palestine, making the last trip in 1875 when he was ninety years old. It was an era when travel was difficult, dangerous, and, at best, exhausting. On one of Montefiore's visits an epidemic raged throughout the city. He camped on Mount Scopus at night but spent the days within the Wall.

Montefiore began sixteen different enterprises in Palestine to help alleviate poverty and hardship. He built houses and institutions and tried to teach Jews crafts and trades. His ventures were singularly unsuccessful, in part because the Jewish community was notoriously split and disorganized. Also, when things went wrong, Sir Moses rarely inquired after the causes but went on to new projects. A typical example is the cotton manufacturing plant he founded in Jerusalem in 1854. He dreamed of turning the city into the Manchester of the Middle East. So great were his expectations that he built a school for girls nearby to teach them how to sew and make use of all the cloth (as yet unwoven). Ten looms and an Irish manager arrived from England, and for the next two years Sir Moses supported eighteen families of young men who were learning the trade. The Irishman complained that the Jews were lazy; the Jews complained that the Irishman did not want to teach them; the cloth produced was of inferior quality. Manchester was safe; Montefiore was unhappy. He fired the Irishman—with three years' severance pay—and brought a devout Orthodox Jew from London to run the business, a man who knew nothing about weaving. Naturally this venture soon collapsed.

Dealing with the different segments of the Jewish population in Jerusalem must have required the patience of a saint. A story is told that during one of Montefiore's visits he was granted permission by the Moslem authorities to enter the area of the Temple Mount. Many Orthodox Jews, to this day, will not walk there because strict purification rites can no longer be observed and also because one might accidentally tread on the original site of the Holy of Holies, where only the High Priest had been allowed to set foot, and only on the holiest day, Yom Kippur, the Day of Atonement. Sir Moses thought that he could solve that problem by not putting his foot down on the sacred ground: he was carried by litter on the shoulders of several Arabs! Some rabbis did not appreciate this compromise and announced that they would put a *herem* on Montefiore, that is, excommunicate him. Later they changed their minds and Montefiore, in the synagogue on the following Saturday, said a special prayer, *Mi sheberech*, for the rabbis. They were honest men, he reasoned, who were not afraid to anger him even at the risk of losing his financial support.

Among all the anecdotes one must not lose track of Montefiore's important role in the development of Jerusalem. The concept of moving away from the protection of the Wall to live outside the Old City in spacious, clean surroundings turned into reality with the help and encouragement of Sir Moses, and the move changed forever the face of the city.

The total population of Jerusalem grew from about nine thousand at the beginning of the nineteenth century, to nearly seventy thousand on the eve of World War I. The Jewish community grew faster than all others, and before they began to emerge from behind the Wall in the 1860s, the population of the Jewish Quarter quadrupled to reach about nine thousand. Many subsisted on charity from abroad. When the Crimean War broke out in 1853, the flow of money from Russian Jews stopped, no pilgrims arrived, and commerce was at a standstill. The Jews sent letters to their brethren in Western Europe asking for help. Montefiore was among the many who responded.

Shortly before that time, Judah Touro died in the United States and left fifty thousand dollars to benefit poor Jews in Palestine. Touro, the son of a cantor in Newport, Rhode Island, was a well-known philanthropist who had contributed money to such projects as the Bunker Hill Monument in Boston and the Touro Hospital in New Orleans. But only in the last few years of his life did he become involved in Jewish affairs. The change came about under the influence of his adviser, Gershom Kursheedt. Touro named Montefiore one of the executors of his will, and Sir Moses thought of using the money to build a hospital outside the crowded Old City. The site on which the windmill stands and the slope below it seemed like a suitable location. First Montefiore acquired a *firman*, a royal decree, which allowed him to purchase land. Then he began to negotiate with a former pasha of Jerusalem, who owned the above-mentioned plot of land. The pasha kept changing his mind about the price and went through the typical empty gestures common to trading in the Levant: "Here, my friend," he reportedly said to Montefiore. "You can have this field for nothing, you apple of my eye. You can have anything of mine, my wife, my children . . ." The final price was a thousand pounds, a princely sum in those days. Montefiore moved his camping tents here from the Russian Compound area, and issued orders to erect a fence, dig a cistern, and build two small houses for his future use. A cornerstone for a hospital was then laid in the ground-breaking ceremonies, and a ring of Judah Touro was buried with it.

When Montefiore returned to Jerusalem in 1857 it became obvious that the Rothschild Hospital, built in the Jewish Quarter in 1854, was adequately serving the needs of the community. Besides, several people, including Dr. Simon Frankel whom Montefiore sent to Jerusalem in 1843, felt that a hospital located "so far" from the Old City might endanger the lives of patients, as the gates were locked when either an epidemic or riots broke out. Plus, the need for housing was more acute than ever. So a change was made in the plans, and almshouses for the poor were constructed. Known as Mishkenot Sha'ananim, "Tranquil Residences," they are one of the next stops on this walk.

First the windmill was built at a cost of £1,450; the machinery was imported from England and brought up to Jerusalem on the backs of several camels. It was meant to supply inexpensive flour for the future tenants of the area. In those days people had to buy wheat, store it, and take some of it to the mill every month to have it ground. It is said that owners of other mills in town were worried by this modern addition and they hired a person known to have an evil eye to cast a spell on the mill. While at first the curse seemed to have no effect, a few years later the mill stopped functioning—some say for lack of wind; others claim that more modern mills offered better service. What probably happened is that due to the usual lack of maintenance some parts broke down and were never replaced. Still, one mustn't underestimate the power of the evil eye!

Many years later, in 1948, the roof of the mill served as an observation point for the Jews in this quarter, until some British Royal Engineers blew off the top of the building. It has since been repaired and now the mill is used as part of the memorial to Sir Moses. Almost every day buses bring schoolchildren from all over the country to visit this historical location.

The two residential sections that we are about to visit are Yemin Moshe and Mishkenot Sha'ananim, built within thirty years of each other. We will visit the more recent section first, to save you from climbing up and down this hill twice.

Before the middle-class neighborhood called Yemin Moshe was built in 1892, difficulties arose. On the land that Sir Moses had bought in 1855 some squatters had settled in shacks made out of Russian kerosene cans. When a group of founders was established to build permanent houses here, the squatters refused to leave even when they were promised new quarters in another area. Finally, with the aid of the Turkish authorities, the squatters were removed. It was one of the few cases in which disputes within the Jewish community were brought before the non-Jewish government.

An equal number of Sephardim and Ashkenazim settled here, each in a separate section. The money for building came from down payments made by each family, and from a special fund in London that lent money to the different households—money to be repaid in monthly installments. When Mishkenot was built in the 1860s, there were few people in Jerusalem qualified to supervise construction, so a foreign architect was hired. In Yemin Moshe a local agent was employed. The founders published a Book of Regulations. It noted the steep slope on which the houses had to be built, and expressed the desire to construct fine, solid dwellings, sixty-five for each community. Every house was to have a kitchen and toilet, a paved courtyard, a place for sewage and trash, drains for collecting rainwater, and cupboards with doors. The neighborhood was to have several public buildings and cisterns, and trees were to be planted along the streets. No additions could be built without the permission of the neighborhood's central committee.

In memoirs by former inhabitants we read of healthy, strong children, of women helping one another in difficult times, of picnics and holiday celebrations, and of two traditions living side by side with Hebrew gradually replacing Yiddish and Ladino. For many years this was one of the better neighborhoods in the city, but it began to decline after the Arab Great Rebellion (1936–39), during which Jews were frequently attacked. Between 1948 and 1967 this area, on the edge of no-man's-land and opposite the Wall, was badly damaged by war. It became an inexpensive but dubious shelter to new immigrants from Turkey. Since 1967 the wheel of fortune has turned again, and a new uproar began because poor tenants were being evacuated. We shall discuss this matter later. The neighborhood was first known as Kerem Moshe Ve'yehudit, the "Vineyard of Moses and Judith" (Montefiore). The current name, Yemin Moshe, comes from Isaiah (63:12) and refers to God's having "caused his glorious arm to go at the right hand of Moses." *Yemin* means "right." A tablet over the main gate cites this quote and commemorates the names of Judith Montefiore, Rabbi Nathan Cohen Adler of London, and Montefiore's nephew and heir, Yosef Sebag.

To leave the terrace walk down the dozen stairs in front of the windmill's yellow door, on the Yemin Moshe side. Just before you cross the wide steps called Rehov Yemin Moshe, note the Jerusalem Music Centre, a unique learning and recording studio, down the slope on the right. Across the broad stairway is a green iron gate entwined with vines of purple morning glory. Enter it and you will be on Windmill Street, or Rehov Ha-tahana. The street signs in the quarter are set within the buildings' walls and often appear only on one corner of a given intersection. Look around. Some houses have been rebuilt, some have been left unchanged, and a few are still in the process of reconstruction.

Walk past the green lawn on the right, which is the roof of the children's club. Turn right, down the steps of Ha-berekha, "the Pool"; the vista unfolds before your eyes and you see Mount Zion across the Valley of Hinnom, where the Sultan's Pool used to be. The street sign is typical of this area; handsome graphics on glazed tiles, uniform in design. Note the ramp on the right of the stairs, for carts, carriages, strollers, and donkeys. Cars may not (and cannot) enter the neighborhood.

The first house on the left sometimes has a sign in front that says Dilian Studio. When the sign is up it means "Open House"; paintings and prints may be purchased at reasonable prices. Both Dilians are artists who live—with their four children—and work in this house. In 1963, when this was still a dilapidated neighborhood under the guns of Arab snipers, a talented sculptor, David Palombo, thought of turning it into an artists' colony. Though Palombo was killed in an accident shortly thereafter, several artists, like the Dilians, did move here. After 1967, when the danger passed, the East Jerusalem Development Corporation became involved in what is now considered to be a somewhat controversial plan. Between 1948 and 1967 Turkish immigrants settled here in half-ruined houses. In order to create an artists' colony, houses were expropriated under a law that makes such actions possible for "the needs of the public"—*letzorchei tzibur* in Hebrew. As the area became more desirable, artists were no longer the sole occupants. The value of real estate went up and taxes rose accordingly, making it difficult for artists to survive here. Only about 22 of the 120 houses in Yemin Moshe still belong to artists and there is some resentment toward wealthy Jews who live abroad but have purchased property here, which again raised real estate values and thereby increased the tax burden for the artists and other inhabitants.

From the Dilians' walk down to the next intersection where you will see a street sign that reads Tura, for Touro. On either side are magnificent flower beds, raised above street level. Continue down Ha-berekha past Tura and stop at the next crossing. Look at no. 12, on the lower right corner. Flowers planted in tin cans and old pots decorate the tiny yard, a true picture of the neighborhood earlier in the century. Turn left here on Malki Street. At no. 18 is the Wien Gallery and if you are a serious collector of nineteenth- and twentieth-century masters, you should make it a point to visit this fine establishment where works by Picasso, Chagall, Miró, and others can be purchased at prices that would be considered low anywhere. The Wiens have lived here since 1974. They brought many of their masterpieces with them from New York.

No. 23 is another unrestored dwelling with cacti and geraniums in rusty cans. A huge mulberry tree shades a courtyard behind a stone wall whitewashed in faint blue lime. Proceed up four steps and across Ha-migdal Street, and walk all the way through to the other end of the small park with the three large eucalyptus trees. Notice the red-tiled roofs on the right, so typical of houses built at the end of the nineteenth century. At

Alley, Yemin Moshe

the end of the park go down seventeen steps distinguished by a wide stone banister. Turn right and continue your descent along Ha-metsuda Street. Stop at the intersection with Pele Yöez Street, which was named for a famous work written by a late-eighteenth-century scholar. On the left and across the valley you can see part of the Citadel, *metsuda* in Hebrew.

To the left of the small drinking fountain are four steps, which lead to a stone-paved platform in front of the Van Leers' house. An old cistern that was beneath the platform was converted into an indoor swimming pool by architect Moshe Safdie when he was rebuilding the house. Light enters through the glass-covered openings. Turn left at the fountain, and you will see grass and olive trees—a good resting place—a small park named for Judith Montefiore. On the left, at no. 23, Pele Yöez, are the studio and house of Ruth Matar. Here you can find various ceremonial objects, like spice boxes made of gold or silver, or a hand-painted *ketubbah*, the traditional marriage contract given to a Jewish woman, which spells out her rights. Meant to protect women when the Law was given to Moses several thousand years ago, it would hardly satisfy today's feminists. Matar's versions are objets d'art.

The next house past Matar's is a modest, one-story Persian synagogue with a palm and a crooked pine tree in front of it. A sign, in Hebrew only, says Yismach Moshe, "Moses will rejoice." The section beyond the synagogue was developed later, and poverty-stricken Jews from Iran lived there, near their synagogue.

Turn back, past the Van Leer house and across Ha-metsuda, and continue on Pele Yöez Street. The first building on the left after you cross the intersection is Beit Yisrael, a synagogue founded by Ashkenazi Jews in 1899. Inside, a plaque near the old ark records the generosity—213 pounds and eight shillings—of Israel Moshe Halevi of London, who donated money for the building. The synagogue fell into disrepair first when the community began to dwindle after the Arab riots of 1929 and 1936, and later because of war. After 1967 the synagogue was restored, and many come to pray and study here. A library and a study hall are located in the former basement.

When you continue along Pele Yöez Street you will pass a small terrace with a bench on the left. Walk left

seventeen steps down Ha-migdal—"the tower"—
Street and turn right on Ha-mevasser; the name means
"the messenger who brings good tidings." If you encounter a black cast-iron figure holding what seems
like a lantern, you are in the right place. Look at the
façade of the house on the left. Behind a wall covered
with grapevines there is a barred window and the
palm of a hand that by now you must recognize.
Above the arch of the balcony, carved in the stone, is a
Star of David; also the word *Jerusalem* and the date,
1906, both in Hebrew. Walk past the olive tree planted
in the middle of the cobbled street and at the next intersection (Ha-berekha) look to the left, at the large
iron gate inside a stone arch. This was the main gate to
Yemin Moshe. The foundation stone is above the arch
on the outer, other side of the gate. You can walk
down sixteen steps to look at it, then return to this
crossing. Before you resume walking along Ha-mevasser look at the house on the upper-left, southwestern corner of the intersection, a two-story building
with a balcony with a black grille and the street sign.
Three symmetrically arched windows on the second
floor are well defined in stone; above the middle one
the *hamsikeh* appears once more. Walk past the house
where, over a very high retaining wall, cascades of geraniums, passion flowers, and morning glory come
pouring down. Ha-mevasser terminates with a house
whose front door is covered by a small green awning.
The red-tiled roof is trimmed in bright green.

This is Mishkenot Sha'ananim Restaurant, the only
kosher "Four Forks" French restaurant in Israel. The
food here is good, the service polite, the view enchanting, the private-stock brandy unique, and you never
know which VIP you may run into in this very elegant
and very expensive place.

Walk up the eighteen steps. On the right you can
see no. 7, Yemin Moshe Street, the J. Robert Fisher
Hall. Above it is the brown trellis of the balcony of the
Sephardic Synagogue. The synagogue is open only on
late Friday afternoons and on Saturday mornings. The
main entrance is on Malki Street. The building was
built in 1897 to serve as a synagogue for the Sephardic
families in the area, and has been beautifully restored
since 1967.

Turn left onto the street that runs behind the restaurant. You can sit on the wide banister and gaze at the long row of apartments on the left with the crenellated roofline. This is the first residential quarter built outside the Wall in 1860, Mishkenot Sha'ananim.

E. W. Smith, the British architect who designed Mishkenot, created a mirror image of the Wall across the valley in the parapet along the roof. Although the arches above the doors and windows are more elongated than was customary here, the masonry frames are made of the traditional hard stone used in local building; the alternating short and long blocks create a pleasing effect. The walls are three feet wide, the ceilings in the rooms are almost fifteen feet high.

A few years after it was built, Mishkenot was described by a local writer, Menachem Mendel Rischer:

> Mountains were flattened, and a strong wall with gates and locks was built, and twenty-two houses [apartments] in a row, beautiful and adorned in the manner of English builders from good masonry stones, with paved courtyards in front and back . . . and a *plompi* [pump] was sent from London so they [the residents] will not have to exert themselves and use a bucket. . . . The windows have melted iron flowers and buds . . . and each person and his family were given a large room, and a small one for cooking, and one for storage.

Mishkenot's plan is not typical of later Jewish quarters built with the entrances facing an inner courtyard that could be locked at night for security reasons. Another feature attesting to Smith's lack of familiarity with local conditions is the awning, with its lacelike trimmings, which had to be added on sometime after the completion of the building to provide protection from the sun (the apartments face east). The pipes that support the overhanging roof of the porch still bear the imprint: G. S. Culver, East Kent Metalwork, Ramsgate, England. Montefiore's estate was in Ramsgate.

If you look closely at the solid doors you can see that they are marked by letters from the Hebrew alphabet, beginning with *alef* above the first door on the right. The last apartment is *kaf-bet* or twenty-eight. Contemporary reports differ as to how many units were here; the numbers range from twenty to twenty-six. Wilson's map of 1864 shows this row divided into twenty-eight units, and we do know that some apartments were used as synagogues and study houses for

Mishkenot Sha'ananim

the Ashkenazim and for the Sephardim, each community praying in its own tradition. There was also a
"House of Balm" here, a pharmacy for which no Hebrew word existed then, and a *mikveh*, a "ritual bath."

There are several myths connected with Mishkenot,
including descriptions by people who "saw" a hospital
with forty beds here; the beds were empty because the
patients were afraid to stay in this "wilderness." Another tale informs us that Montefiore had to pay people to live in the apartments, and even then they spent
only the day here—at night they returned to the safety
of the Jewish Quarter within the Wall. In fact, Sir Moses did send money twice a year to the families resid-

ing here, a small gift of three pounds accompanied by a request that the apartments be kept clean. During the cholera epidemic of 1865 about 15 percent of the population of the Jewish Quarter was reported to have died. No one fell ill in Mishkenot. This helped convince people that clean air and water were very beneficial, and thus increased the desirability of this area. It encouraged people to move outside the Wall. Four more units were added here in 1866, probably the ones where the Jerusalem Music Centre is now located.

Walk along the long line of apartments, and in front of the fourth door look through the fence for the first tree, a small pine. A low stone wall bears inscriptions in memory of Avraham Michael Kirschenbaum, who fell here in the war of 1948, in front of his house. He was "twenty-two springs old."

Continue to the small gate house and enter it. On the right, in the middle of the roofline, is a memorial tablet to Judah Touro whose money was used to build Mishkenot. At the top of the stairs on both sides are water cisterns, but the *plompi* is gone. Beautifully restored after 1967, Mishkenot Sha'ananim functions today as a guest house for visitors from abroad—artists, scholars, and writers who come to work in Jerusalem. It is a truly wondrous place.

The theme of water runs like a leitmotif through Jerusalem's history, and not a hundred yards away from Montefiore's *plompi* are the remains of an ancient aqueduct that carried water to the Second Temple. To see it, turn left when you come out of Mishkenot's gate house and walk back a few steps in the direction of the restaurant. Just before you reach the back of the restaurant, on the right, is a large, stone-paved terrace. When you stand at the edge of the terrace closest to the Old City Wall, the aqueduct, covered loosely by flat stones, is at your feet.

Turn back once again along the lane and go past the gate house of Mishkenot. The walk continues through blazing purple bougainvillea to a tall, white monolith just beyond the southeastern corner of Mishkenot. Go up a few steps to look at the memorial created by sculptor Igael Tumarkin. Surrounding the base of the stone there is a pile of farm tools and munitions. The inscription, carved into the stone in Hebrew and Arabic, is the oft-cited passage from Isaiah (2:4). It was quoted by Sadat, Begin, and Carter when the Egyptians and Israelis signed a peace treaty in Washington on March 26, 1979: "And they shall turn their swords into plowshares, and their spears into pruning-hooks. Nation shall not lift up sword against nation, neither shall they learn war any more."

With the monolith on your left, walk down to the red-and-white posts that make the side road a dead end to car traffic. Look both ways before crossing Derech Hevron, the ancient road to Hebron. On the left there is a sign announcing the construction of the Film Archive Cinémathèque. Near the sign, to the right of the path that goes down to the valley, there is a small Jerusalem Foundation marker for Wolfson Garden. Turn to face the marker, and with the memorial across the street on your right now look at the upper-left-hand corner of the building in front of you, the one with the arched windows and large TV antenna. A cable begins there and a boxlike object projects over the edge of the flat roof. The box is rusty and hard to see because of the vegetation; you may wish to walk a few steps down the path leading to the valley to get a bet-

Cable, old Ophthalmic Hospital (Spanish Colony)

ter look. The cable stretches all the way across the Valley of Hinnom to Mount Zion, and thereby hangs a tale. To have it related, walk up to the building, now the Spanish Colony, at no. 15, Derech Hevron, where you can enter the cafeteria on the lower-left side, or else walk past the entry to the empty lot that separates this building from the ruined one up the street. The cafeteria offers a good selection of dishes at a buffet lunch, or just something to drink. You can read the next couple of paragraphs on the terrace garden.

No. 15, Derech Hevron, the damaged building, and the one across the road were all part of the British Ophthalmic Hospital, founded by the Order of St. John in the last two decades of the nineteenth century. (See page 57 for the history of the Order.) The hospital treated mostly Arabs who suffered from trachoma, the highly contagious and often blinding eye disease. The services of the British doctors were in great demand and the waiting room of the clinic established in 1882 across the road was always crowded. Arab patients would arrive from their villages and sleep outside the gates, which were opened at 1:00 A.M. There was pushing and shoving until patient number 100 was admitted. Then the doors were locked and no one could enter or leave the building. The waiting often lasted ten hours.

The three buildings were damaged in 1917 but escaped lightly in the 1948 war. The hospital remained in Jewish hands after the cease-fire in that last war. The Order decided to sell it to the Israelis and build another hospital in East Jerusalem where most of their patients lived. It is interesting to note that the Jordanians wanted the hospital relocated in Amman—Jordan did little for the development of Jerusalem—but the Knights of St. John have a history of more than eight hundred years in the Holy City. Supported by the Arab City Council, the new hospital was finally built north of the Old City in a section called Sheikh Jarrah.

From the steps of the garden in back of the restaurant you can see the box and the cable, remains from the War of Independence in 1948. In May of that year, the Israelis were trying desperately to break through to the besieged Jewish Quarter in the Old City. West Jerusalem was also surrounded by Arabs then, but the situation in the Old City was far worse. On May 18 the

Israelis occupied Mount Zion and hoped to use it as a bridgehead to the Jewish Quarter. Arab snipers sitting on the ramparts just a few feet away made it difficult to deliver supplies across the valley and up the mount. A cable was then laid on the bed of the Valley of Hinnom, and there it remained during the day. At night, with the help of a crank located on the roof of this building, the cable was stretched taut high in the air, beginning here and ending at the Gobat School on Mount Zion. Bread and guns were ferried over in the box, and the wounded soldiers were evacuated from the front line on return trips. The box was built to accommodate a stretcher.

The view across the valley is spectacular. The western part of the Wall is on the far left, where one can also see the clock tower of St. Saviour and the red roofs of Casa Nova. To their right is the minaret in the Citadel. The first building outside the southwestern corner of the Wall is the Greek Orthodox Seminary with the light blue shutters; just below it and to the right is the former Gobat School, where the cable ends. On the slope above the turn in the road is the Protestant Cemetery. The Dormition Abbey and its bell tower loom behind. To the right of the mountain, beyond the Valley of Hinnom, is another ridge, the Mount of Offence, where a stone wall surrounds a small, dark green wooded area. The village that clings to the slope is Siloam.

Between you and Mount Zion the Hinnom winds its way to join Kidron and together they continue to the Dead Sea. Nestled at the foot of Zion, below the road, is the Orchestra House, in a newly renovated building. A settlement of impoverished Jews, Shama'ah, was built in that vicinity in 1900. Some Arab families joined them and they coexisted peacefully until the 1929 massacre of the Jews of Hebron. As the dead and the wounded were brought to Jerusalem along Derech Hevron, the frightened Jews moved to less isolated parts of the city. The houses were badly damaged in 1948 and most have been torn down since.

There are many caves in the valley where exiles, rebels, and political and religious refugees have found shelter over the centuries. Gypsies lived in them in the early nineteenth century. There is also an ancient burial ground, the cemetery of the Karaites, a heretic sect that broke away from the mainstream of Judaism in the eighth century. Farther down the valley, not visible from here, is the Field of Blood, known by its Aramaic name, Haceldama. According to Matthew, after Judas betrayed Jesus he gave the thirty pieces of silver to the priests, who refused to put it in the treasury because it was the price of blood. Instead, they used it to buy a burial place for strangers "whereof the field was called the Field of Blood to this day."

There are plans to restore the damaged building next to the Spanish Colony. It was in the process of being torn down to make room for a large hotel when protests began about the destruction of historic buildings. Ten years and four architects later, current blueprints call for incorporating the former Ophthalmic Hospital buildings into the new hotel; the box and cable will be repainted and made accessible to the public. Before you leave take note of the beautiful tile floors, different in every room, with borders reminiscent of Oriental rugs. On the way out look for a plaque, near the handicraft store, in memory of Genevieve Lady Watson, Dame of the Order of St. John, who worked in the hospital and died in Jerusalem in 1936. Her husband was Sir Charles Watson, a well-known British explorer.

Cross the street and enter no. 12, the former outpatient eye clinic, currently the House of Quality. The name comes from the "seal of quality," *ot hamutzar* in Hebrew, an award given by a special board that evaluates design and workmanship of the goods produced or displayed here. You can watch artists and craftsmen at work: glassblowers, weavers, or silversmiths. There are about fifteen studios on location; 150 other artists, all from Jerusalem, display their works in David Palombo Hall, named after the sculptor killed on Mount Zion in a road accident. Here you can buy batiks, silk prints, weavings, dresses, pottery, jewelry, glassware, and wood carvings. There is a coffee shop on the first floor, additional display space on the second. Over the doorways in the inner courtyard are coats of arms carved in stone, in memory of the Knights of St. John.

You now have two choices; our walk is nearing its end. If you are not tired you can add a late-nineteenth-century railway station and *khan* to the walk, and visit

the Church of St. Andrew, an interesting 1920s structure—which means a detour of about three-quarters of
a mile. If you prefer a shorter version, turn left and
walk down the road past the monolith and continue
from there, on page 182.

Turn right for the somewhat longer walk, and cross
the street again. A bit up the road, glance over the
stone banister at a new vista. Beyond the village of Siloam is the tall bell tower of the Russian Church of the
Ascension on the Mount of Olives; next to it on the
right are the arches of the Intercontinental Hotel; below, covering the slope, is the Jewish cemetery.

When you walk a few more steps up the hill you
will pass by an iron gate at no. 20. There you see the
house that Shlomo built, but beware of the dogs: at
any given time there are at least four large ones roam-
ing the property. Shlomo moved here in the late 1950s
when he was a student at Hebrew University. He had
become disenchanted with Jerusalem landladies who
were always complaining about the number of show-
ers a person took—water was a scarce commodity
then—and who also displayed too avid an interest in
their tenants' "affairs of the heart." Shlomo found this
abandoned guardhouse near the 1948 Armistice line
then, and he is still renovating it.

Continue up the hill to the traffic light. You are now
climbing the slope of Givat Hananiah, the Hill of Evil
Counsel, or Abu Tor, depending upon whether you
are Jewish, Christian, or Moslem. In Hebrew the hill is
named after Hananiah, the High Priest who was buried
here late in the Second Temple Period. Christian tradition tells of the summer house of Caiaphas, the High
Priest, on this hill. Here Caiaphas asked Jesus: "Art
thou the Christ, the Son of the Blessed?" (Mark 14:61.)
When Jesus answered in the affirmative Caiaphas tore
his robe, a sign of mourning, because he had heard
what he considered to be blasphemy. Others present
shared his view, hence the origin of "evil counsel."
(The Armenians believe the house of Caiaphas was on
Mount Zion. To add to the confusion, there is another
Hill of Evil Counsel not far from here.) The Arab
name, Abu Tor, means "father of the bull." In the days
of Saladin, a brave warrior who always rode a bull was
"given" this hill after he helped secure the victory over
the infidels, the Crusaders, in 1187. In the late nine-

teenth century the Jews built some houses here and called the section Beit Yosef, after Yosef Navon, who helped build the railway to Jerusalem.

A story is told by Dov Yosef, the military governor of Jerusalem during the 1948 siege, about the Christian Arab families who lived on this hill. In anticipation of the Second Coming these families always took along an extra plate when they went on picnics, in case Jesus should suddenly join them; on their houses they hung signs saying "Maybe today."

Turn right at the intersection of Hebron Road and Yosef Navon Square, which leads to David Remez Street. The building on the left is one of the few modern buildings from the Mandate Period in which the British broke their own law requiring that all houses be built of stone. This 1920s concrete building was the Government Printing Office.

On your right is the highest point on this rocky hill, where the Roman legions of Pompey camped in 63 B.C. In 66 A.D. Roman troops again besieged Jerusalem, for four long years, but could not capture her until Titus built a wall around the city and prevented the Jews from smuggling in fresh supplies. Josephus describes the wall, four and a half miles long, which went west from the Mount of Olives and Siloam to "the tomb of Ananus [Hananiah] the high priest, embracing the hill where Pompey's camp had been."

Straight ahead is the Jerusalem train station, which has barely changed since its grand opening in 1892. The building, one of the few "Italian Renaissance" types in Jerusalem, is modest and symmetrical, and its arched doorways are accented by fine masonry work. The corners of the building are both emphasized and strengthened by quoins. The triangle of the roof and the "wings" on either side of the second story are later additions that detract somewhat from the integrity of the original lines.

For centuries the road from Jaffa, the main port of entry to the Holy Land, was barely more than a path. After a dangerous sea voyage on slow sailboats under threat of piracy, passengers had to be taken ashore by small rowboats because the harbor was full of boulders, forcing larger vessels to anchor at a distance. Once on terra firma voyagers had to face Turkish bureaucracy, and only then did they begin the slow journey to Jerusalem, which took a day and a half. On horse, on donkey, or on mule, they climbed up through rocks and thorns. They were frequently assaulted by bands of marauding Arabs, and they had to pay tolls and road taxes that were arbitrarily imposed by greedy pashas.

When the Suez Canal was opened in 1869, Emperor Franz Josef came to Jerusalem, and the Turks leveled and widened the road so that his carriage could reach the city. The wheel never became part of the Islamic world; the carriage was the first such vehicle in the Holy City since perhaps the day of the chariot.

Plans for a train line began in 1855 when Sir Moses Montefiore tried to persuade several of his London colleagues in The City to invest in a railroad that would connect Jerusalem to the coast, but nothing came of it. The Sublime Porte would not guarantee a minimum 6 percent profit on top of providing the land for the line. Several other attempts failed until the concession was given to Yosef Navon, a thirty-year-old descendant of a prestigious Sephardic family (his grandson became president of Israel). Navon had a hard time raising local capital and at the end had to sell the rights to a French company that became known as Société Ottomane des Chemin de Fer de la Palestine. Halfway through the project, even before the railway reached the difficult mountain terrain, the society ran out of money. Some French Catholics came to the rescue, hoping to facilitate the journey of the pilgrims. The station could not be built close to the Old City because of the topography; it was next to impossible to bring the line across the Valley of Hinnom. The project took three years to complete; the station was inaugurated with pomp and circumstance in September 1892. For his efforts Navon received the French Legion of Honor, a Turkish medal, and the title *Bey*, the equivalent of "His Highness."

The train made life easier for all travelers, and after a few years it even ran fairly regularly. There were exceptions, though, as evidenced by contemporary humor: "Why do you complain about the service?" a young man asks his friend. "It is now three-fifteen and the train is here, only fifteen minutes late." "This is yesterday's train. Today's will arrive in twenty-six hours."

At present a train departs for Tel Aviv and Haifa

twice a day; it usually takes two hours to get to Tel Aviv, three to Haifa. The scenery along the route is dramatic, especially in the first hour as the train makes its way through Wadi Sorek. Perhaps because of the station's location, trains never became an integral part of the city's life.

If you are facing the station, turn right and go along David Remez Street (named after Israel's first Minister of Transportation) until you reach a late-nineteenth-century *khan*. It was used as a storage area for cargos that arrived by train, and also as a "parking" place for camels. The old *khan* has been converted into a theater that features concerts and plays, and it has become one of Jerusalem's favorite night spots. At the Poire & Pomme restaurant, you can eat either indoors or out on the terrace that overlooks the inner courtyard's olive trees and grinding stones. The restaurant specializes in crêpes, but also serves homemade soups, omelettes, and pasta.

Turn right when you leave the *khan*. The next, pre-1865, building is the British Consulate, open Monday through Friday. Like most other major countries, Britain maintains two consulates in Jerusalem; the other is in the former Jordanian part of East Jerusalem.

Continue along the stone wall until you see a driveway with a "no entry" sign for vehicles—a red circle with a white line through it. On the right is the Scottish Hospice and Church of St. Andrew, named after one of the first followers of Jesus, a fisherman born on the shores of the Sea of Galilee who later became the patron saint of Scotland. In the eighth century St. Andrew's relics are believed to have been brought to the Pictish King Angus, via Constantinople, and buried in the town on the North Sea that now bears the saint's name. Andrew is said to have been crucified in Patras on a cross shaped like an X—hence the origin of St. Andrew's Cross.

Before you enter the church, note the decorative blue tiles in the small doorway of the hospice and in the water fountain. The foundation stone was laid by Field Marshal Viscount Allenby on May 7, 1927, to commemorate the British victory in the Holy Land a decade earlier. The church was designed by Holliday.

St. Andrew's Church

It is interesting to note that like other architects who were brought to Jerusalem from abroad in the 1920s and 1930s, he too tried to integrate local motifs into his designs. This is a successful attempt: the building is low, its mass is broken both by domes and by a stripped version of a Crusaders' tower, and by a few (inevitable) arches. The simple lines repeat themselves within the pure, white church. Light comes in through blue and green Hebron glass panes in the symmetrical windows. The seats are wooden with blue kneeling cushions. There are many memorial tablets in the church, and an interesting Bride's Bell. In the floor near the altar is a memorial in honor of King Robert the Bruce who asked, before he died in 1329, that his heart be buried in Jerusalem since he had not fulfilled a vow to visit the Holy Sepulchre. While carrying the heart in a box to the Holy City, Lord Douglas was attacked and killed by the Moors in Spain. The box was recovered and buried in Melrose, and six centuries later the citizens of that town gave the tablet here "in remembrance of the pious wish" of the king. The chairs in the nave bear the names of parishes in Scotland.

People who have stayed in the hospice recommend it highly.

Walk to the end of the driveway and at the bottom turn right onto the dead-end street that takes you past Tumarkin's white sculpture to Derech Hevron.

Turn left and walk down the ancient route that connects Jerusalem with Bethlehem and Hebron. About a hundred yards past the monument, almost hidden by small olive trees on the left, you may notice an old arch, part of the aqueduct we saw before.

The road turns right and crosses the Valley of Hinnom as it did in 670 A.D. when the Bishop of Arculf, a pilgrim, wrote of a stone bridge built southwest of Porta David, the Byzantine name for the city's western entry, now Jaffa Gate. Follow the road until you are in the middle of the bridge. When you face Mount Zion, on your left is a Turkish water fountain, a *sabil*, which has recently been cleaned by the Jerusalem Foundation. One hopes that soon the flow of water will resume so that weary Jerusalem-walkers will be able to quench their thirst as travelers did in the days of Suleiman. One also hopes that people will stop throwing trash into this lovely monument. Inside the *sabil* the inscription testifies that the great Sultan Suleiman "ordered the building of this blessed fountain" in 1536.

Go a few steps back in the direction of Mishkenot and turn right where the parapet of the bridge ends just in front of a flight of stairs. Enter Mitchell Garden—the name is on a stone marker. The bridge, or dam, should now be behind you, Yemin Moshe on the left, the Old City Wall on the far right. If you look toward the back of the *sabil* you can see the plaster that is still covering the wall of the dam. The plaster prevented the water from seeping through the stones. The part of the valley closest to the dam was known as the Sultan's Pool. Both the pool and the valley have interesting histories. There are many benches along the path where you can sit and read; our final destination is the low row of shops at the end of the path, Hutzot Hayotzer, on the northern edge of the valley.

Gai Ben Hinnom in Hebrew means the "valley of the son of Hinnom." It is first mentioned in the Bible as the border between Benjamin on the north and Judah on the south, at the time when Joshua divided the land among the Twelve Tribes of Israel. (Joshua 15:8, 18:16.) At that time Jerusalem remained a walled Jebusite stronghold. Some three hundred years later, around 1000 B.C., King David conquered the city. The valley acquired its ill repute in the days of the kings of Judea, who "did that which was evil in the sight of the Lord"—like King Menashe, who "made his children to pass through the fire in the valley of Hinnom." (2 Chronicles 33:6) The Molech stood in this valley then, the terrible god who demanded human sacrifice. Made of copper, with outstretched arms and the head of a bull, a fire roaring in his belly, he accepted human offerings. When a child was put into his insatiable arms, loud drums were beaten to drown the screams of the helpless victim. Tophet was another name for this place; it may have originated from *toph*, which means "drum" in Hebrew.

The sins committed in this locale—Gai Hinnom— gave birth to the concept of *gehenom*, "hell" in Hebrew, where the wicked burn and suffer, while the just feast on the meat of the Leviathan in the Garden of Eden. Via the Greek of the New Testament (Matthew 5:22) the word *gehenna* entered French and English.

In Arabic it is *jehennum*. The Moslems, though, call this the "Valley of the Violin," Wadi Rababa, perhaps because of its shape.

The Sultan's Pool is the name of the water reservoir that used to cover the area from the new stage that you see to the road. The pool was created by the dam that stopped the flow of rainwater from continuing on to the Dead Sea. The pool may have first been formed when Herod's masons were searching for stones for his ever-growing building projects in the first century B.C. Josephus writes of the Serpents' Pool, which may have been in this location. In the Crusader Period this was known as Lac Germain, named for a citizen, Germain, who was concerned with supplying water to all the people: he had bowls chained to three marble tanks from which anyone could drink. The name has been translated, incorrectly, as the German Lake. Suleiman the Magnificent's first project in Jerusalem was the improvement of the water supply. An aqueduct that brought water from Solomon's Pools was repaired, as was the reservoir here that bore his name. For a brief period the Sephardim in Yemin Moshe called the body of water el Rio de Montefiore. Children used to swim in the pool in early summer when the water level was high. The pool was five hundred feet long, two hundred feet wide. The upper valley was used as a thrashing ground—bits of pottery were smashed here and recycled as gravel; and once a week the cattle market was held here. In the southeastern corner, closest to the dam and Mount Zion, stood a veterinary hospital in the beginning of the century.

Where you see another marker that says Mitchell Garden, go out through the stone gate. Across the street is a house with the sign Eliel Dror Street. Walk to the right and, where the main part of the road begins to climb uphill, take the narrower branch, which goes right to where you see the back of Hutzot Hayotzer (with barred windows, and green flower boxes along the edge of the roof). When you reach a millstone at the bottom of a street of wide steps, and see the James Felt Lane sign, you will know that you are in the right place.

Hutzot is the Hebrew word for "outskirts" or "street," and *yotzer* is a "creator," thus this attractive shopping mall is called the "Street of the Craftsman." It

is all that remains of a late-nineteenth-century neighborhood, Jorat el-Anab. A *jora*, as every Jerusalemite
knows, is an "open sewer" or a "pit," and *anab* is the
Arabic for "jujube." Jujube trees used to grow here and
the fresh fruits were sold in the city markets. In this
"Pit of the Jujube Trees" lived a mixture of poor Arabs,
Christians, and Jews. The latter were mostly Sephardim
who either worked in the slaughterhouses or were ap-
prentices at various workshops and printing presses.
This area was on the border between 1948 and 1967.
Most of the extant shops were repaired and reopened
in 1971. The grinding stone, amidst a flowering bush,
comes from the Berman flour mill that stood in Jorat
el-Anab. It was one of the first mills in the city operated by steam power, a modern marvel in the 1890s. Yehoshua Berman, who operated it, was known as *la
barba blanca*—the white beard—by the Ladino-
speaking residents of Yemin Moshe.

The shopping hours at Hutzot Hayotzer vary, so you
might wish to consult a newspaper or a tourists' guide.
Here you can find many artisans at work in the studios
behind their shops. Wander through whichever store
strikes your fancy. The following is a partial list, not a
survey.

Michael Ende is a silversmith who creates charms,
rings, and ceremonial art objects. Each piece is individ-
ually hand-chased and molded. Some larger pieces can
be taken apart and each unit becomes a separate object, like a turret with tiny doors, or a box with hidden
drawers. Ende is a fine craftsman of unique, if expensive, pieces. Others who specialize in decorative and
religious art objects are Hadany and Jackson.

You can watch Ya'acov Dar throw pots at his wheel,
or select an unusual semiprecious stone or a mineral-
ogical specimen at Roup's Rock Shop, where 80 percent of the raw materials are imported but cut and
polished at the shop. You can choose a bag, a belt, or
sandals at Or Hayotzer workshop. And don't miss the
Jerusalem Tapestries of Georgés Goldstein, woven in
front of your eyes; they reproduce works of famous
artists or are based on Goldstein's own designs.

Jewels are a good buy in Israel as both the crafts-
manship and the design are of high quality. Uri Ramot
uses ancient Roman glass in fine, modern designs.
Each of his necklaces, rings, and pendants is one of a

Grinding stone, Hutzot Hayotzer

kind. Gideon Flanter settled here in 1969, before the area became fashionable. His creations are a combination of silver and different gems. The shop also carries appliquéd tapestries. Among other silversmiths who work here are D. U. Alsberg, Avi, and D & B. The latter are David Hooper and Benny Bronstein, who teach at the Bezalel Art School. Bronstein likes to show the mechanics of his trade in his jewelry—springs, locks, latches, and bolts.

There are several art galleries on this lane: Blum, Israel Art Centre, Morris. Farther up the lane, on the right, is Galerie Vision Nouvelle, which displays works by contemporary European artists. The Hamiache family, which owns the gallery, came to Israel from France in 1971, and they maintain the French connection: prints arrive here directly from the publishing house and are of high quality. The last shop on the right is the Engel Gallery, which carries works by many well-known local artists: Levanon, Reuben, Agam, Stern, Steimatsky.

Tired? Hungry? On the left is The Café, where you can enjoy a cold drink or a light meal on a spacious terrace under an orange awning. Great view! There is a Chinese restaurant in the basement in case you long for wonton soup.

Across the street and a few steps to the left is the stop for many bus routes. Or you can get a taxi at Jaffa Gate. (This whole area is due to be redeveloped, so exact directions may be futile.)

If you wish to return to the YMCA or the King David Hotel, go back down to the millstone at the bottom of the lane, walk up thirty-three steps, and turn right at the paved road. In front of you is the bullet-pocked Tannous Building. Basically you have to walk to the left and up the hill. You will soon recognize the King David and see the latticed back wall of the garden of the French Consulate. Walk in the direction of the *tricolore*, past the consulate built by architect M. Favier. It is a classic 1930s building, International Modern in rose Jerusalem stone.

You should be on Paul Emile Botta Street, named for a French consul of the last century, a well-known Assyriologist. Pass the Pontifical Biblical Institute and the Paz gas station on your way to King David Street.

Walk

5

Street of
the Prophets

○

The treasure of the world is Jerusalem. . . . The
dew which descends upon Jerusalem is a rem-
edy for every sickness. . . .
Barhan ed-Din el-Fazari
Lecturer in Damascus, circa 1300

This walk begins rather ingloriously with one of Jerusalem's first public toilets, built by the British in the early 1930s. Just off Zion Square, located behind no. 44, Jaffa Road, no. 4, Harav Kook Street, is a true monument in the realm of *pissoirs*. Very streamlined *moderne*, it is built in a style reminiscent of architect Erich Mendelsohn's work. The "Ladies" entrance is marked by a neatly engraved bronze plaque in English, Hebrew, and Arabic; it's the original sign from British Mandate days. To the right is a more recent marker that says "W.C. Men" in the aforementioned languages; a man's head with a pipe in his mouth also appears on the sign. The "W.C." is a British legacy; a 1944 Webster's Collegiate Dictionary defines W.C. as "a closet or room containing a hopper for defecation fitted with some device for flushing the bowl with water."

The battle of Hygiene versus The Call of Nature has a long history in Jerusalem. In the sixteenth century we find a complaint by the Ottoman authorities about ladies who come to the holy mosque of el-Aqsa pretending to be pilgrims but in fact stay in the courtyard "for relieving nature," thus creating problems for the sweepers. In the late nineteenth century the city hired a man every summer whose sole duty was to walk through the streets with a bucket of lime and ladle it into corners where people "lay their waters." The battle is still raging, with Hygiene not always gaining the upper hand—as many a corner in the Holy City will testify.

Inside the ladies' section there are two types of toilets, with and without seats. The flushing mechanism is activated by pulling the handle that hangs on a chain. This releases the water in the small tank above the seat known as "Niagara."

To reach the next compound up Harav Kook Street, stay on the right-hand sidewalk and walk through the

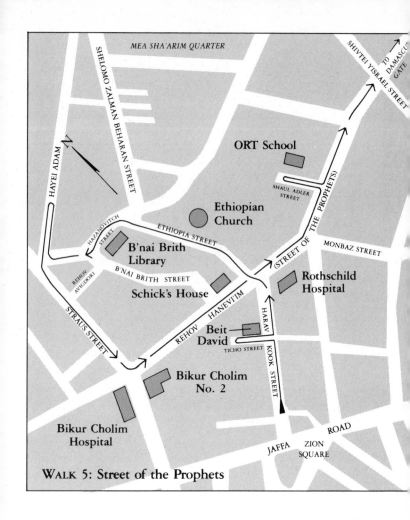

WALK 5: Street of the Prophets

gap in the wall to the small unpaved lot. You will be passing between a pine and a pepper tree and entering the courtyard of no. 6. On the right are several workshops: one produces aluminum shutters as announced by the glass and metal sign just off the street. Next to it is the Solomon Press; the sign is in Hebrew only, but you can see and hear the press through the open door. An old gentleman (a real character) who works here is ready to talk about the good old days when the Solomon Press, established in the Old City in 1860 and the second Hebrew press in Jerusalem, published the first newspaper in the city, *Halevanon*, beginning in early 1863.

The small red-tiled-roof building that is flush with the sidewalk is the Borochoff Synagogue. It bears the name of the Bukharan family who purchased the building from its Arab owners in 1895. As you continue up Harav Kook note the two oculi with clear molding frames and wrought-iron pattern on the side of this architectural gem in simple stonework.

Maskit is located in no. 8, a handsome two-story building set back from the street with an ample yard, now used for parking. In the symmetrical façade, the windows are enhanced by stone molding. The door lintel is ornamented by scrollwork, and lions' heads are carved into the wooden section of the door. The delicate wrought-iron-work and the glazed canopy are recent additions that blend well with the façade.

The building was the seat of the Italian Consulate probably through the first three decades of the twentieth century. In the 1940s it functioned as a small hotel; later it was occupied by the *Jerusalem Post*. Maskit, the current occupant, is one of the finest stores in the country. It was founded with the help of Ruth Dayan, whose idea it was to preserve and encourage the arts and handicrafts that the new immigrants brought with them to Israel. During the 1950s masses of refugees poured into Israel—from Iraq to Yemen, Morocco to the Persian Gulf—bringing with them unique weaving, silversmithing, embroidering, and leather-tooling skills. Since then Maskit has expanded; it now provides an outlet for many talented artists and artisans. This is a great place to shop for pottery, batik, one-of-a-kind dresses, or jewelry made with semiprecious stones like agates or amethysts or with pieces of ancient Roman or Byzantine glass. In the courtyard behind Maskit in summer is a small open-air café with gaily colored umbrellas, tables, and cushioned chairs covered with Maskit-type fabrics. This is a pleasant place for a coffee break or a cold lunch on a hot day.

If you stand in the backyard with the Maskit building behind you, straight across is the rather undistinguished back of the building where the *Palestine Post*, later to become the *Jerusalem Post*, was published for many years. The building was badly damaged in February 1948 when a bomb placed in a British army lorry exploded in front of it. Four people were killed but the *Post* came out that very morning, printed on a neighboring press. The paper has now moved to the new industrial section of Romema. It is still Israel's only daily English newspaper.

When you leave Maskit take a look at no. 12, on the right, a modest two-story building where the Manufacturers' Association is located. For many years Dr. Eliezer Brown practiced dentistry here. In 1921 he was one of thirteen dentists in the city, and was listed in *All Jerusalem*, the city's first edition of a phone and address book *cum* "Yellow Pages." There were only a hundred telephones in the city at that time! (Dr. Brown, to make a personal aside, was my paternal grandfather.)

One building up and across the street is a large two-story building, no. 9, whose well-ordered façade is marred by the addition of a balcony protruding in the center. On the side of the balcony is a sign in Hebrew and English: "Central Committee, Knesseth Israel." The building stands at the corner of Harav Kook and a small alley named for Dr. Avraham Ticho. Cross the street and walk down the alley to the first doorway on the right. Enter and you will find yourself in a paved courtyard of Beit David, the House of David.

This was the fourth Jewish neighborhood established outside the Old City, just after Nahalat Shivah (page 135). The land was purchased in 1872 and two years later a synagogue was completed, along with ten apartments, places for poor Ashkenazi students of the Torah to live rent-free for three years at a time. The money was given by David Reiser, also known as "the Yanover," after the Polish town from which he came. Most of the above information and the names of the donor and his wife are engraved on the plaque on the wall above the door opposite the gate. Between the gate and the door, in the center of the yard, is the mouth of a water cistern, a standard feature in every old Jerusalem court. Behind the stone rim you can see the remains of a hand pump, the great invention that replaced the bucket-and-rope routine. The inscription informs us that this model was imported from England and made by Lee Howl & Co. This courtyard is the prototype of many other Jewish developments in the city: the entrance to each apartment is through this inner court whose gate was securely locked at night. None of the original apartments had direct access to the street.

The second story was added later on, as indicated by the finer masonry. The addition was made in 1902

Courtyard of Beit David

to house the headquarters of Va'ad K'llali, or "Central Committee," which was in charge of distributing *halukkah* money. *Halukkah* means "division," in this case referring to money that came from Jewish communities abroad to be distributed among the unemployed, i.e., many of the Ashkenazim of Jerusalem. Giving money was not considered charity, but rather a duty; those who lived in the Diaspora felt obliged to support their brethren who "represented" them in the Holy Land where daily life was so harsh. It is an ancient Jewish concept. In the late nineteenth century disputes arose as to how the money should be doled out. Warsaw Jews, for example, felt that they had first dibs on money sent by Polish Jews, and eventually the whole community split into *kolelim*—sections belonging to certain towns or countries. When "American" money began to arrive and there were few Jews from the United States living in the city, this committee was

founded with a representative from each *kolel* to ensure fair share. The committee became an important
institution of negotiation with the Turkish authorities.
This assumes, of course, that the various sects were
not always too busy fighting among themselves.

When you leave the courtyard, turn right to the ad-
joining house where the inscription on the stone
plaque informs us that it was built in 1926 for Avraham
Hacohen Kook, the Chief Ashkenazi Rabbi in the Holy
Land. The house has a marvelous arched stairway that
spans the garden. Prayers can often be heard here.
Rabbi Kook tried to establish a central, universal *yeshivah*, where the teaching of the Talmud would be tied
in with the studies that have become customary over
the years—Halachah and Ma'aseh (traditional law and
common practice). He approved of Zionism even
though it was a secular movement, because he saw
that it brought young people back to the Holy Land,
who—he hoped—would eventually follow in the
ways of the Lord. He was reasonable, loving, learned,
and modest, and his following was tremendous.

At the very end of the alley and slightly to the left
stands the house of the late Dr. Avraham Ticho, Jerusalem's most famous eye doctor. In 1912 he began his
fight against trachoma; to his hospital—which was located on the ground floor of this building—flocked
Arabs from all over the Middle East. You can mount
the flight of steps to the flat where the nameplate, surrounded by floral designs, says "Anna Ticho" in italics.
Anna, Dr. Ticho's wife, continued to live here until she
died in 1980, at age eighty-six. She was a great lady
and a fine painter who specialized in black-and-white
views of Jerusalem and the Judean hills; charcoal was
her preferred medium. Meir Ronnen of the *Jerusalem
Post* eulogized her thus: "Like the great Chinese artists,
Ticho evolved her own very personal set of cyphers
for drawing figuratively in a completely non-figurative
manner; she was above mere realism."

Walk down to what remains of the garden of this
house, built by an Arab and known as el-Rashid's villa
in the 1870s. We have a wonderful description of what
this place was like then from Myriam Harry's book
about her childhood, *La Petite Fille de Jérusalem*. The
garden reached all the way to Jaffa Road then and it
was like a Persian orchard, a *bustan*. Fruit trees

bloomed among flower and vegetable plots. In the spring irises mingled with fire-red roses, and under the silvery-gray olive trees purple artichokes grew. Grapevines wrapped themselves around the fig tree, entwined like lovers. The ground floor of the house was Arab in style, with pointed arched doorways, domed rooms, and deep window seats. The second floor was European with only thin decorative grilles across the windows, and open balconies from which one could observe the traffic—donkeys, horses, camels—heading from the port of Jaffa to the Old City. In the garden lived a collection of stray animals that Myriam cared for: cats, dogs, doves, a deer, and even, at one point—to the great delight of the boys in the orphanage next door—an ostrich.

The likes of Myriam's family could have been found only in Jerusalem: the father was a converted Russian Jew called Moses Shapira; the mother a German Lutheran deaconess who longed for snow and fir trees. Shapira had an antique shop on Christian Street where he sold Holy Land souvenirs to tourists, and old books and manuscripts to collectors and museums. "Correspondent to the British Museum" said the sign above his store. He traveled far and wide in search of antiques; when the pickings got slim he began to manufacture his own. Eventually he came up with "the oldest written text in the world," which was displayed at the British Museum in 1883, and even Prime Minister Gladstone came to see it and chat with Shapira. But soon thereafter the manuscript was exposed as a forgery and the international scandal that ensued shook the learned world of archaeology. Disgraced, Shapira shot himself in a Rotterdam hotel called Bloemendaal, "Valley of Flowers." Shapira's family left Jerusalem shortly after his death; it was from Paris that his daughter later wrote her charming account of a Jerusalem childhood. The state of the garden today, like that of the house, leaves much to be desired. Still, it is pretty in winter and spring when the rains turn it green again, and we can shut our eyes and picture the blazing colors of the flowers of Myriam Shapira Harry's days, and perhaps even see the ostrich.

Stand with your back to the front door of the house, where all the clutter is. Straight ahead, just beyond the end of the garden, is the building where the Austrian

Consulate used to be at the beginning of the century. On your left, if you climb up the pile of dirt, you can see the back of the Sokolow School. You should be able to discern the lines of the original, older building to which more rooms and a second story were added. Like the Ticho mansion, this house also belonged to an Arab, Abed el-Rahman, who sold it around 1882 to a society that established an orphanage in it. Poor Jewish orphans were the first to fall victim to missionaries, and this was a modest attempt to meet the needs of the orphans and teach them useful trades. At first only six boys lived here but their numbers grew by the end of the nineteenth century when the second story was added. When some German donors wanted the children to learn German, the ultra-Orthodox objected, claiming that teaching secular subjects was tantamount to "a third destruction"—a reference to the destruction of the First and Second Temples. The children from this institution were the ones who used to climb over the fence to chase Myriam's ostrich around the garden.

During the War of Independence the school building served as the headquarters of Mishmar Ha'am, the "Civil Defense," whose duties included water distribution during the siege of 1948: when the Arabs had cut off the supply of water to the city, the old cisterns were sealed and then emptied in turn by water trucks. In every neighborhood lines formed for the daily quota—a quarter of a bucket per person. Mishmar Ha'am also supervised the activities of all "dangerous" people in the early part of 1948 after several incidents in which British army lorries, filled with explosives, were left in front of nonmilitary targets. The famed Ben Yehuda Street explosion resulted in the death of fifty-four civilians caught asleep in the predawn hours. Checkpoints were established to control the flow of people from one zone to another. Jewish prostitutes had to report to this building three times a day—not for moral rehabilitation but to repeat the rumors they had picked up from British soldiers. All's fair in love and war.

Return to Ticho Street and turn left when you reach Harav Kook. On the other side of the street is the Esther Gottesman Recreation Centre, a very modern bureaucratic-looking building.

In the courtyard are two basketball hoops. The

ubiquity of the national sport! The Gottesman Centre has replaced the old Biblical Zoo, which used to be here in the 1940s. The word *zoo* might be a bit misleading: the number of animals was rather limited. A pool with several turtles was the main attraction, plus a couple of monkeys, some deer, rabbits, several hens running loose, and a few handsome roosters with long brown tails. The zoo has moved twice and is now located in a pine grove near Tel Arza. It makes a good outing for children.

At the northern edge of Beit David, up the hill, there is a small municipal parking lot. It has replaced a Jerusalem landmark, the bakery of Mrs. Patt. For many years she operated a café and pastry shop here that was patronized by students who used to take bus no. 9 nearby, up to Hebrew University on Mount Scopus. Yaacov Dori, the commander of the Haganah and later Israel's first chief of staff, worked secretly in a room in the courtyard. In an empty cistern members of the underground drilled. Once, when the British came to search for arms, Mrs. Patt hid the cache of guns in a batch of dough; they were not discovered. With bureaucratic tact, the building was leveled a few years ago on the day of Mrs. Patt's funeral.

Harav Kook Street ends at the parking lot. Walk a few steps to the left and cross Hanevi'im Street to the corner of Ethiopia Street. If you look back toward Jaffa Road, against the background of many undistinguished tall office buildings, you can see the cupolas of the Ticho house on the right. Continue the walk on Ethiopia Street, named for the church we shall soon visit. The sidewalks here are less than one foot wide, and you will be walking with your back to the oncoming cars on the one-way street.

This late-nineteenth-century street is perhaps the most charming in Jerusalem. Behind tall stone walls— a necessary precaution a century ago—lie hidden elegant dwellings set in typical Jerusalem gardens. Most of the houses were built in the 1880s by wealthy Arab families, like the Husseinis and the Nashashibis, and they present a fine example of luxurious private building of that period. By the beginning of the twentieth century these houses were rented to Jews. Many of the leaders of the community lived here: politicians, teachers, the intelligentsia. Several institutions moved to the neighborhood: the Bezalel Art School, the Teachers' Seminary, a large orphanage. In fact, so many young people filled the street, many of them "Bohemian" students, that this was considered the "Latin Quarter" of Jerusalem.

The first courtyard on the left that we can look into is no. 3, with the big old fig tree reaching over the wall. The house used to be shared by the Levy and Feigenbaum families; the late Professor Arieh Feigenbaum's brass plate is still on the gate. Feigenbaum was a well-known eye specialist. His name means "fig tree" in German, and for many years the doctor and the tree lived side by side on the premises.

When Dr. Chaim Weizmann came to Jerusalem with other members of the Zionist Committee in 1918 after the British occupied Palestine, he stayed in this house, and the Spanish consul who was residing next door at no. 5 lent additional furniture to make life more comfortable for the distinguished-looking gentleman who, thirty years later, was to become Israel's first president.

Across the street is no. 4. You cannot see the house from the street, only a tin-covered garage and cars with CC—Consular Corps—plates. Judge Gad Frumkin used to live here; you will read about him later on. Behind the pepper tree and close to the road is no. 6, where the Sarkisians, an Armenian family, have lived for many generations. Stand with your back to the garage and look at no. 5 on the other side of the street. It's flush with the sidewalk and has a balcony with fine wrought-ironwork and many flowerpots. The houses on either side of no. 5 are set back from the street, thus forming a pattern—consistent throughout Ethiopia Street—that offers more privacy to the residents.

It is probably at no. 5 that the German Evangelical Institute for the Study of Antiquities in the Holy Land in Jerusalem functioned between 1902 and World War I, under the directorship of Dr. D. Dalman. Over fifty theologians worked here then, and the building contained a library, an archaeological collection, and a public lecture hall. By 1918 the Spanish consul was here.

Today Jacob Pins resides in the upper story. Pins is an artist who left Germany in 1936 and lived on a kibbutz before coming to Jerusalem in 1941. He is well known, not only for his paintings and woodcuts but also for his fine collection of Oriental art. A self-taught expert on the subject, he has managed to assemble a large collection with very little money. His speciality is Japanese woodblock prints, particularly the long, narrow "pillar prints," which are quite rare. Mr. Pins plans to leave his collection to the Israel Museum, where part of it has been exhibited. His apartment is enchanting: the ceiling of the large living room is paneled in wood, the floors are covered with Persian rugs, on the walls hang masks and a few Pins originals, and statues of Buddha stand here and there. The total effect is most elegant, as befits a fine scholar and artist.

Back on the right side of the street and past no. 6 is a green gate with the sign Hadassah Medical Organization; the first narrow passage you see between two stone walls leads into a neglected garden and in the rear a pink stone building with green shutters, which is now living accommodations for medical students. When the shutters are closed you can see the white stone window dressings on the ground floor, which stand out against the rose stone walls. Note the old-fashioned shoe scraper near the steps, on the left.

From 1906 to 1914 the American School of Oriental Research—known today as the Albright Institute of Archaeological Research—was located here. The school was the brainchild of Professor Joseph Henry Thayer of Harvard University. It first opened in 1900 in the Grand New Hotel in the Old City and moved here in 1906, to "its own hired house." The school closed during World War I, and in 1917 "the school building was tendered to the Red Cross which occupied it through the remainder of the struggle," according to Bulletin no. 1 of the American School, which also shows a photograph of this house. It did not have a second story then; the pillars at the entrance and the porch are also later additions. The fence that separates this courtyard from the Ethiopian property next door existed then and the tall cypresses behind the house were mere saplings.

To the right of this house, behind the wall, you can see part of no. 4, the former Frumkin house. You can climb some broad steps on the opposite side of the garden to get a better look. This is a peaceful place, where you might want to sit and read about the judge. In his memoirs Gad Frumkin tells of the World War I years, which he spent in a house with a spacious garden and water fountain that was located next to the American School and across the street from Dr. Feigenbaum. The judge was the son of Dov Frumkin, editor of *Habazeleth,* a Hebrew newspaper established in 1863. Gad was born in the Old City, in a courtyard in the Moslem Quarter shared by a nanny goat, some hens, and a white donkey on which Frumkin the Elder used to ride. The printing press was on one floor; the family lived on the second story, which overlooked the Temple Mount and the Mount of Olives. The Husseinis were their landlords, and relations were most cordial. The family moved out of the Old City to a house near here, and the move brought young Frumkin in touch with Zionist newcomers and with others who grew up in agricultural settlements. He envied them their vigor and sense of purpose and felt that the members of the old *yishuv*—the Jews who had lived in Jerusalem for generations—did not have the creative powers of the newcomers because no one ever prepared them for an active, productive life. He began to write about these problems in *Habazeleth* and, as early as 1907, called for an effort to establish commerce and industry in the city.

When, in Constantinople, the "Young Turks" came into power, Gad Frumkin's hopes rose for publishing a modern newspaper, free of censorship. There were celebrations in Jerusalem with fireworks, music, and long speeches: "Long live Liberty, Justice, and Equality." Gad wrote an article about the festivities, urging young Jews to study Arabic and Turkish so that they could become involved in the new political life of the Ottoman Empire. Dov Frumkin, still editor, crossed out the last few lines of the article. Furious, the son rebelled. How could he preach freedom and equality when he could not even express his own thoughts in the paper? He soon left his father's world of publishing and went to Constantinople to study law so that he could participate in Turkish democracy. He returned to Jerusalem at the outbreak of World War I and settled in this house with his young wife. When the country came under British administration at the end of the war, there were few people as qualified as Frumkin to lead the new judiciary system. For almost thirty years he served on the bench of the Supreme Court under the Mandate.

Go back out to Ethiopia Street and look at no. 8, immediately on your right. Over the door of the balcony on the upper story is the Lion of Judea, carved in the stone; it's the emblem of the Ethiopian royal house. Together with several other houses nearby, this place was built by Emperor Menelik II early in the twentieth century to produce rental income for the church next door. An orphanage was located here, and later the Nursing School of Hadassah.

A few steps down and across the street is no. 9, Ethiopia Street, where the offices of the American Jewish Committee are located, as well as those of several U.S. colleges. The gate is usually open, except on Saturday. You can sit in the well-cared-for garden—large cacti, oleanders, grass—and look at the façade of the building, which continues on the left, behind the low wall, as no. 7. The balcony originally was in the center of the house; thus no. 9 is part of the old house to which another wing was added. This can be clearly seen to the right of the drainpipes, where the stone is newer and the grillwork on the windows is different. Note the attractive windows of no. 7, on the left, set off in stone moldings.

Conrad Schick's map of 1894 leads one to assume that the British Consulate occupied this building at that time. Later, Dr. Arthur Rupin lived here, a man instrumental in the agricultural development of the country. Today the library of the American Jewish Committee is located in what was the salon of the house, a beautifully proportioned room with a carved wooden ceiling decorated in gold. A white marble floor with black squares adds to the elegance of the room.

The adjacent building on the right side of the garden has great arched windows framing colorful, ornate panes. It is no. 11, and you might read about it while sitting in the garden. There used to be a placard on the house indicating that here lived "Eliezer Ben Yehuda, the Reviver of the Hebrew Language and

Compiler of the Great Dictionary, 1858–1922." Ben Yehuda came to Palestine in 1881, changed his name—it used to be Perlman—and became a Turkish citizen. When his first child was born he fired their part-time Arab maid so that the baby would hear only Hebrew spoken. Among the new words that Ben Yehuda coined for the small child were bicycle, doll, towel, jam. Gloves were "houses for the hands" and a clock was an "hour indicator" until new words were made up. In his crusade to make Hebrew a living language once again, Ben Yehuda preached, wrote, begged. His fiercest opponents were the ultra-Orthodox Jews, who still oppose the secularization of Hebrew even though it had been the vernacular in Biblical times and was constantly used in letters and documents and by poets and philosophers in the Diaspora for two thousand years. The Turks also were suspicious of Ben Yehuda's activities, fearing any new ideas that might lead to nationalism; at one point he was even arrested. But in the end he won. It is hard to believe today that in 1902 there were only ten households in Jerusalem in which Hebrew alone was spoken. Cecil Roth summed up Ben Yehuda's campaign: "Before Ben Yehuda Jews could speak Hebrew; after him they did."

His wife, Hemda Ben Yehuda, also left her mark on Jerusalem. She gives this address as her residence, a separate listing from her husband's, in the 1921 *All Jerusalem* address book. She used to write a fashion column for the local press.

Turn left when you leave the courtyard and look at the façade of no. 11. The unattractive concrete balcony, recently redone, has the original handsome wrought-ironwork, and the old wooden shutters still protect the windows of the second story. On the right jamb of the arched main entry you can see the holes of the memorial placard to Ben Yehuda, which is replaced periodically and torn off again by the ultra-Orthodox of nearby Mea Sha'arim. Today, veteran sculptor David Ozeransky works behind the gaily painted door on the left.

Cross the street to the large iron gate set back from the narrow sidewalk, which is the entrance to the compound of the Ethiopian Church. Despite the sign announcing the hours when the church is open to the public, the gate is locked at times. On the gate's lintel is the royal motto, an inscription from Revelation 5:5 in Geez in honor of Emperor Menelik II who was instrumental in building the church: "The Lion of the Tribe of Juda . . . hath prevailed. . . ." In the middle of the inscription is a cross with a circle around it and a crown over it. Two lions stand guard on the sides. Some thirty centuries ago the Queen of Sheba came to visit King Solomon, a visit that, according to Abyssinian chronicles, resulted in the birth of Menelik I, the founder of their kingdom. Upon the departure of the Queen of all the Ethiopians from Jerusalem, King Solomon presented her with a flag on which the Lion of Judea was depicted; this became the royal emblem.

By the fifth century A.D. the Ethiopians—also called Abyssinians—adopted Christianity, and through the years pilgrims from the kingdom came to Jerusalem to pray and to live here. By the beginning of the nineteenth century their fortunes declined: they were poor, few in number, and many of their rights in the Church of the Holy Sepulchre were usurped by the Copts in a fight that still goes on today. In the 1880s, however, money and support began to arrive from Ethiopia. New quarters for the Patriarch were purchased in the Old City, and a large area was acquired on this street which the Ethiopians call Dabre Gannet—"Mountain of Paradise."

Inside the gate is a peaceful garden: a small lawn, olive trees, geraniums, and cypresses. On the benches, like shadows, old men sit and pray. Only three dozen priests are left in the city, but the community still maintains a school in the compound.

The round church is dedicated to Mary. One source says that architect Conrad Schick designed it. The dark purple dome sits on a drum decorated with pillars and arches on the outside. On top of the dome is a large Ethiopian cross. The foundations of the church were laid in 1882 and the building was completed ten years later. The church is built around a central altar that is in a separate, circular structure. The dome, which represents heaven, is supported by pink marble columns with blue decorations. Everywhere are pictures of Ethiopian and Coptic martyrs and saints. Leave a donation, especially if the church was opened just for you. "Every man according as he purposeth in his heart, so let

Entrance to Ethiopian Church

him give; not grudgingly or of necessity: for God loveth a cheerful giver." (2 Corinthians 9:7.)

Walk around the church's balcony, starting at the steps on the right. You should be able to recognize Emperor Menelik's house, no. 8. Inside the compound, near the steps in back of the church, is a small one-room building with two rosettes and a decorative cross above the door. This is a special Beth Lehem, from the Hebrew for "House of Bread," common to Ethiopian churches where bread was prepared to be used in services. Face the House of Bread with the church behind you and no. 8 on your right. On the left, beyond a wall and six pine trees, is a house identical in size and design to no. 8. It was built in the same year, 1906, by Empress Taitu. On the façade is a rising sun. Now a municipal Mother and Child Clinic, it was the location of the Bezalel Art School when first built. As you continue on the balcony, note the lemon grove and oleander bushes, and the small bell tower next to the vine-covered water cistern.

Turn right when you leave the Ethiopian compound. Across the street, past Ben Yehuda's house, is the gate to no. 13, which is in the back. A small arch spans the narrow passage, and steps lead to the roof of another house. Va'ad Ha'ir, the Central Jewish City Committee, was located here. There is a ravishing garden on the right. The projecting balcony, best seen from near the gate, rests on ample arches and is filled with flowers and clinging vines. Continue on Ethiopia Street to the front gate of no. 15 and look at the metal grille over the gate where you can see an Arabic number: a 1 followed by a backward 7, then an open 9 and a 0—1295. The Arabs number their years beginning with 622 A.D., the year of the Hegira, which marks Mohammed's flight from Mecca. This house was built in 1878 A.D., which one can figure out by taking lunar years into account, or by checking the *Encyclopaedia Britannica*. Pass no. 17 on the left, followed by Beit Hannah—a boy's club operated by the B'nai B'rith Women of Canada—which is set back from the street in a well-kept garden.

Stop in this fine urban aggregate. Stand with your back to the stairs which lead to the garden of Beit Hannah. The two-and-a-half-story building on your right, on the edge of the Ethiopian property, was built in the 1880s to house monks. Today it is shared by a religious school for girls and a tricot knitwear workshop. It has an interesting façade of arched and circular windows that seem to alternate at random. Across the street is no. 2, Shelomo Zalman Beharan Street, Beharan being one of the founders of the Mea Sha'arim quarter that lies at the other end of this street. (It is a fascinating neighborhood, designed by Conrad Schick and built a century ago. The inhabitants still maintain the values and appearances of eighteenth-century East European ghetto-dwellers. It is not part of our walk.) The sign on no. 2, in red Hebrew letters, says: "Daughters of Israel, the Torah commands you to dress in modest clothes which cover all parts of the body, according to the Law." Even if you are not a "daughter of Israel" don't venture there in a short-sleeved dress. On Saturdays this intersection is blocked to prevent car traffic because it disturbs the Sabbath. (Northeast of here, on the Ramot Road, cars are often pelted with stones on Saturdays. The fiercest battles in the Holy City seem to be between ultra-Orthodox and non-Orthodox Jews.) Here, with the road closed, large families come out on Saturday afternoon for a stroll, dressed in their Sabbath best. The children are scrubbed clean; little girls wear long stockings, and their hair is braided with colorful ribbons (little boys wear their hair long until they are three years old, then it is shorn). Everyone speaks Yiddish.

Opposite the former Ethiopian monks' house is no. 5, Hazanovitch Street. It's built of concrete and dates back to the early 1920s. The bougainvillea vines are as old as the house. The last house on this triangular intersection is no. 6, Hazanovitch, next to Beit Hannah, where Dr. Avigdori used to live. The fine lines of the house are marred by pipes, tanks, an enclosed balcony, and a yard full of trash and thorns. With no. 6 on your left and no. 5 on your right, walk along Hazanovitch Street. No. 3 is a hastily constructed apartment house from the period of acute housing shortages in the 1950s and 1960s. A lone tree stands on a neglected lawn, typical of the "Levantine"—or sloppy—maintenance of the house.

The street veers to the left. Follow it and step into the small parking lot and sit on the low stone retaining wall. The building in front of you is the B'nai B'rith Library; it was completed in 1903.

There were no public libraries in the city until the second half of the nineteenth century, when an English-language reading room attached to the British Consulate opened a small lending library in the Old City. In 1875 a group that called itself Tiferet Yerushalayim, the "Pride of Jerusalem," made an attempt to found a Hebrew library where secular reading material would be available. The group members were known as the Maskilim, the "Enlightened." As Sir Moses Montefiore, then ninety, was visiting the city for the seventh and last time, they named the library for him and his wife. Sir Moses donated five pounds, a rather miserly sum from a man who gave generously to far less worthy causes. Perhaps he had some misgivings, knowing Jerusalemites well by then. For a while all went smoothly. Jewish periodicals and Hebrew newspapers were gathered and made available to the reading public. But soon an uproar began, led by the Haredim, an Orthodox group, who feared anything that smacked of enlightenment or moved toward secularization. When sacred texts, like the Talmud, were discovered on library shelves side by side with secular writings by "heretics," the Beit Din, the "Rabbinical Court," issued a verdict forbidding anyone from using the library. When echoes of this battle reached London, the tired old Montefiore asked that his name be removed from the library. It closed shortly thereafter, in 1877.

A second attempt was made in 1884 when another library opened in two small rooms on Jaffa Road that were originally meant to be a grocery store. It was called Beit Hasfarim Le'vnei Yisrael, the "House of the Books of the Children of Israel." Scholars like Ben Yehuda and Luntz were among the founders; Yitzhak Horowitz was the librarian; and Ephraim Cohen-Reiss eventually became the treasurer of the empty coffers. Due to lack of funds and interest, and an abundance of disputes among the founders, this library too had to close.

The People of the Book finally pulled themselves together, realizing that irreplaceable treasures had been lost for lack of a central book depository. The year 1892 marked the four hundreth anniversary of the expulsion of the Jews from Spain; a library was established and named after Don Yitzhak Abrabanel, the leader of the Spanish exiles in 1492. Books were collected from all over the world; Ben Yehuda's library and eight thousand volumes that Yosef Hazanovitch sent from Bialystok formed the core of the collection, which found temporary shelter in the Amiel house near the Russian Compound. It was a free lending library and its doors stood open eight hours a day. When it outgrew its quarters, the land where you are now standing was purchased in 1900. The first wing of the library—a reading room on the ground floor, books on the second floor—was completed a couple of years later.

This was considered to be the National Library until the main collection was moved to a new building at the Hebrew University campus on Mount Scopus after 1925. But even then the books that remained in this location continued to provide a key to the world-at-large, especially for those of us who grew up near here. Author David Shahar, born in 1926, writes in *The Palace of Shattered Vessels*: "I liked the librarian mainly because of the gateway he opened for me four or five times a week: in the long school holidays I was capable of finishing almost any book in one day's reading. . . ." One was allowed to check out only one volume a day. Another prominent Israeli writer was a young patron of this library: Amos Oz, author of *Michael, My Michael, The Hill of Evil Counsel*, and many other books.

The library has been cleaned and repaired by the Jerusalem Foundation in recent years and it still functions, with a large reading room and a special children's section. You are looking at the rear of the building, so you may wish to walk through the well-tended garden to look at the handsome façade. Come back to the parking lot if you do.

The building across the street, no. 2, Hazanovitch, is veritable Bauhaus—stucco exterior, glass corner, curved rear wall. Built in 1921, it serves as the headquarters of Hapoel Hamizrachi, a progressive religious party that believes that its members should work to support themselves, though without neglecting their religious studies.

Walk past no. 2, Hazanovitch, and turn right. Note

the two-story building with the fading blue decor; it improves when you look at it from the small park, Na'amot Square, where the second floor, resting on *pilotis*, forms a sheltered passage—very 1930s International Modern.

On the other side of the street is no. 22, a massive building that serves as the Headquarters of the Pension and Insurance Fund of the Union of Construction Workers—so says the large sign in Hebrew to the right of the building. The small red sign next to it, on the building itself, points to a hole in the ground with a heavy lid over it—not a garbage can but a *bor bitahon*, a "safety well," a place to deposit suspicious-looking objects that might contain explosives. Russian is often heard here as the building also houses the offices of Immigrant Absorption. Built of huge prefabricated blocks that look like marble, and having small slits for windows, the tall building predates the era of energy consciousness.

On this site stood an old house in which the second Hebrew-speaking nursery school in the city opened in 1904. At that time the battle for the revival of the "Holy Tongue" was raging. At the nursery school people marveled at the sight of children who played and sang in Hebrew, the language of prayer.

When you stand facing the Construction Workers' building, on your left you'll see the Hadassah Vocational Guidance Institute in the old Nathan and Lena Straus Health Centre built "for all Races and Creeds." Nathan Straus was a Jewish philanthropist from New York. The fine white stone building is surrounded by grand old pines. The taxi station with the bright yellow sign does not add much to the area's appearance.

With the cabs behind you and the tall Construction Workers' building on your right, walk a few steps down Hayei Adam. It means "Life of Man," which is the name of an eighteenth-century book by Avraham Danzig. Within seconds the landscape changes dramatically: the institutional bureaucratic edifices of the twentieth century are left behind as you enter a hamlet ambience. The vistas that open up before your eyes are of French Hill and Mount Scopus on the east. On the left are the red-tiled roofs of Batei Wittenberg, built in 1886. On the right are modest two-story houses in the vernacular of the last decades of the nineteenth century; the balconies on iron projections were added later on.

A personal note: Worth a mention but not a detour is a house halfway down Hayei Adam. It was designed and built almost a century ago by Eliahu Berman, my grandfather. My mother was born there, and I was born and brought up there. A girls' orphanage since 1955, the house has been ruined by crude glass and concrete additions. The garden and many of the pine trees are gone.

Walk back up the steep hill to where Hayei Adam begins and turn left on Straus Street. Across the street is no. 17, Beit Hahistadrut. The large white building with a block of windows on the top floor is still bricked up, a reminder of the days when a Jordanian shell could be launched from the east and hit the building. Beit Hahistadrut, the Headquarters of the Trade Unions, stands on an internal Jerusalem "border": beyond it Straus Street begins to go downhill and meets Mea Sha'arim and Geula Streets in an area controlled by Orthodoxy. On the Sabbath the road is closed to traffic. Walk past no. 20 on the left and the Edward and Helena Mitchell Auditorium on the right. The deserted minaret behind the parking lot marks a traditional grave site of a friend of Mohammed. It is called Nebi Oq'sheh.

Cross Rehov Avigdori. At no. 18, Straus Street, look behind the gray gate into the tiny courtyard of Arazim, a public school with large, high-ceilinged, sunny rooms. When it opened in the 1930s it was called Gymnasia Sokolow for a Russian Zionist leader in the early days of the movement. One of the school's more illustrious alumni is former Chief of Staff Motta Gur, who in 1967 led his paratroopers to the Temple Mount and won the battle for Jerusalem. Gur claims that his military career began here when he organized a group of friends to come and break some school windows because the school refused to supply students with adequate sports equipment. Years later, he writes, as he passed by here on the eve of the Six Day War, he was hoping that the windowpanes would not be broken again.

No. 16 is an apartment house with vertical pilasters throughout, and stepped, almost streamlined recessions. The street here is lined with apartment houses, most of which were built in the 1930s when this was a more fashionable neighborhood and "tall" four-story apartment houses were a novelty. The street had just been paved then and was named Chancellor Street for the British high commissioner at the time (Sir John Chancellor, 1928–31).

No. 14, Straus Street, where pink oleanders and blue *ofreet* shrubs bloom, was built half a century ago. It is a modern-looking building with clean lines cluttered now by the improvisations of different tenants. For many years various Berman cousins who own the building lived side by side with noted physicians: Drs. Gross, Eiges, and Helena and Moshe Weizmann. Helena was a pediatrician; Moshe, a scientist overshadowed by his brother Chaim, who later became Israel's first president. Their mercurial nephew Ezer is a former Israeli minister of defense. The building had a tennis court in the back in its more gracious days.

Next down the street are nos. 10 and 8, which used to be the San Remo Hotel, so named to commemorate the meeting of the prime ministers of the Allies in 1920. It was at San Remo that plans were drawn up for a treaty with the defeated Turks and Britain was handed the Mandate for Palestine with a stipulation to establish a Jewish "National Home." The two-story building is decorated with a mélange of Eastern details with *moderne* articulation. Across Straus Street on the right is Beit Haropheh, the Israel Medical Association, a windowless white stone building. A finely carved bronze caduceus—the traditional symbol of medicine—appears above the entry in the convex façade.

You are about to cross the axis of this walk, Street of the Prophets, Hanevi'im Street, which branches off Jaffa Road and forms an alternate route to the Old City, ending at Damascus Gate. In the last decades of the Ottoman Period it was known as "the back road," Hospital Street, or Street of the Consuls. As the names imply, many hospitals and consulates moved to this area when Jerusalem began to expand beyond the Old City Wall. Note the fine cypresses and pines that line Straus Street as it continues downhill toward Jaffa Road.

Cross the street and enter the court of the building with the sign—in oversize graphics—that says Bikur

Cholim Hospital, Building No. 2. Built in 1894, this used to be a German hospital operated by the Diakon- issen Kaiserwerther Schwestern, the "Deaconesses Sis- ters from Kaiserwerth," who moved here from their quarters in the Old City. The development of clinics and hospitals in this area closely resembled the pattern established within the Wall half a century earlier: when one religious order offered medical services that drew all citizens to it, other religions—anxious to protect their folds—followed suit. This hospital, before it was taken over by Bikur Cholim next door, was Ziv Hospi- tal, part of Hadassah after 1948.

Where the two wings of the building meet the fa- çade is cut across by a projecting first story. Architect Theodore Sandel, a German Templar who lived near Jaffa, used a mass of Eastern and Western architectural details. The attic roof with iron grillwork has a pyrami- dal cupola tower. A dove, the symbol of the Deacon- esses Sisters, is carved on the keystone of the main portal. Note the central bifore window, and the oddly shaped, oddly grouped upper-story quadratic set of windows on the left. The building is girded by hori- zontal stone stringcourses that clearly mark the divi- sions of each story—a feature common to many of Sandel's buildings.

Across Straus Street, on the right, is the other Bikur Cholim Hospital; it isn't part of this walk. It too was de- signed by Sandel, and was completed in 1925. The main entrances of both hospitals face each other across Straus Street; the interesting doorways are set within imposing frontispieces.

With your back to the Bikur Cholim No. 2 building, turn right on Hanevi'im Street. On your right, within the hospital grounds, is a "B'rith Hall" where circumci- sion ceremonies take place. Beyond it is a green hut, a patient rehabilitation center, followed by a concrete building with small barred windows—the hospital's former morgue. Across the street is a stone wall with a gray iron gate, no. 47, which is the Catholic Ecole Française de Jérusalem, run by the Sisters of St. Jo- seph, who founded the first convent in the city in 1848 and then moved here in 1887. It too is not part of our walk.

An empty lot on the right separates the morgue from nos. 43–45, a building defaced by blue spray-paint advertising "Jerusalem wild flowers, wholesale." In former days this may have been part of the German Hospital, as the dove of the Deaconesses Sisters is carved over the small side gate. On the right side of the building is a projecting window with the Latin Cross of Jerusalem on its façade. Note the intricate iron grille over the main door, and the rotting wooden shutters, which must be as old as the house.

Cross over to no. 64, Hanevi'im Street, opposite the small gate with the dove. Walk into the compound through the iron gate with the cross above it. The garden is charming, with large cacti—*sabras*—beyond the water cistern. In two old bathtubs more flowers grow. In the far left-hand corner of the compound is the house where the British painter William Holman Hunt lived when he returned to Jerusalem for the third time in 1873. A painter of the Pre-Raphaelite school, he first came to the Holy City in 1854 and painted some of his most famous Biblical scenes, like *The Scapegoat*. In the 1870s, he either built or purchased this house, which he later left to a Russian woman who worked for him.

In 1924 the poetess Rachel lived in this compound; she was a beautiful young woman, blonde with blue eyes. When she first arrived from Russia, she tilled the fields of Kinneret and Degania on the shores of Galilee. In Jerusalem she taught Sephardic girls agriculture. She composed passionate songs, some to an unknown lover, others exalting the land. She suffered from tuberculosis for many years, and wrote most of her verse in the last years of her life.

> If I had a son,
> A small child,
> Wise, with ebony curls.
> To hold his hand
> And slowly walk
> Through the garden paths.

She died childless in 1931 at age forty-one.

Another renowned woman, Dr. Helena Kagan, spent many years here. A pediatrician, she became a legendary figure in the city where she practiced for more than sixty-five years until she died in 1978: no one, Arab, Christian, or Jew, was ever turned away from her door without receiving medical care. Former patients fondly tell of her inoculating them in this courtyard, where needles were sterilized on a large *primus*, an archaic local version of a kerosene burner.

Turn left when you leave the compound. No. 62 was built in 1924 by Dr. Propper. Set back from the street, the front entrance—an arch supported by two columns—is marred by later additions, fortunately well hidden behind the trees in the garden. Look across the street at no. 43, with the now defunct Mandarin Gallery. To the left of the building is a gate with a Russian inscription over it and the emblem of the Russian Orthodox Church on either jamb. The date is 1891 and this was the entrance to a hospice for Russian nuns.

"In every house a doctor," or so it seems on this former Hospital Street. The corner house, no. 60, Rehov Hanevi'im, served for many years as the residence and radiation clinic of Dr. Izmozik. This is a good example of local construction: The quoins of the square building are of a harder type of stone that is used to add strength and stability. The horizontal stringcourse between the floors is a common local feature; Arabs often built one-story houses hoping to add on to them later on. In order to attain a more finished look, a molding was attached to the edge of the roof. The molding became a tradition and was used even when both stories were built at the same time. Note the idiosyncratic "pediments" above the windows, the central wrought-iron balcony, the green shutters, and the crowning open-worked roof rail. The offices of the Ata Corporation are currently in this building.

Cross B'nai B'rith Street and proceed to No. 58; the number is on the left of the green gate. On a projecting block above the gate, supported by four corbels, engraved in the stone is: "THABOR, Psalms 89:13, 1882." Conrad Schick, a Swiss scholar and lover of Jerusalem, lived here. He named his house after the mountain that, together with Hermon, rejoices in the name of the Lord. Construction began in 1882. At the upper-left-hand corner of the gate-house façade you can see two small rosettes embedded in the stone. The house is a whimsical combination of local elements and stylistic touches from Europe. On the second story the corners are strongly emphasized with a Schick favorite: the "Horns of the Altar." Stone dentils adorn

the cornice along the roofline. In the middle of the ga-
ble sits a small oculus. The house today belongs to the
Swedish Theological Seminary, where Hebrew, Bible,
and the history of the Holy Land are taught. For many
years, *The Thaborian*, a Protestant publication, was issued from here.

Schick came to Jerusalem in 1846 with three other
"brethren" sent by Herr Spittler of Basel. Founder of
the College at St. Chrischona, Spittler dreamed of
spreading Christianity through the revival of Apostle
Stations; Jerusalem was to be the first mission. The
brethren, trained as craftsmen, were to live together
and teach native youths useful skills with a bit of religious training on the side. Although the project failed,
the four remained in Jerusalem and became influential
in her development. Schick first headed the School of
Industry of the London Society for Promoting Christianity Amongst the Jews (see page 78). When Charles
Wilson came to Jerusalem in 1864 (see page 92), it
was Conrad Schick who helped him both with his
knowledge of antiquity and as a liaison with the Arabs,
whose language and customs he had studied. Later, as
an architect, city planner, and archaeologist, Schick
made many important contributions. He cleared the
spring of Gihon, published the Siloam Tunnel Inscription, and excavated the so-called Herodian family
tombs. He drew the plans for Mea Sha'arim, and
among many other buildings he designed Talithakumi,
which was, most regrettably, torn down in 1980.
Schick published more than two hundred papers, articles, and reports on the city. He spent his last years in
this house; he and his wife are buried in the Protestant
Cemetery on Mount Zion.

Walk along the stone fence with the old pine trees
hovering over it, and you will pass by another projec-
tion with a stone tablet with the letters F C and D S,
and 1889 on it. C and S are Schick's initials; the date is
the year the house was completed (F and D may be
his wife's initials). In the keystone of the arch above
the round window are the Greek alpha and omega, for
God who is "the beginning and the ending."

On the other side of Hanevi'im Street is an empty lot
filled with thorns and incidental trash. It was the site of
a girls' school at the end of the last century. Cross Ethiopia Street and continue to the restaurant Mifgash Bav-

"Thabor," Conrad Schick's house

ly at no. 54, Hanevi'im Street. *Mifgash* means "meeting place"; *Bavly* is a person from Babylon, in this case the owner, who often presides over the ample lunchtime buffet. In the tall, shady tree near the entrance you can still see a board where neighborhood kids used to take turns acting as lookouts in the last days of the British Mandate and warning of approaching pa-

trols that used to confiscate arms from the Jews (but seemed to be somewhat less diligent when dealing with Arabs). Anticipating the inevitable clash that began even before the British left Palestine, arms were hidden around the city in caches. Near the bathroom in back of the house there is a cistern, where the vent pipes begin. An arms cache used to be there, underground. The interior of this former residence is typical of the elegant quarters of the Street of the Consuls. The façade features grand arcades beneath a wrought-iron, covered balcony.

Cross the street to no. 37 and see if the guard will let you enter the garden of the old hospital. If not, peek through the gate. The more modern building on the left is the Hadassah Community College. More interesting is the older building in the compound, straight across from the gate, the old Rothschild Hospital. The inscription on the lintel above the front door says "Hopital Israelite Meyer Rothschild." Note the triple window with the triangular pediment and the elegant proportions of the building. The decorative string-courses that separate the two stories—often used by Sandel, who designed the two hospitals we saw earlier—have led to speculation that this too is a Sandel creation.

This was the first Jewish hospital outside the Old City. It moved here in 1888. About a decade later, the author Luntz described it in his yearbook: a three-story building with a pharmacy, laboratories, kitchen, offices, and servants' quarters on the ground—basement—floor. On the second floor were two large rooms, one for male and one for female patients, plus an operating room and more offices. On the third floor was a children's department, a library, a synagogue, and a visitors' room. Others wrote of the spacious garden and noted the improvement over the old (circa 1854) quarters of the hospital in the Old City that held only eighteen beds while the new one had twenty-four. The garden, grassy with old trees behind a stone wall, makes this a shady resting place.

There is a wonderful "only in Jerusalem" story connected with this building. In the 1880s some foresighted Presbyterians began to worry that if the Second Coming were to occur on either a very hot or rainy day, their coreligionists flocking to Jerusalem might find themselves without shelter, an undesirable situation even on so great an occasion. Money to purchase material for a tent large enough to accommodate five thousand pious worshipers was collected in the United States and Great Britain. (How this particular number was reached is anybody's guess.) Linen, poles, and pegs were acquired; the cloth was stamped every few feet "Property of the Presbyterian Church." Mission accomplished, the Presbyterians found themselves with this huge quantity of fabric, awaiting the uncertain date of the Coming of the Messiah. Eventually it was stored in the villa of Sir John Gray Hill on Mount Scopus, now the site of Hebrew University. Next, the makings of the tent found shelter in the American Consulate until the Rothschild Hospital was prevailed upon to store the material in its new and empty basement. Perhaps the paraphernalia would still be there if it were not for an enterprising hospital administrator. One very cold winter during World War I, he decided to use the pegs and poles to stoke the furnace. Next he noticed the shortage of linen, and, feeling that the material for the tent might well rot before the Second Coming, he had it cut into sheets and hospital gowns. When and if Jesus reappeared, he reasoned, let the Rothschilds worry about a new tent then. All this might have passed unnoticed, except for some petty clerk who fought with the administrator and denounced him to the Rothschilds. He was dismissed and left for Paris where he died soon after, some say by suicide. The tent, to my knowledge, has never been replaced.

Before you leave, take a look at the gateposts. The old hospital name is carved in the stone in Hebrew, French, and Arabic. The newer, Hadassah name appears on brass plaques in Hebrew and English. The latest addition is in black Hebrew script on yellow paint, with arrows pointing to a shelter, in case of war.

Continue along the fence of the hospital and you will see a smaller, black iron gate with the words "Entrée Consultation" cut into the arch above it, the former entrance to the outpatient clinic. This hospital came under the management of Hadassah in 1918 and was the organization's main hospital until its new quarters, designed by Erich Mendelsohn, were built on Mount Scopus in 1938.

Pass the padlocked wooden doors farther along the fence. Here was a school for the blind in the early part of the century. Behind the stone wall, where the scent of jasmine is almost overwhelming, you can see the corner house with an impressive balcony. The house belonged to Shlomo Amiel of a well-to-do North African family. Mrs. Abutbul, one of his descendants, still lives in the house. In the 1950s, when the city was undergoing one of its chronic housing shortages, the family rented rooms to medical students who worked in the hospitals nearby. Early every morning the young men got up eagerly and rushed to the back windows to watch the girls at the nearby school in their exercise classes.

With your back to the house, look to the right and across Monbaz Street, named for the son of Queen Helene who came to Jerusalem and converted to Judaism in the first century A.D.; you will see an empty lot. To its right is an 1873 building, originally a German Evangelical school for boys. Start to cross Monbaz Street but stop at the traffic isle, where, when you look to the right again, you will glimpse the green domes in the Russian Compound. On the corner, after you complete the crossing, is no. 33, Hanevi'im Street, the Zion House, where Bibles in different languages are sold by Protestant missionaries. They occasionally have the dubious honor of having their shop defaced by fanatics.

Look across at no. 48, Hanevi'im Street. Note the wonderful, almost-hidden tile street sign in three languages to the left of the gate—a Mandate era legacy. The American Consulate was in this building at the turn of the century. Today you find a gallery here, a restaurant with a garish yellow sign (Karme Teman), and the Yemenite Falafel Center—the sign is in Hebrew only but you cannot miss the portrait of a Yemenite nor the smell of the hot frying oil. Falafel is a Near Eastern specialty: cakes of ground chick peas are mixed with spices, deep-fried in oil, and served wrapped in pita, the flat bread of the region. This tiny, spotless place, with standing room only, serves very good falafel.

On the right side of the street, which becomes very steep here, you pass a "romantic ruinscape," a long stone building with irregular arcades where cars are parked amid fig trees and wild-growing shrubs. Next down the hill, behind lime green and bright orange doors, flora and fauna may be purchased in the newly opened shops. The Mount of Olives provides a scenic background on the eastern horizon.

Large mirrors, an ungainly traffic device on the marked curve, indicate no. 29, Hanevi'im Street, where in an old house the offices of Dan and Raphael Ben

Dor are located. The two brothers are well-known architects who came to Jerusalem in the 1920s. If you peek through the hole in the red-painted door, you can see pieces of ceramic works amid lush greenery in a tiny courtyard. To the right of the door, a few feet off the ground, is a ring embedded in the stone—handy if you wish to tether your horse! The building was part of a Protestant children's hospital—eight beds, two cribs—that opened here in 1872 and was financed by a noble German family. It appears on Schick's 1894 map as Kinderhospital Marienstift. The physician, Dr. Charles Sandreczki—at times listed as Dr. Max Sander-ezki—was a Roman Catholic Pole who had served with the French Foreign Legion in North Africa. He later became a Protestant and came to Jerusalem in 1851, where he worked with the Church Missionary Society. It seems that he committed suicide in 1892; the hospital closed in 1899.

Cross Hanevi'im Street. Through a gray iron gate, no. 44, you can see the Public Works Department, which has been here since the early 1920s. Turn left at the shedlike structure onto Shaul Adler Street, and continue along the blue iron fence. Try the first gate; if it is locked, continue until you see the pillbox. Enter the courtyard of the ORT Vocational Training School and turn right to get to the front of the building, which faces Hanevi'im Street.

On this site stood a splendid array of tents in 1898, with rugs and elegant furniture supplied by Thomas Cook and Son. Four extra special tents were sent over by the Sublime Porte in Constantinople, all in honor of Wilhelm II and Augusta Victoria who came to Jerusalem to consecrate the Church of the Redeemer (see page 63). After the most royal visit, this "classical" villa, a dash of Renaissance in Jerusalem stone, was built for the German Probst by an architect named Palmer, apparently the same Frederick Palmer who came to Jerusalem in 1846 with Conrad Schick and "managed" the Gobat School for several years—although he was "no more than a soap boiler by profession" then. Palmer obviously made a lot of progress, as evidenced by this house: its harmonic proportions, the symmetry, the enclosed centerpiece of the façade, and the windows are all sheer "neo-Palladian." In deeply inset panels to the left and right of the central frontispiece are

German Probst's house, now ORT School

German inscriptions: *Eine Feste Burg*, and *ist unser Gott*— "A strong fortress is our God." The windows of the upper story are still bricked, a protection from Jordanian shelling in 1948. On the white board in the yard is another reminder of the conflict: a *yizkor*, a "memorial," to students of the ORT School who fell in the Arab-Israeli wars.

When the British occupied Jerusalem in 1917, they took over enemy property throughout the city, and into this German house moved Sir Ronald Storrs, the new military governor. Storrs soon invited Charles Robert Ashbee, an architect interested in arts and crafts, to act as his civic adviser for culture and aesthetics. Many of Ashbee's contributions are still with us, like the tile street signs. It is said that he was the one who convinced Storrs to pass a regulation that only stone be used in construction in the "Holy City." One night when her husband was away, wrote Janet Ashbee in her journal, Sir Ronald invited her to dine with him in this house. The gesture was not as risqué as she may have imagined, as rumors have it that Sir Ronald's appetites leaned more toward young Arab boys. At some later date under the Mandate, a training school for Arab women was located here.

When you leave the grounds of ORT, on the right, at the very end of Shaul Adler Street, are two buildings, no. 3 and no. 5, similar in style to the Probst house. They belonged to the German Evangelical Society's high school, which moved here around 1910. Today offices of the Municipality's Family Services are in those buildings.

Return to Hanevi'im Street, turn left, and walk downhill past a pink and gray stone wall, colors more commonly seen in Tel Aviv. No. 40 (and no. 38) on the left is an imposing building built by a queen, Empress Zaudito of Ethiopia. The land—according to K. Pederson, a student of Professor Ben-Arieh at Hebrew University—was purchased from another Ethiopian woman who was married to a Ustinov. (Peter's father was born in Jaffa.) She must have been Peter Ustinov's grandmother. The building, the former Imperial Ethiopian Consulate General, was completed in 1938. On his flight to England in 1936 after the Italians occupied Addis Ababa, Emperor Haile Selassie stopped here. He arrived dressed as a British officer, covered with medals, accompanied by dark beauties and heavy crates rumored to have contained gold.

In the central, upper part of the heavily rusticated façade is a mosaic rendition of the familiar lion. Below it, in a smaller pediment of the same design appears a crown with a cross and an inscription in Geez that is the motto of the royal house of Ethiopia. Grand arcades, an open loggia, attached columns, and triangular pediments with colorful mosaics lend an exotic air to the façade. Modern additions deface the building; some of the elegant windows are blocked; balcony space is used for storage and laundry.

Cross Hanevi'im Street, and a few yards up the hill is a large iron gate, no. 25. Inside are formal symmetrical gardens with circular beds of pine, cypress, and pepper trees. The handsome one-story house is on a high ground base with a neoclassical portico. Four piers with a cast-iron balustrade mark the central roofline. On Schick's 1894 map this is listed as Haus der Englischen Judenmission—the English missionaries used to spend their summers in this villa, away from the putrid alleys of the Old City. The building beyond the house, on the right, appears on Charles Wilson's 1876 map. This whole area, including the children's hospital, belonged to the Protestants. Today the Finnish Messianic Center is located in no. 25; in the 1950s, glass was produced here by the Phoenicia factory.

Continue downhill, past no. 23, where behind a doorway set off by two imposing columns Israel Press Clipping Ltd. operates. Go through the next gate into a typical Jerusalem courtyard of an extended family, where additions were made as sons or daughters got married and moved into their own apartments, still sharing the cistern and the yard space of this Berman family compound. The arched windows in the main building on the left are classic examples of local construction: twin arched lintels under a larger relieving arch that takes the pressure of the weight of the wall off the windows. The small round opening over the windows, here purely decorative, was essential in the days predating glass panes: in winter the wooden shutters were closed and air circulated through the round hole. Note the heavy white quoins, the rusticated stone used for the building, and the fine portal, all marred by recent additions.

When you leave, turn right, walk down to the end of the block and look across the street. No, you are not in Florence. What you see is the tower of the Italian Hospital and Church built in the style of the Palazzo Vecchio. Building began before World War I but was completed only in the 1920s. Today it is part of the Ministry of Education. The enormous compound is typical of many monumental edifices built by churches in the city since the middle of the nineteenth century. During the same period, Jews were trying to meet their housing needs by building modest residential quarters of which Beit David and Batei Wittenberg are good examples. The Arabs, who sold the land to both the Christians and the Jews, were using their newly found wealth to build private villas, such as the Ticho house or some of the buildings we saw on Ethiopia Street.

At the intersection where Hanevi'im crosses Shivtei Yisrael Street, you can turn left and you will see the bus station for nos. 1, 3, 11, and 29. (A block farther to the left is the Mea Sha'arim quarter.) Or you can continue down Hanevi'im Street for a few blocks to reach Damascus Gate with its large taxi stand. If you wish, you can return to Zion Square (where this walk began) by walking up Hanevi'im Street to the corner of Harav Kook, turning left there toward the center of downtown Jerusalem.

Walk

6

The
Jewish Quarter

Sufferers from venereal disease or leprosy
were debarred from the City at all; from the
Temple women were excluded during their
monthly periods. . . .

Josephus, First century A.D.

Bus: No. 1
Starting Point: the Dung Gate

A dung gate in the Holy City, and at the foot of the Temple Mount? The name comes from the Hebrew *sha'ar ha'ashpot*, and one theory has it that in Biblical times one gate through which garbage was removed took on this somewhat unpoetic name.

We first encounter a "dung gate" in 445 B.C. when Nehemiah, cupbearer to King Artaxerxes of Persia, asks permission to leave the Babylonian Exile and return "unto the city of my fathers' sepulchres, that I may build it." (Nehemiah 2:5.) When he comes to Jerusalem, he grieves to see how the city, destroyed by Nebuchadnezzar in 586 B.C., still "lieth waste." Three days after his arrival Nehemiah sets out secretly to inspect the city walls, hoping not to arouse the "wroth" of Ammonite and Arabian neighbors.

> And I rose in the night, I and some few men with me; neither told I any man what my God put into my heart to do for Jerusalem; neither was there any beast with me, save the beast that I rode upon. And I went out by night by the valley gate, even toward the dragon's well, and to the dung gate, and viewed the walls of Jerusalem, which were broken down, and the gates thereof were consumed with fire. [Nehemiah 2:12–13.]

The dung gate that Nehemiah encountered lay south of its present namesake, in the City of David. Across from the present Dung Gate, at the edge of the road and left of the kiosks, there is a post with a street sign that says Ha'ofl Road. Look over the banister: the City of David lay on the spur that goes down from the Temple Mount to the valley below. It was an ideal place for a city, protected as it was on three sides by the valleys of Kidron, Hinnom, and Tyropoeon, and near the only spring in the area, the Gihon. Bronze Age remains from the early part of the third millennium B.C. indicate that a settlement existed here even then, and further excavations have revealed that the city had already been fortified by a wall for a thousand years before becoming the City of David circa 1000 B.C.

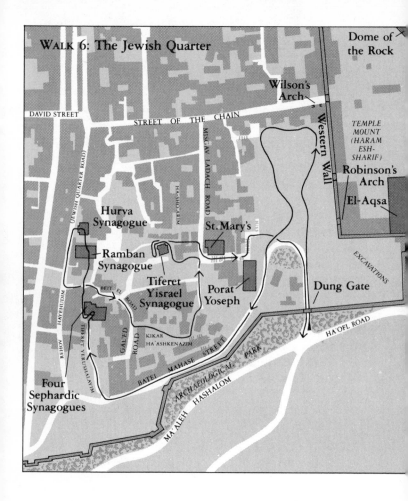

WALK 6: The Jewish Quarter

Dome of the Rock

Wilson's Arch

DAVID STREET

STREET OF THE CHAIN

Western Wall

TEMPLE MOUNT (HARAM ESH-SHARIF)

Robinson's Arch

El-Aqsa

JEWISH QUARTER ROAD

MISGAV LADACH ROAD

HA-SHO'ARIM

Hurva Synagogue

Ramban Synagogue

St. Mary's

Tiferet Yisrael Synagogue

Porat Yoseph

BEIT EL ROAD

HAYEHUDIM

EXCAVATIONS

Dung Gate

REHOV

TIFERET YERUSHALAYIM

GALED ROAD

KIKAR HA'ASHKENAZIM

HA'OFL ROAD

Four Sephardic Synagogues

BATEI MAHASE STREET

ARCHAEOLOGICAL PARK

MA'ALEH HASHALOM

Return to the Dung Gate where the retaining walls in front of it, on either side, form fine benches. From here you can read of the origins of the city and enjoy the vista.

Under the guidance of Yigal Shiloh, archaeological excavations continue at the place where the City of David once stood. From there the city climbed north, to Mount Moriah where King Solomon built the First Temple. The mountain, now called the Temple Mount, was also known as Mount Zion—not to be confused with the present Mount Zion, which was then the Western Hill. As the city grew, more and more houses were built on the Western Hill; this Upper City was roughly where the Jewish Quarter is today. The Tyropoeon Valley separated the Upper City from the Temple Mount. It was much deeper then, not yet filled with debris. The Dung Gate and the plaza in front of the Western Wall are both in this valley, which begins at Damascus Gate.

With the Dung Gate behind you, look to the far left to see the Mount of Olives with its tombstones from three thousand years of Jewish burials. The low arcaded structure at the summit is the Intercontinental Hotel. There are many churches on the mountain that commemorate the events in the life of Jesus; they are better seen from other places.

On the ridge to the right of Olivet we see a two-story white house amidst a grove of dark pines. On the slopes of this mountain some of Solomon's "seven hundred wives, princesses, and three hundred concubines" made offers and sacrifices to their foreign gods, thus offending God. The hill is called the Mount of Offence, Har Hamash'hit in Hebrew. The houses of the village of Siloam cover the slope today.

Straight ahead is another hill, sometimes called the Hill of Evil Counsel. On it you see several tall antennae and a large building on top of which flies the light blue flag of the United Nations. The white house was built by the British for the high commissioner in the 1920s on what they called Government Hill. After the 1948 war United Nations Headquarters moved to the house. When, on June 5, 1967, Jordanian troops crossed the Armistice Line and occupied the building, the Israelis realized that their neighbors on the east had chosen to join the Egyptians in war.

On your far right is Mount Zion, the buildings on it mostly hidden by the Wall that juts toward the south. The mountain is the "popular" site of the tomb of King David, which shares a building with another "popular" site, the Room of the Last Supper. Not to be outdone, the Moslems built a mosque next door. The mountain is uneasily shared by Armenians, Franciscans, Greek Orthodox, and Benedictine monks. An old cemetery, a Chamber of Martyrs and the Museum of the Holocaust, *yeshivot*, and a nightclub that features Hassidic music and dances represent the Jews on the mount. On the southwestern slope lies a Protestant cemetery. Physically, the mountain is dominated by the Dormition Abbey, which was built by the Germans in the beginning of the century. I have been told by the gatekeeper of the Armenian cemetery that before the year 2000 it will be overshadowed by a taller Armenian church, although the building process has been delayed due to a shortage of funds—not an atypical occurrence in the Holy City. The dome that can be partially seen on the left slope of Mount Zion marks the location of St. Peter in Gallicantu.

The slope from the abbey to the Dung Gate, next to the southern section of the Old City Wall, is filled with archaeological remains, many from the Second Temple Period: houses, ritual baths, cisterns, an aqueduct, all marked and dated. There are also Byzantine and Crusader towers. If you look down beyond the banister and the olive trees, to the left of the stairs, you can see a broken pilaster next to which is an old Roman or Byzantine street pavement that continued north to Damascus Gate. The remains are all part of the National Park, cleared and marked since 1967. They are open to all, and are well worth a visit. The archaeological gardens continue on the other side of the Dung Gate, to the east. The olive trees were brought here in 1979.

Turn to face the Dung Gate. The lowest gate in the Wall, it sits 2,460 feet above sea level. Only a single rosette can be seen above the pointed arch tympanum of the portal. The original opening was only half as wide as it is now. The Jordanians enlarged it after 1948 to allow vehicles to enter the southwestern part of the Old City; Jaffa Gate and Zion Gate were blocked. The new lintel is a crude block of concrete; an equally unattractive iron sliding door can be seen on the other side of the entrance.

The Crusaders called the gate located here Postern of the Tannery. On the left when you face the gate, jutting out of the Wall are the remains of a tower from that era—about ten courses of crudely hewn ashlars. The gate was also known as Siloam because of its proximity to the village. In the eighteenth and nineteenth centuries several writers mention that this gate, which was usually blocked, was opened when there was a drought to speed up the supply of water coming from the spring of Gihon, water that was brought to the city on donkeys. In recent times the Arabs called the gate Bab el-Magharbeh, after the North Africans who inhabited the area near it.

After you enter the gate, you will see on the right archaeological excavations that were started in 1968 under the direction of Professor Benjamin Mazar. Eventually they will become part of the National Park belt and will be open to the public. (You can call the Society for the Protection of Nature at 222357 for information about English-speaking guided tours of this most interesting dig.)

Walk up the road to the triangular rose bed in front of the security inspection booth and look down to the right at the excavations in which remains of every era have been found, from fragments of vessels dating back to the kings of Judea in the eighth century B.C. to a Moslem palace from the eighth century A.D. In layer upon layer lies the history of the city. What you see on the surface, near the Wall to the right, are mostly Omayyad structures (660–750 A.D.). The silver dome is the Mosque of el-Aqsa first built in 715 A.D. The Moslems called the enclosure on top of this mountain Haram esh-Sharif, the "Noble Sanctuary." On both ends of the Haram stand graceful minarets, somewhat marred by modern-day megaphones through which the faithful are now summoned to prayer. Below the right-hand minaret is the angle formed by the two enormous walls, the southwestern corner of the Temple Mount. The foundations and the supportive walls were built by King Herod around 20 B.C. when he enlarged the Temple enclosure. The larger, lower ashlars that we see today are Herodian, finely bossed and with recessed margins. The quality of the masonry deteriorates from the superb Herodian stones to a markedly less grand style, the most recent being more commonplace.

Three small windows and a larger, quadrilateral one are just under the minaret. Below them a fragment of a molded arch projects from the wall, remains of broken ashlars. The arch, almost fifty feet wide, spanned the Herodian street below it and supported a monumental set of steps that went up from the street to the Royal Portico which stood along the southern end of the Temple Mount. An American Biblical scholar, Dr. Edward Robinson, first noted the remains of the arch in 1838. It has since been named after him, Robinson's Arch. His theory was that the arch formed the beginning of a bridge which connected the Temple Mount with the Upper City behind you, where the Jewish Quarter is at present, across the valley that was deeper then. Recent excavations have shown that there wasn't a bridge here, just a flight of steps with small shops under it. Until 1968 the accumulated dirt and rubble covered the wall almost up to the level of Robinson's Arch. The color of the newly revealed courses is lighter.

To the left of the arch is a ramp that leads to the Mugrabi, or Moors' Gate. It is the only gate to the Haram esh-Sharif over which the Israeli army and Moslem guards together keep watch. Under the Mugrabi Gate is one of the original entrances to the Temple's courtyard, probably Sha'ar Kipunos, which is mentioned in the Mishnah. The Arabs call it Bab el-Nabi, "Gate of the Prophet," believing that when the Prophet Mohammed was carried to Jerusalem on his Night Journey by his winged, legendary horse el-Buraq, he tied the horse up at this gate. Although the Koran does not mention Jerusalem by name, according to Moslem tradition Mohammed ascended to heaven from the Temple Mount.

At the far right side of the Western Wall, in the women's section (a partition separates them from the men, in accordance with Jewish tradition), there are a few steps that lead up to a small space under the ramp. There the lintel of the Herodian gate can be seen, made of one stone, about twenty-four feet long. In recent years the ramp has served as a buffer zone between the Ministry of Religious Affairs, which controls the Western Wall to the north and would like to declare the whole area a Holy Place, and the archaeologists on the south, who continue to excavate.

At the inspection booth you are expected to open your bag to show that you are not carrying weapons. Just beyond the booth are two signs, white graphics on blue. One asks you—in Hebrew, English, and French—to dress and act modestly. You are approaching a Holy Place—no bare shoulders, and don't try to take photographs on Saturdays or on Jewish holidays. The second sign, in the above-mentioned three languages, and with Russian added at a later date, prohibits all Jews from entering the Temple Mount, but not for security reasons: "Entrance to the area of the Temple Mount is forbidden to everyone by Jewish Law owing to the sacredness of the place. The Chief Rabbinate of Israel." The origins of this ban go back to the period following the destruction of the Second Temple in 70 A.D. when the rabbis felt that Jews could no longer purify themselves before entering the area since the ritual required the use of the ashes of a red heifer—consult the Mishnah for further details. Also, since the exact location of the Holy of Holies is now unknown, one might accidentally step where the High Priest alone was allowed to enter only on Yom Kippur. This rabbinical ban is not observed by most visitors.

The plaza in front of the Western Wall was cleared three days after the Israelis entered the Old City in June 1967. Some six hundred Arabs of North African origins who lived here were evacuated from their houses to other parts of the city. By morning bulldozers had demolished most of the buildings. It was, perhaps, inevitable that a large space that can accommodate tens of thousands of worshipers would be created in front of the Western Wall. Off and on, since Roman times, Jews have been prevented from praying near the Temple area by pagans, Christians, and Moslems alike, at the place that symbolized their past glory, their independence.

In the days of the Temple, the Western Wall was merely the outer, supporting wall of the western edge of the Herodian platform. But as it had been sanctified for nearly two thousand years, the Ministry of Religious Affairs decided that all rules that govern synagogues have to be observed here. In the area between the iron fence and the Wall men and women pray separately. (It is interesting to note that until 1948 there was no division between the sexes: Moslems would allow no changes in the status quo, and a partition, or even a bench, was considered as a change.) There are no uncovered heads here, no immodest dress. And in the rest of the plaza, no food is allowed, and no trees can be planted as long as the Temple remains unbuilt.

The Western Wall looks smaller now, even though several more of its large Herodian courses have been exposed since 1967. When the space in front of it was only ten feet wide, the Wall loomed tall and imposing. When one looked up there was a ceiling of blue skies where one felt the close presence of God in an intimate, personal temple. On the other hand, to get to this *mur des pleurs* one had to walk through a multitude of beggars in the Mugrabi Quarter, avoid being bumped by harassing Arabs on their donkeys, and pass by the watchful eyes of British policemen.

In the first week that the Western Wall became accessible to the Israeli public, beginning on June 14, 1967, nearly half a million people made a pilgrimage to see it, to touch it, to pray in front of it. An ancient custom was renewed: leaving special notes, *tzetalach*, to the Almighty in the cracks, between the giant stones. Any requests lodged in the Wall are sure to get special attention. There are always worshipers here, and Bar Mitzvah rites are observed in the manner of the different communities. On Friday nights and on holidays dancing breaks out here, often engulfing the crowds. The Wall is no longer "The Wailing Place of the Jews."

Architect Moshe Safdie has drawn plans to reshape the plaza into "a series of ascending piazzas" with some small places for individual worship that reach down to the original level of the Herodian street on the southern, excavated side of the Wall. The idea comes from Josephus who, in *Antiquities*, wrote: " . . . for the city lay over against the temple in the manner of a theatre . . ." The plans, having encountered objections from the religious authorities and others, have been temporarily suspended.

At the northern end of the Western Wall, to your left when you are facing the Wall, are three vaults. The largest arch that leans against the Wall is called Wilson's Arch and is part of a series of piers and arches over which a causeway crossed the Tyropoeon Valley connecting the Upper City to the courtyard of the Second Temple. In 70 A.D., after four years of war, the Roman legions burned the Temple. A meeting was then arranged between Titus and the Jewish leaders. Writes Josephus, who witnessed the events:

> The partisans and their chiefs, beaten in the war all ways and shut in by a wall that left them no possibility of escape, invited Titus to a parley . . . he took his stand to the west of the Outer Temple; for here . . . there were gates, and a bridge linked the Temple with the Upper City; this now separated the party chiefs from Caesar. On either side stood a dense crowd—Jews round Simon and John on tiptoe with hope of pardon, Romans eager to see how Titus would receive their appeal.

Titus, according to Josephus, spoke to the Jewish leaders. "Your reckless impetuosity and madness," he said, "destroyed your people, your city, and your temple" and offered to grant them their lives if they surrendered: "I will punish what cannot be cured and spare the rest for my own use." The Jews asked to be allowed to leave the city and go to the desert. Titus, "furious that men no better than prisoners should put forward demands," refused. The battle raged for another month; the Upper City and the Royal Palace were then taken and burned, and the defenders were killed or taken prisoner. Titus ordered that the city be demolished; the Second Commonwealth came to an end.

As mentioned before, the valley became almost filled with debris of Titus's—and others'—destructions; the causeway survived as an ordinary street (see page 103). In 1864–65 Charles Wilson explored the then subterranean vaults when he was working with Charles Warren of the British Royal Engineers on the Ordnance Survey of Jerusalem (see page 92). Thus the largest arch is named after Wilson. You can enter the vaults through an arched door on their left side, located in the three-story building with the Israeli flag and large antenna. Visiting hours: Sunday, Tuesday, Wednesday from 8:30 to 3:00, Monday and Thursday from 12:30 to 3:00, and Friday from 8:30 to 12:00. Wander inside the vaults, where you can peek down two of the shafts that were dug by Warren and Wilson—fantastically deep—and see how far down the Western Wall continues. The Ministry of Religious Affairs has declared part of this area under the vaults to be holy, and several Arks of the Law have been placed here. At any one time you can see men at prayer here, tourists of all creeds, shapes, and colors walking around, and an occasional stray cat. Women leave this area separately so that they will not enter the men's section in front of the Western Wall.

Take another look at the building on top of Wilson's arch. It is a Mamluk building built by Seif ed-Din Tankiz in 1328 as a religious school, and later became the Mahkama, the Moslem Court of Law.

Farthest from the Western Wall, along the same northern side of the plaza as Wilson's Arch, there is an

underpass that was recently reopened. It goes to Rehov Ha'gai, or El-Wad Road, the street that continues
north to Damascus Gate along the route formed by the
Tyropoeon. Interesting remains of arches and pavements from earlier periods can be seen here, and all
are clearly identified. At the bottom of one shaft you
can see the continuation of the Roman or Byzantine
street that we noticed outside the Dung Gate. Don't go
out to El-Wad Road; return to the Western Wall plaza.
This walk will now continue to the center of the Jewish Quarter, and the benches in the underpass or just
outside it are good places to sit and read the next couple of pages.

It is difficult to write about the Jewish Quarter because it is still in the process of being rebuilt. The authorities in charge of the reconstruction and the
planning of new buildings have tried to retain much of
the character of the old quarter. The 1970s brought
fine stone buildings, new shops, clean and evenly
paved roads. But the masonry has not yet been softened by age, nor has the quarter acquired the patina
that comes with the passage of time. The area is in a
state of incompletion, its present mood impossible to
capture.

Most historians believe that before the Crusaders'
conquest the majority of the Jews lived where the Moslem Quarter is today, near the Damascus Gate. Some
Jews may have lived in the southern part of the city,
close to the Western Wall. The Jewish community was
not very large when the Crusaders arrived; it may have
numbered only fifty families, as many Jews had left the
city during the eleventh century, a period of wars and
revolts. Contemporary sources tell of Jews locked up
in their synagogue by the Crusaders and burned together with the building. There is also evidence that
other Jews were taken prisoner and sold into slavery.
After 1099, when life became more peaceful in Jerusalem, some Jews were allowed to return; apparently
they settled near the Citadel of David. Saladin, in his
efforts to rebuild the city, encouraged Jewish immigration after 1187. By the second half of the thirteenth
century, after the final defeat of the Crusaders, Jews
were living in what is known now as the Jewish Quar-

Alley, Jewish Quarter

ter. The word *quarter* is misleading, as the area grew from only one-twelfth to one-eighth of the Old City.

Most of the houses in the Jewish Quarter belonged to Arabs; some were *waqf*. (*Waqf* is property left for the benefit of a religious Moslem institution.) Since most Jews were not allowed to own property and had nowhere else to go, their landlords did little to maintain the houses and were mainly interested in collecting rent. As the number of Jews in the city increased, living conditions grew worse. This was especially true in the nineteenth century: in 1800 there were about 2,250 Jews in the city; by 1870 the figure rises to 11,000. (Moslems increased from 4,000 to 6,500 in that time span, Christians from 2,750 to 4,500. These figures were compiled by Professor Yehoshua Ben-Arieh in *A City Reflected in Its Times*, Jerusalem, 1977.)

By the middle of the nineteenth century there was a chronic shortage of water because cisterns could not meet the needs of the area's population. Few in numbers from the start, the cisterns were often leaky and unclean, neglected by the Moslem landlords. Poverty was the norm in the backward, provincial Jerusalem of the late Ottoman Period. In houses of learning and in synagogues the men spent their days praying and studying while their wives struggled to feed their families. Many subsisted on the *balukkab*, money that came from Jews in the Diaspora. Crowded, poor, and suffering from water shortages, the Jewish Quarter was the dirtiest part of a city not known for its cleanliness, and it was prone to outbreaks of epidemics.

In the 1860s Jews began to settle in new neighborhoods outside the Wall. By the beginning of World War I, 16,000 lived in the Jewish Quarter while 29,000 lived in new sections of the city. During the war, exile, conscription, starvation, and emigration depleted the total number of Jews. Riots and pogroms in the years between the two World Wars made life unsafe in the Jewish Quarter; by the early 1930s only about 5,000 remained. At the outbreak of hostilities in 1948, the Jews in the Old City numbered about 1,700, mostly old men, women, and children. In May, after weeks of siege, the Jewish Quarter surrendered. About a third of the houses were damaged in the fighting, and most synagogues were destroyed after the evacuation. The reconstruction of the quarter that began in 1967 after the city was reunited is still continuing. This makes it difficult at times to give accurate directions—the area is still in a state of flux.

Now you can begin to walk again. When you leave the underpass, on the right is a smooth reddish stone house with lucite half-domes over its balconies and black iron railings. In it is the residence of architect Moshe Safdie. Porat Yoseph Yeshivah, which he designed, dominates the southwestern corner of the plaza, to the left of his house.

Leave the area through the same inspection booth through which you entered, and turn right. Follow the road as it forms a U above the miniature rose garden and continue to climb up the hill past Porat Yoseph. Where the road begins to narrow, hugging the southern section of the Old City Wall, there are several houses on the right, some new or rebuilt, some older. You will be on Batei Mahase Street. No. 9 is the private residence of Dr. Itzhak Nebenzahl, Israel's remarkable state comptroller; it is a monumental building. At no. 7 the Great Rabbinical Court meets—note the plaque, in Hebrew only, on the right side of the vaulted passage. The third floor of the building is newer, nicely joined to the lower ones by an ornamental parapet. At no. 5 the arches were inspired by the Ottoman style of the city gates. At the next building the "Houses of Shelter" begin—Batei Mahase in Hebrew. They form the southern edge of the Jewish Quarter. We will see them again later on this walk. A small fig tree grows out of the wall, in front of the street sign in three languages on beautiful tiles.

At the point where the Old City Wall turns sharply to the left toward a corner called Burj Kabrit in Arabic, or "Sulphur Tower," you see a large construction area. At the farthest end is a modern apartment building, Gulbenkian House, in the Armenian Quarter. Beyond the Wall on the left you can see the top of the conical roof of the Dormition Abbey and its clock tower.

In 1976 the site was being cleared for building an amphitheater. After removing tons of earth, as the bulldozers were reaching the lowest point of the slope, they uncovered the top of a vault. "We threw down a rock and didn't hear it land," says Moshe Safdie, "and we knew that we had problems." The archaeologists were delighted to have these problems; they continued to dig. They found six impressive barrel vaults about thirty feet high and over ninety feet wide. The vaults are part of the underground construction of the "Nea" Church.

The sixth-century historian Procopius described this magnificent complex—church, hospice, hospital—which was consecrated in 543 A.D. and destroyed by an earthquake in the eighth century. Wrote Procopius in *The Buildings of Justinian*:

> At Jerusalem he built a church in honour of the Virgin . . . the Emperor Justinian ordered it to be built upon the highest of the hills, explaining of what size he wished it to be. . . . The hill was not of sufficient size to enable the work to be carried out according to the Emperor's orders, but a fourth of the church, that towards the south wind and the rising sun . . . was left with no ground upon which to rest. Accordingly those in charge of this work devised the following expedient. They laid foundations at the extremity of the flat ground and constructed a building rising to the same height as the hill. When it reached the summit they placed vaults upon the walls and joined this building to the other foundation of the church; so that this church in one place is built upon a firm rock, and in another place is suspended in the air. . . . [*Palestine Pilgrims' Text Society*, vol. 2, pp. 139–41.]

The sixth-century Byzantine Madaba map shows a large building in this general area, and explorers in the late nineteenth century mentioned subterranean vaults here without realizing that they were part of the "Nea" Church. *Nea* means "new" in Greek. In 1970, near Batei Mahase, remains of a massive wall and a large apse were uncovered and assumed by Professor Nachman Avigad to be part of the "Nea." In 1975 archaeologist Meir Ben Dov found another part of the outer church structure just on the other side of the Wall from where you are standing, north of Burj Kabrit. In 1977, when Avigad was clearing the vaults, a large Greek inscription was found above a cross, both in plaster relief. The inscription attributes the construction of the church to the generosity of Emperor Justinian.

Professor Avigad has been in charge of the excavations in the Jewish Quarter. New foundations have been dug all over the quarter since reconstruction began in 1967. This has given archaeologists a rare opportunity to explore this area and the finds have changed many previous theories concerning the extent of the spread of the city to this western hill, the Upper City, in the days of the First and Second Temple. A book edited by Yigael Yadin, *Jerusalem Revealed* (Jerusalem, 1975), contains an excellent collection of articles about the archaeological explorations in the city between 1968 and 1974. After the amphitheater is completed, it will be possible to see the vaults again. Reckless characters have been known to go down and explore the area even as it is.

The walk continues up the hill, past no. 3, where Yeshivat Hakotel is located.

The last house at the corner of Batei Mahase Street has a sign in Hebrew and English above a contemporary iron door set within an older arch: "Metivtah Gedolah, Beth Harashal, Yeshivah High School [and] Beth Midrash. Founded by the Council of the Sephardic Community." *Harashal* comes from *Harishon Le'zion*. "The First in Zion" in Hebrew, which is the title of the Sephardic Chief Rabbi. For many years he was the only Chief Rabbi under the Ottomans, since the Ashkenazi community was insignificant here.

Turn right at the corner where the street sign says Tiferet Yerushalayim Square. *Tiferet* means "glory." On the wall is a line of red panels in varying shades that give directions in three languages. Continue past a new building in red Jerusalem stone—with archaeological remains strewn in front of it—to a wooden staircase that will take you down below street level to the courtyard of the Four Sephardic Synagogues, open to the public daily from 9:00 to 4:00, Friday from 9:00 to 1:00. Before entering the beautifully restored complex one must lament a few 1979 additions: air conditioners that ruin the windows, several gas tanks, and a large brown sign with white graphics in Hebrew that offers information about renting a hall here.

The Four Sephardic Synagogues begin with the Yohanan Ben Zakkai Synagogue, which you enter to the left of the steps. We don't know the exact date of the building of this synagogue but it was early in the seventeenth century. Sephardim and Ashkenazim used to worship together at the Ramban Synagogue (which will be our next stop) until 1586, when it was closed down by the Ottoman authorities. Jews and Christians were forbidden to build new houses of prayer then, or to worship God in public in accordance with what the Turks called "their foolish tradition." This may account for the modest exterior of the Four Synagogues; they are indistinguishable from the surrounding domestic architecture, made to look ordinary so as not to provoke unwarranted attention from the hostile authorities.

Despite this attitude, Jews were still better off under Moslem rule than they were in Christian countries. After the Spanish Expulsion in 1492 the Sephardic community in Jerusalem grew. When Palestine became part of the Ottoman Empire in 1517, Jews benefited from the improved economic conditions that followed stabilization and the end of wars. According to early Ottoman tax records, about a quarter of the Jewish males in the city were rabbis (meaning scholars) and the rest were craftsmen or owners of small shops; none were in the "high income brackets." Most of the Jews were Sephardim then, and they retained their majority until the last decades of the nineteenth century. As the Sephardic community expanded, so did this complex. The earliest synagogue is the one in which you are standing, Yohanan Ben Zakkai, named after a sage who was smuggled out of Jerusalem in a coffin in the last days before the Roman destruction of 70 A.D. He later surrendered to the Romans in order to establish a school where Torah would continue to be taught even after the fall of the city. Three more interconnected synagogues were gradually added to the Ben Zakkai: Eliyahu Hanavi, Central, and Stambuli.

What we see today is a restoration of the old synagogues, of which only the original walls and vaults remained. In 1967, after nineteen years of Arab occupation, ten feet of dirt had accumulated here because the space had been used to stable donkeys. The paving stones had been torn off the roof, so rainwater penetrated the fill of the thick walls and the plaster became moldy and had to be removed. Dan Tanai was the architect who reconstructed and restored the four synagogues in this complex.

The elongated hall of the Ben Zakkai has three cruciform vaults in the Byzantine manner, but the diagonal ribs stop short of meeting so as not to form a cross on the ceiling (a cross is an unacceptable shape in a synagogue). In the eastern wall two arks can be seen behind doors designed by the late Bezalel Shatz. They are inside a framework restored along the lines of the Gothic stone arches of the old arks. A double ark is very rare and it is possible that the concept was transferred here from the Ramban Synagogue, where the structure of the hall dictated twin chambers. Between the two arks are marble Tablets of the Law from an Italian synagogue in Livorno. Over the arks is a mural by Jean David that at first glance seems to clash with the elegant simplicity of the restored hall; perhaps, though, it recaptures the more ornate nature of the original synagogue. The seats are traditional to Sephardic synagogues; the *bimah*—pulpit—is a modern, airy design. The black marble lines are remains of the old floor. Parts of the walls, arches, and other outstanding architectural details were left unplastered to show the texture of the stone.

The glass of the windows that face the outer courtyard is opaque and decorated with spiral designs. While the glass is new, the pillars, the delicate capitals, and the rosettes are from the old structure, as are the arches above each window, which end in a Moorish peak called a "camel's back." As noted outside, the beautiful windows are spoiled by air conditioners that have been installed recently.

The women's gallery is on a balcony behind a wooden grille in a niche in the western wall, near the main entrance. Sephardic women did not attend services often; many did not know how to read Hebrew (Ladino being the vernacular). The Sephardim call this hall *El Kahal Grande*; *Kahal* means "congregation" in Hebrew.

Look up at the southern wall, on the right when you face the arks. In a square window high above the arches you can see a jug of olive oil and a *shofar*, the ram's horn that is blown on the High Holidays (Rosh Hashanah and Yom Kippur). Both items replace the ones lost in 1948 that, according to a popular tradition, remained from the days of the Temple. This *shofar* will be used to announce the coming of the Messiah.

Leave through the farthest door in the north wall, opposite the window, on the other side of the *bimah*. You will find yourself in the Central Synagogue, sometimes called Kehal Zion because of a legend about a tunnel that connected it to King David's tomb on

Mount Zion. This narrow hall used to serve as the entrance to Ben Zakkai and Eliyahu Hanavi until the growing community required another synagogue. At the apex of each of the cross vaults here is a plaster relief medallion in a different motif. The ark was in the niche in the east wall. The wall opposite overlooks the inner courtyard; the portal has two asymmetrical windows on its sides. Over one window a square is filigreed in stone, over the other a circle. Corbels and three arches support the small balcony.

Continue through the small door in the north wall, and enter the Stambuli Synagogue, which was founded by Turkish Jews and named after the city that many of them came from. It is the largest and least symmetrical of the four halls, basically square, with a dome that sits on a drum supported by pendentives. The windows in the base of the dome filter in rays of sunlight in many colors. Architect Tanai says that the windows resemble those of Spanish synagogues in the twelfth century, colored glass medallions inserted in latticed stone frames. Beautiful! The gilded ark, from Ancona, and the *bimah*, from Pesaro, were both rescued from old Italian synagogues that were destroyed in World War II. Heavy and highly ornate, they fit in with the tradition of the Stambuli, the most lavishly decorated hall in the past.

This synagogue has a separate entrance from the street, reached by a steep staircase. Because of the steps, the ark is not in the center of the east wall, but left of the steps. In the northern wall, on your left when you face the ark, is an open niche where the *genizah* used to be—a storage chamber for worn-out sacred texts. When the chamber became full, the holy pages could not simply be discarded. Instead they were collected in some two dozen sacks to be carried by procession and buried in one of the Jewish cemeteries. The procession was a joyous occasion. Since local Moslems and Christians shared the Jewish belief that it would assure a year blessed with rainfall, they joined their neighbors in song and dance. Torah scrolls were carried under silk canopies usually reserved for wedding ceremonies. Leader of the parade was *Harishon Le'zion*, "the first in Zion," the Chief Rabbi of the Sephardim. In front of him walked his *kawwass*—a Turkish guide assigned to the highest religious and diplomatic officials—splendidly attired in the manner of the Orient, carrying pistol, sword, and a tall cane with a silver head. Candles were lit, rose water sprinkled from the rooftops, horns blown, and the prayer for rain recited. It was a colorful, gay event in the drab Holy City of the Late Ottoman Period, in which everyone participated because of the importance of rainwater.

To see the synagogue named after the Prophet Elijah, go back to the Ben Zakkai and enter the last door in the north wall, across from the main entrance. Once, when a tenth male was needed to form the *minyan* required for a service, Elijah appeared in the form of an old bearded man to join the worshipers here. He later revealed his true identity to the rabbi in a dream. Because of this the synagogue is called Eliyahu Hanavi; "his" chair used to stand near the ark and a small candle, an eternal light, burned over it.

The sixteenth-century ark, somber, solid, with designs carved into the wood, was rescued from the synagogue in Livorno. Again, because of structural limitations, the ark is off-center. The main women's gallery is in the west wall, the one opposite the ark. This room used to be a study hall before it became the second synagogue of the Sephardim in the early eighteenth century. It is similar in shape and architectural details to the larger Stambuli. It had a wooden roof that was replaced in the 1830s.

> As we are on the question of repairs, we must say something about the Jewish Synagogue. One year ago only, seeing the liberal disposition of Mehemet Ali and Ibrahim Pasha, they dared to speak about their Synagogue. They asked that their House of Prayer, being in a ruinous condition and in danger of falling in, might be repaired. So, those who did not even dare to change a tile on the roof of their synagogue at one time now received a permit and a decree to build. . . . They built the Synagogue all of stone, and in place of the wooden roof they erected a Cupola. . . . The Cupola was also very low for they feared the stability and certainty of the government.

So wrote a Greek Orthodox monk around 1838 (*Journal of the Palestine Oriental Society*, vol. 18, 1938). His name was Neophytos, of Cyprus. The changes that took place in the 1830s are discussed on page 78.

There is one guard at the synagogue who takes great

pleasure in telling legends related to Eliyahu Hanavi. If you miss him, or rather he misses you, there is a pamphlet you can buy at the door that contains a lot of information. Before you leave, it ought to be mentioned that this complex served as the hospital for the wounded in 1948 before the Jewish Quarter fell. The restoration and rebuilding of the Four Synagogues were done with love and care. Architect Dan Tanai and all those connected with the project must be congratulated. This was the first historic site in the Old City restored after 1967.

The next paragraph is an adaptation of an 1892 description from the memoirs of Ephraim Cohen-Reiss, a teacher at the Lemel School. It tells of the inauguration of the Chief Sephardic Rabbi Yaacov Shmuel Eliashar.

> The *kawwass* of the rabbi of Constantinople brought the *firman* [permit] and medal of honor from the Sultan. Together with the community's dignitaries Eliashar walked to the house of the Governor of Jerusalem, led there by two local *kawwasses*. After the *firman* was read, the soldiers raised their guns [saluted] and on the way back to the Ben Zakkai Synagogue the Arab proprietors of the cafés poured coffee at his feet, a sign of admiration. At the synagogue the leaders of the Ashkenazi community were also present, and the teachers from Lemel [a progressive school where the instruction was done in Hebrew over the objections of the ultra-Conservatives]. The children sang in Hebrew and even the *Mithnaged* Rabbi from Brisk, an extremist in the fight against modern culture, moved his lips along with the song. Eliashar wore a new coat so he could say *Sh'hechiyanu* [a blessing thanking God for letting one "see this day"]. Because of the participation of the Ashkenazim, Eliashar spoke in Hebrew [Sephardim spoke Ladino, Ashkenazim Yiddish]. It was customary during this ceremony to slaughter a sheep in the courtyard and the *shochet* [ritual slaughterer] used to dip his hand in the blood and press it against the lintel to ward off the evil eye. In deference to the *Maskilim* [the enlightened, modern Jews], both Sephardim and Ashkenazim, this custom was not observed in 1892.

After you mount the steps and leave the courtyard of the Four Synagogues, turn right and follow the road as it goes under a flat-roofed overhead passage. When you emerge take note of the shop called Mystical Corner on the right on Beit El Road, because the walk will continue from this point after we see the Ramban and Hurva synagogues.

Across the street is a large arch with the Sidnah Omar Mosque on its left. In front of the arch is a flat roof with five large flower containers. Walk toward the roof and you will see on the right, under the letters Synagogue Haramban, a set of stairs that go down below street level and end by an iron gate. Unless you get here at 6:00 A.M. for *Shaharit*, the morning prayer, or return at 6:30 P.M. for *Ma'ariv*, the evening prayer, you may not be able to enter this historic place, but you can at least see the courtyard through the latticed gate and look at the old pillar. This is the Ramban Synagogue, the oldest extant synagogue in the Jewish Quarter. Its history goes back to 1267. You can read about it sitting on the stairs, or go back up to street level, turn right, and walk up the broad staircase where the flowerpots are to the roof of the Ramban. If it is a hot day and you are looking for shade, turn to page 254 and walk to the Hurva courtyard, where there is always a shady spot for reading.

Jews continued to come to Jerusalem on pilgrimages even after the destruction of the Second Temple in 70 A.D. and we know of synagogues that existed in the first century. In 333 A.D. a Christian pilgrim from Bordeaux wrote that of the seven synagogues on Mount Zion only one remained. During the Early Moslem Period there are references to prayers and ceremonies on the Mount of Olives, where the *Shechinah*, the Divine Presence, had remained.

In the introduction to the Jewish Quarter, we already mentioned the small number of Jews in the city in the eleventh and twelfth centuries. In 1267 the Ramban, Rabbi Moshe Ben Nachman, who is also known as Nahamanides, came to Jerusalem. This famous scholar and commentator on the Bible had been invited by churchmen in his native Spain to debate the relative merits of Christianity versus Judaism. When he won the argument, the seventy-two-year-old sage wisely left Spain to come to Jerusalem. From here he wrote a letter to his son, a copy of which is reproduced inside the synagogue. It is a moving and informative document and I have taken the liberty of translating it from the original Hebrew.

God bless you my son Nachman that you should see the well-being of Jerusalem, and see the sons of your sons, and that your table should be full like the table of our Forefather Abraham.

From the Holy City of Jerusalem I write this letter to you, as with thanks to the Rock of my Salvation [God] I was fortunate to arrive on the ninth day of the month of Elul [September 1, 1267] and where I stayed, in good health, till the morrow of Yom Kippur [about one month] then to go to Hebron to lay upon the graves of our Forefathers, and to acquire a burial place for myself there.

What shall I tell you of the affairs of this land? Much is deserted, destruction is everywhere, and one Holy Place is more desolate than the other. Jerusalem is in greatest ruin, Judea being worse than Galilee. But even in her ruin the city is very good, her citizens close to two thousand of whom there are three hundred Christians, refugees from the sword of the sultan. But Israel [Jews] are not among them, since they escaped when the Tartars came, except those who were killed by their sword. Only two brothers buy dyeing [a license to work as dyers—a traditional Jewish craft] from the governor, and a few others join them at their house on Saturdays, to form a *minyan* [ten adult men required for services].

And we urged them on, and found a ruined house that was constructed with marble pillars and a beautiful dome, and we took it for our synagogue for the city is lawless, and whoever wishes to benefit from the ruins can do so. And we volunteered to repair the house and already started the renovations, and sent to Shechem [Nablus] to bring back the scrolls of the Torah which were smuggled there when the Tartars came. And in this house we shall erect a synagogue, and pray here, for many come to Jerusalem, from Damascus and Aleppo, and Egypt, and all the districts of the country, to see the [ruined] Temple and to cry over it. And He who has granted me to be able to see Jerusalem in her ruin, will grant us seeing her built and restored when the glory of the *Shechinah* will return. And you my son, your brothers, and the house of your fathers, may you all benefit in the good of Jerusalem, in the comfort of Zion,

> as is the wish of your father,
> who worries and sighs,
> who observes and rejoices
> Moshe Bar Nachman

The Ramban describes a desolate city torn by the conflict between Christians and Moslems, sacked by Tartars, her walls and fortresses torn down. The present

Jewish Quarter, where the German knights lived during the Crusader Period, was obviously sparsely populated when the Ramban arrived in 1267 and "found a ruined house."

For almost three centuries the Ramban remained the only synagogue in the city, and several pilgrims described it. It had an elongated hall, divided by four pillars, with a dome and a cistern. Light came in only through the entrance; candles had to be used even in the daytime. Sixty scrolls were kept in two chambers in the east wall. At one point a schism occurred within the community and a man who owned the property abutting the synagogue converted to Islam and built the mosque next door to spite his former coreligionists. This *muskita* is described by Rabbi Obadiah of Bertinoro in 1488. In the sixteenth century complaints were registered by Moslems that the noise coming out of the synagogue disturbed their prayers and the peace of other Moslems who resided nearby. Eventually, in 1585, the Ramban Synagogue was closed by orders of the governor of Jerusalem.

In the following years the space was used for different purposes—as a flour mill, as storage space for the mosque next door, and at one time for making cheese and drying raisins. According to the historian Yehoseph Schwartz, there was still a dome here in the 1800s, but it collapsed toward the end of the century. In 1967, when the Israelis reentered the Jewish Quarter, they cleared the space and a celebration was held here to commemorate the seven hundredth anniversary of the Ramban's modest synagogue.

Since then the building has been simply and painstakingly reconstructed under the supervision of Dan Tanai. This was never a grand building, and even the original structure was built of materials in secondary use. The pillars are from the Roman or Byzantine Period, and lack the classic bases. The capitals are not adorned with the usual carving and may have been the bases of other pillars turned upside down. The four pillars support half-vaults that form a long and narrow room. A fifth pillar may have stood in the middle of the room, where the *bimah* is. The deep double niches in the east wall—the direction Jews face when they pray—fit an earlier description of a Holy Ark that was like a chamber. Tanai writes that he decided not to reconstruct a dome since the dimensions of the old one were not known. The size of the original court-yard is also not clear but it was in the same location as the present one. Tanai opened two windows and a door in the south wall, into the yard, to let in natural daylight.

When you stand on the flat roof of the Ramban with the flowerpots behind you, you can see a plaque on the right that lists the significant dates in the history of the Ramban and of the Hurva Synagogue next door. (Slight variations in dates occur partially because of long construction periods; one source may refer to the ground-breaking, while another is referring to comple-tion.) Plans are in the making for reconstructing the Hurva, whose remains we are about to visit. If this hap-pens, you may still wish to read the history of the syna-gogue, then walk around the minaret and turn right on the Jewish Quarter Street, continuing the walk on page 259. If the rebuilding process has not yet started, note the small doorway to the left of the large arch. A set of steps leads from the door to the courtyard in which a skeleton of a building remains. Walk to the right, to what was the large hall of the synagogue. The recon-structed arch, now on the right, is one of four that used to support a large dome. This arch alone was re-built after 1967 to give some idea of the former size of the building. *Hurva* means "ruin" in Hebrew, and it is an apt name for this place that was destroyed, for a second time, in 1948.

The history of the Hurva begins at the end of the seventeenth century when Messianic dreams were still fermenting among the Jews of Eastern Europe. In 1700 Rabbi Yehuda Hassid—the "Pious"—left Poland with a group of disciples to settle in Jerusalem, in hopes of hastening the coming of the Messiah through prayers and fasting. On his way to the Holy Land Rabbi Ye-huda traveled through many Jewish communities, where he collected pledges of support for a new syna-gogue in Jerusalem. When he and his thousand follow-ers—this number varies with the sources—arrived in the city, he moved to this courtyard, which had been purchased for him; it is even possible that a small Ash-kenazi synagogue already stood here. There was a 1680 purchase document in the Moslem court and

Ruins of Hurva Synagogue

Arabs referred to this place as *deir esh-Shiknaz*, the "courtyard of the Ashkenazim."

It seems that some of Rabbi Yehuda's disciples had borrowed money from their Arab neighbors even before his arrival, in anticipation of funds from abroad. Unfortunately, Rabbi Yehuda either caught cold or was bitten by a snake three days after he came to Jerusalem, and he died. It is said that this sad event—either the chills or the sting—took place at the Pool of Siloam where Jews used to bathe. The pool was known as the *mikveh*—ritual bath—of Rabbi Yishmael Cohen Gadol, a martyr killed by the Romans.

Without Yehuda Hassid's name and prestige his disciples were unable to collect the money that had been pledged in Europe. The debt to the Moslems, with accumulated interest, grew larger as the hope to repay it diminished. The Arabs lost patience. On November 8, 1720, on Shabbat *Lech Lecha* (the weekly Torah portion for that Saturday, which began with God telling Abraham "Get thee out . . ."), the Arabs broke into the Ashkenazi synagogue, tore up the Torah scrolls, and burned the building, and this place became known as the Ruin of Rabbi Yehuda Hassid, the Hurva. All Ashkenazim were banned from Jerusalem then, and they moved to Safed and Tiberias. For the next hundred years, if an Ashkenazi came back in secret to Jerusalem, he would dress in Oriental clothes and pretend to be Sephardic.

Things began to change in the early nineteenth century. After earthquakes, a plague, and a pogrom in Safed, many Ashkenazim left and came to Jerusalem. A new law canceled debts that were more than forty years old, and the Qadi of Jerusalem ruled that this area belonged to the Ashkenazim. During the time of Mohammed Ali, one Avraham Shlomo Zalman Zoreph—"the goldsmith"—went down to Egypt to seek permission to rebuild a synagogue here. Assisted by the Austrian and Russian consuls, he submitted an elegantly written petition that Ali liked. The sultan issued a *firman*, a royal decree, which restated that *deir esh-Shiknaz* was Jewish property and that a synagogue could be built there. Singing songs of praise to the Lord, young and old and even "the dignitaries of the generation" rolled up their sleeves and began to clear the accumulated rubbish. A year after the *firman* was granted, in 1837, Menachem Zion Synagogue was finished. The name means "Comforter of Zion."

More and more Ashkenazim were coming to live in Jerusalem, and they soon outgrew the small synagogue. In 1839 the city was back in Ottoman hands, so permission for building a larger place of worship had to come from Constantinople. After many requests, bribes, help from the British ambassador to Turkey, and pressure from Sir Moses Montefiore and other British Jews, a *firman* arrived in 1855.

A couple of years later, when digging to lay the foundations began, a marble pillar, presumably from the Ramban Synagogue next door, was unearthed—a good omen. The cornerstone was laid by Baron Alphonse de Rothschild. The synagogue was officially named Beit Yaakov, after the baron's father, James, but remained known by its popular name, the Hurva. It took more than seven years, until 1864, to complete the building because the community lacked sufficient funds. Money was raised in Palestine and abroad, and even poor Jews contributed. "He buys his world [place in the next world] who buys one stone" was the fundraising slogan, based on Jewish belief that one can reach salvation with one good deed. It is interesting to note that one of the largest contributions for this Ashkenazi synagogue came from the Sephardic family of Señor Yehezkel Rueven of Bombay.

Assad Afandi, a Greek architect from Constantinople who was supervising repairs at the Haram esh-Sharif, designed the synagogue in the Byzantine style. The large hall was almost square; the pendentives were inserted between the four arches to support the decorated round dome, along whose interior ran a balcony. The tall dome became a landmark in the city skyline.

A two-story ark stood in the eastern wall, a "masterpiece" sent from Kherson in the south of Russia. It was so large that twelve camels were required to carry it from the port of Jaffa to Jerusalem. Two sets of Corinthian pillars flanked the bottom half of the ark, which was covered with baroque wood carvings of flowers and birds. On the top part, between sets of Ionic pillars, were the tablets with the Ten Commandments. Two large bronze candelabra were the gift of the Imperial Court tailor of St. Petersburg. The *bimah* stood on a pink marble base. There was also a *mareh shaot*, an "hour indicator," in the building—there was no word in Hebrew then for clock. The building costs were more than fifteen thousand pounds. Contemporary newspapers described it as a splendid place, built in a "European" manner.

By the end of the nineteenth century there was a

whole array of buildings in the courtyard, housing several different institutions. There were study houses: *batei midrash, yeshivot, talmudei Torah*. On their first day of school here little boys were showered with sweets, gifts from an angel in heaven they were told. Travelers found free lodgings here for three days. A committee of "Wise Men" and the *Beit Din Zedek* or religious court, sat in this place. Seven cisterns helped ease the chronic shortage of water, and it was distributed to the poor free of charge. There were two ritual baths here, not always spotlessly clean: "This must truly be a Holy Place," remarked one user, "or else everyone who washed here would get sick from the filth." The large synagogue held 300 men and 150 women, whose seats were spread over five different galleries.

Sir Moses Montefiore prayed at the Hurva in 1866 and 1875. Years later, under the British Mandate, another English Jew, Sir Herbert Samuel, was appointed to be the first high commissioner to Palestine. He came here in 1920, on his first Saturday in Jerusalem. The *haftarah*, a passage read from the Bible that changes weekly, was from Isaiah: *Nachamu, nachamu ami*—"Comfort ye, comfort ye, My People." Special events were observed here. A eulogy was delivered in Hebrew after the death of Queen Victoria; prayers of thanks were offered after the Balfour Declaration; the flags of the first Jewish brigades, from World War I, were deposited here. It was the vigorous center of the life of the Ashkenazi *Mithnagdim* (or *Prushim* as they are called in Jerusalem).

The synagogue was damaged during the fighting in 1948 and destroyed after the surrender of the quarter. The place was looted, the scrolls were burned, the walls and arches torn down. In 1967, when the Jews returned and began to remove the debris, fragments of a tablet were found with the inscription "This is the Gate of the Lord. The Righteous shall enter it."

Plans have been made for rebuilding the Hurva. One, now aborted, called for a "colossal" synagogue with a gold crown on top. More realistic plans have recently been drawn by British architect Sir Denys Lasdun. One hopes that the single arch with the mosque overlooking it and the pink-grained remains of the *bimah* will be left as they are. This is a place in which to remember the past, a testimony to the futility of war.

To leave the courtyard of the Hurva, stand with the arch on your left, in front of the steps that lead up to Talmud Torah Etz Hayim—the faded sign is over a square wooden door, to the left of the steps. On the right is a dark vaulted corridor; walk through it and you will know that you are in the right place if, after you are out on the street, you turn around and see five rosettes in the arch of the gate. Also, if your eyesight is good, you may be able to see a tiny green disk with "87/ΛV" on it.

You are now on the Jewish Quarter Street, Rehov Hayehudim. From 1948 to 1967 the Arabs renamed it Tariq el-Munadileen, "Road of the Warriors." The street is in the midst of reconstruction, with Arab masons, Jewish contractors, and debris-bearing donkeys everywhere. Across the narrow street from the entrance to the Hurva and slightly to the right is a large arcaded building. In 1972 Peter Bugod won a competition for his design for this building, whose construction was delayed because of the rich archaeological finds discovered below street level. Upon completion of the building, the public will have access to the site where the flagstones of the Cardo can be seen: they are remains of the street that traversed the city from north to south. About seventy-five feet wide, the Cardo was lined with two rows of columns that supported the red-tiled roofs of the porticos. No Roman strata were found during the excavations. The remains—shards and coins from the street, drains, pottery from under the pavement, Corinthian capitals and bases, some *in situ*—can all be dated to the Late Byzantine Period. This has led Professor Nachman Avigad, who directed the excavation, to propose that the southern part of the Cardo may have been built by Emperor Justinian at the same time as the "Nea" Church.

One hopes that when all the construction is finished the street will come alive again. For many years Rehov Hayehudim was the nerve center of Jewish commercial life—noisy, crowded, smelly, but alive. Here food was sold, and merchants called out to passersby to come and examine their wares. Cotton spinners worked silently, while the clatter of the tinsmiths' and cobblers' hammers resounded through the street. From the grocery stores came the smell of ground coffee, soap cakes, goat cheese, pickled herring, and black and green olives. Piles of watermelons almost blocked this narrow artery. Dogs barked, children cried, old men leaned on their staffs and haggled over the price of some overripe vegetables. Deliveries were made by pushcarts and donkeys, as in the *suq* today, adding to the confusion. But one must not overromanticize the past and must recognize that the street, like the quarter, was poverty-stricken. It was unpaved and filthy; the stench of the sewer often had the upper hand over the pleasanter aromas of fresh bread and spices. And everywhere there were beggars.

Return to the entrance of the Hurva and continue, with the gate on your left. After you walk past a large round window almost on street level, the minaret, and the small pocket garden with bright flowers, you will see a small square with an olive press, behind which are a police station and several galleries. Turn left here, on Beit El Road. Look at the first gate on your right: it has a lovely hand, a *hamsikeh*, carved over the arch, to ward off the evil eye.

You should now be able to see the underpass on the right and the Mystical Corner where earthly souvenirs are sold by a real Jerusalem character, an elderly gentleman named Mr. Cohen. ("*Vemens bist du?*" he wanted to know when I told him my great-grandparents used to live on Rehov Hazehirdim. "Whose are you?" in Yiddish.) Beyond the four steps Beit El Road becomes a narrow lane on the right. Before entering the lane, stop in front of the iron door on the left; it's painted yellow with three small Stars of David on it. On the plaque above the door and on the lampcover it says, in Hebrew, that Beit El, Congregation of Hassidim and Mekubalim Yeshivah, was founded in 1737. This group was dedicated to a communal, austere life of prayer and mystical meditation and was led by the Yemenite Rabbi Shalom Sharabi. Sharabi, rumored to be assisted by the Prophet Elijah, composed complicated texts that only the most learned students of Kabbalah, or Mysticism, could understand. His disciples meditated and fasted to hasten the arrival of the Messiah. One of them was Yehoseph Schwartz, whose book *Tevuot Ha'aretz*, a comprehensive account of life in Palestine in the first half of the nineteenth century, was the first Hebrew book printed in Jerusalem, in 1844.

Leaving the synagogue on your left, follow Beit El—which means the "House of God"—Road to where it forms a T. Take a few steps to the right where the alley ends in front of an enchanting door behind which is Eliyahu Hanavi Synagogue, which we have seen earlier in this walk. The modern door, created by artist Shraga Weil, has the synagogue's name embossed next to the handle. A beautiful old corbel is above the finely molded, arched doorway. Turn back and continue down Beit El Road, which splits here at a tiny square with an orange tree in its center. The re-

Gate with *hamsikeh*

Gal ed, a memorial

taining wall is shady even at high noon. It's a good resting place. The large bronze door on the right is the street entrance to the Stambuli Synagogue. Sculptor Buki Schwartz based his design on the theme of the *menorah*.

Walk down the right, narrower part of the fork; a red sign with black graphics, "Arts and Crafts Batei Mahase Square," points in the correct direction. There is also a street sign high on the wall on the left, Gal'ed Road. If you can imagine this lane dirty and with a muddy pavement, you'll get a feeling for a typical nineteenth-century alley in the Jewish Quarter. Take the first left turn—Arts and Crafts again shows the way—and you will find yourself in a modest square with a delicate pepper tree, an iron chain, and a simple memorial stone, a *gal ed*. Forty-eight people were buried here, killed in the last weeks before the Jewish Quarter surrendered. It was impossible then to take the bodies out to a cemetery; in 1967 the remains were moved to the Mount of Olives. The inscription on the wall, in black Hebrew lettering, is well placed in what might have been a window. You can see the same style of stonework in the arch above the inscription, in the doorway, and in the "flying buttress" on the right.

Walk past the memorial stone and suddenly, after a maze of vaulted lanes, you will enter a large, open space, a most unusual feeling in the crowded Old City. This is Kikar Ha'ashkenazim, also known as *der Deutscher Platz*, the German Square. From the start it was left open to help alleviate the crowded conditions in the quarter. Today, splendidly repaved in Jerusalem limestone, it lies drenched in sunshine, almost devoid of people. Only small children chase one another among ancient capitals and bases. At times prayer chants drift through open windows onto the square.

The colossal relics were found in different excavations in the quarter. Beneath a Herodian floor was found the base of the Attic-style column. The lower diameter of the base is six feet, and the column it supported may have been more than thirty feet high. The Ionic capital and column segment are also impressive in both style and workmanship, and date back to the period before the destruction in 70 A.D. It was surprising to find remains of such size in the Upper City; it's an indication of the existence of enormous buildings. A popular explanation is that some may have come from the palace built by the Hasmonean. Professor Avigad writes that columns of such proportions were most typical of temples (*Qadmoniot*, vol. 5, nos. 3–4, 1972).

While a few trees have been planted here lately, the square is almost barren, as it must have been over a century ago when water was scarce, expensive, and difficult to conduct. Trees were a luxury in the arid city.

The first house on your right is Beit Rothschild,

named after Baron Wilhelm Karl de Rothschild of Frankfurt, an Orthodox member of the illustrious family, who gave the money to build it. It is an elegant urban place in pink stone with arches across its two-storied façade. The lower-story loggia is above a set of broad steps. Architects work within, in finely reconstructed vaulted chambers. The house was damaged in 1948, but now, restored to its original beauty, it holds the offices of the agency in charge of rebuilding and developing the Jewish Quarter. In the middle of the upper story is a coat of arms of the Rothschilds.

On the southern end of the square, on your left if you face Beit Rothschild, is a block of apartments, with cupolas over the roof at evenly spaced intervals. A sign says Yeshivat Hakotel. These are the original Batei Mahase, "houses of shelter" or "refuge." The concept comes from the European *shtetl*, where houses of shelter offering asylum to the poorest Jews were common. The apartments were built in 1858 by Kolel Ho"D, the community of Jews who came from Holland and Deutschland (thus Ho + D). One unusual feature of Batei Mahase is that the Jews managed to buy the land on which they are built. It was almost impossible for Jews to buy property, even after the Crimean War when Turkey liberalized the laws that forbade foreign nationals from owning land. Today *yeshivot* have moved to the former dwellings.

On May 28, 1948, John Phillips, an Englishman, captured with his camera the tragic face of war: old men, women, children clutching their pitiful bundles; thirty-five weary, weaponless Haganah fighters, all gathered in this square near Beit Rothschild before evacuating the quarter. The dome of the Tiferet Yisrael Synagogue—our next stop—though slightly damaged, still dominated the skyline. Phillips's photographs are published in his book *A Will to Survive* (New York, 1977).

To leave the square, walk to the corner diagonally across from where you entered it. There is a set of stairs to the right of Adi Gallery that go down to Misgav Ladach Road. The name of the street means "refuge for the downtrodden," and it was the name of the first Jewish hospital that stood here, built by the Rothschilds in 1854. Turn left at the bottom of the stairs and just past Mamedot Israel Road, on the left, you

Beit Rothschild

will see a courtyard at no. 48 filled with the creations of sculptress Leah Majaro Mintz. After you pass Haye Olam Road and the large wooden and glass doors of Hechal Wohl on the right, you will come out from under the covered street to a small square. On the right a magnificent vista appears: el-Aqsa against the background of the Mount of Olives.

Enter the large double vaults on the left into an area with several shops and studios, and cool, wide stone benches. You might be approached by someone from a *yeshivah* called Aish Hatorah, the "Fire of the Torah." Most likely he will be an American dedicated to "the battle for Jewish survival," part of a group that is determined to explain what Judaism is all about to the sinner and the ignoramus in hopes of returning errant Jews to the ways of the Lord.

If you are hungry or thirsty, you can walk up the set of steps in back of the *yeshivah*, on your right when you stand with your back to Misgav Ladach Road. There you will find the Quarter Café, a clean cafeteria that serves tasty food and isn't too expensive. The great view of the Temple Mount is free.

Next to the steps to the café is a plain-looking iron door—brown with glass panes. Behind it is one of the most exciting discoveries of Professor Avigad: the remains of the burnt house from 70 A.D.

In the corner of one of the rooms an iron spear was found leaning against the wall as if left ready for use, and

Sculptress' courtyard

against a wall in the small kitchen, we found the skeletal arm of a young woman who apparently did not manage to escape when the house went up in flames, collapsing upon her. This was the sole instance of human remains left from the disaster which overtook the house. One of the stone weights bears the Aramaic inscription "[Of] Bar Kathros" . . . [*Jerusalem Revealed*].

Kathros was a family of priests mentioned in the Talmud.

On the far side of the vaults, away from Misgav Ladach, is another small square with massive remains of a large structure on the left—cement poured over ruined walls. The base of an ancient column lies amidst green shrubs. Walk straight up the street on the right and pass by Ha-Shoarim Road and two studios with signs in Hebrew only. On your left you will see three arches of varying sizes, and a set of twenty-six stairs behind the smallest arch. These stairs will take you up to the main entrance of the Tiferet Yisrael Synagogue, the "Glory of Israel," inaugurated in the fall of 1872, destroyed in the spring of 1948. The remains look almost theatrical: among roses and delicate vines against the background scenery of the Temple Mount sits an enormous ruin that appears to be cast in plaster of Paris. The façade, or what is left of it, is most elegant: the triple-arched entry is articulated with a dentil entablature framing the deep arches. The central arch rests on pairs of engaged columns, all carved of light red Jerusalem stone.

The popular name of this synagogue was Nissan Bak, after the man who was instrumental in its founding. The Baks were a family of Hassidim who moved to Jerusalem after riots and a major earthquake destroyed their home and printing press in Safed. In 1841 Yisrael Bak, Nissan's father, reestablished his press in the Old City. It was the first Hebrew press in Jerusalem. Only the Armenians had a printing press then, dating from 1833. The Baks were a hospitable family, and many other Hassidim stayed at their house when they came to Jerusalem. As their numbers grew they needed a large place of worship. With the help of Rabbi Yisrael Friedman of Ruzhin and Sadigora in Galicia, this plot of land was purchased in 1843, at which point a Moslem grave was discovered on it. After many delays the Qadi of Jerusalem gave permission to move the bodily remains to a Moslem cemetery but riots began when another Arab claimed that the spirit of the deceased visited his dreams and bemoaned the contemplated move. The wise Qadi solved the problem by having the same spirit appear in his dream with a change of heart. It seemed that Abraham, the Forefather of both Jews and Moslems, could not bear to see his children fight, and asked the dead man to agree to the move!

This problem solved, Nissan Bak went to Constantinople to try to get a building permit. Soon he ran out of money for the appropriate *baksheesh* and his request was not granted. So he went to Vienna and drew up a petition that he threw into the carriage of Emperor Franz Josef. Why the emperor? Because many of the Hassidim were under his "protection," as they originally came from Austria. With the help of Count Pizzamano, the Austrian consul to the court of the Sublime Porte, a royal *firman* was finally issued in 1858 to build "the said synagogue."

The plot continues to unfold like the libretto of an *opéra bouffe*. The Hassidim own the land, *sans* tomb, plus *firman*. But they don't have money. In fact they are so poor that they cannot even risk sending the customary *shlihei tzibur*, "fund raisers," abroad for fear that they would not be able to cover their own travel expenses. But slowly the word spreads; donations start to arrive; and construction begins. In 1869 when Franz Josef visits Jerusalem he comes to see the building, which is still roofless for lack of funds. "Where is the synagogue's roof?" inquires the emperor. "It has taken off its hat in honor of Your Highness" is the diplomatic reply. The emperor, well known for his previous help to Jews, donates the money for the dome. In 1872, some twenty-nine years after the land was first acquired, a grand ceremony marks the completion of the synagogue.

Below street level was a large ritual bath, a thirty-five-foot-square *mikveh*. In the great hall the dome was supported by a drum that had many windows, and a balcony ran the length of the drum on the inside. The pendentives were decorated with pictures of birds and animals, and the *bimah* was high, with a wrought-iron railing. The building was three stories high without the dome, making it one of the tallest in the Old City.

Some say that the Greek architect who helped design the Hurva drew the plans for this synagogue too; others claim that the architect was the same man who built the Russian Cathedral. Judging from old photographs there were many basic similarities between this place and the Hurva, so it is likely that the same hand designed both. The synagogue was destroyed after the Jewish Quarter surrendered to the Arabs in May 1948.

Across the street is the Karaite Synagogue. To the right of the gate is a brass *mezuzah*, shaped like a Torah scroll. The word *pa'amon*, "bell," is written on the wall in black letters. To the left of the gate is a sign that says: "The Karaite Jewish Community in Israel, The Anan Ben David Synagogue, Founded in the 8th Century C.E. [Common Era] Reconstructed in 1978 (5738)."

Kara means "read" in Hebrew. Members of this sect followed the written Scriptures but refused to abide by the Talmudic law, which is based on oral interpretations. It is said that Anan Ben David started this schism in Baghdad in the eighth century because his brother was chosen over him for the office of the exilarch. His followers began to move to Jerusalem in the tenth century, and it was probably two centuries later that they built this synagogue, which is completely underground. There are three possible reasons given for this odd location: the Moslems did not allow building synagogues with windows, it was safer to be inconspicuous, or a custom was followed of praying to God from a low place: *"Mema'amakin kraticha, Yah."*

The Jews considered the Karaites to be heretics, but at one time conditions became so bad under the Moslems that they decided to hold a joint meeting in the safety of this building. The Karaites seized the opportunity to take revenge on the Jews who usually shunned them. They hid some books, holy only to Jews (perhaps the writings of Maimonides), under the steps so that they would become desecrated when the Jews unwittingly stepped on them. Miraculously, the Jewish rabbi who was leading the way tripped and rolled down the steps and did not commit a sin by walking over sacred texts. His followers investigated the bizarre incident and discovered the holy books. For their trickery the Karaites were cursed that their male numbers should never again exceed one dozen in Jerusalem. In 1948 there were only two Karaites living here when the quarter fell, but newcomers from Egypt have now revitalized the sect, and the "spell" seems to be broken. The restored synagogue is usually closed to the public.

Retrace your way back down the twenty-six steps, through the vaults and past Aish Hatorah Yeshivah to Misgav Ladach Road. Just where you come out from under the vaults you will see a sign that says "Archaeological Garden" across the street. Enter the portal to the left of the sign, which is the street entrance to a Crusader center known as Saint Mary's of the German Knights. After you walk in, under the second vault on the right on a yellow background, you will see the architectural plans of this complex hanging on the wall: church, hospice, hospital, as they once were, plus a brief history that also tells of the rediscovery of the site amidst the ruins of the Jewish Quarter in 1968. Sometimes the gate is closed, but you can still enter the lower part of the complex. Here is a summary of the provided information.

During the Second Crusade, German knights who did not speak the languages of the other Crusaders moved to this sparsely populated section of the city. In

1128 they built this complex to serve German-speaking pilgrims. In 1190 the Germans formed their own Order of the Teutonic Knights, separating themselves from the Hospitallers. After the fall of the Kingdom of Jerusalem in the thirteenth century this church was partially destroyed, and eventually some other structures were built on top of the ruins, hiding all evidence of the once-thriving church. In 1968, when some of the rubble was removed from the area, these remains were discovered and the site was cleared.

The church, almost on street level, was Romanesque in style. It had three apses in the east wall with windows that overlooked the Temple Mount and Olivet. The central apse had a wider window, now rebuilt, and the other two apses had elongated windows, divided in two, as you can see on the left side. The two side aisles were narrower than the nave. As you face the windows, note the blocked arched one in the north wall, on your left, still has patches of blue paint on it, remains of secondary occupation. Behind this wall was the hospice.

To see the rest of the site you have to leave through the main door, turn left, and left again to a long staircase called Ma'alot Rabbi Yehuda Halevi, named after the great twelfth-century Spanish poet. "My heart is in the East and I am in the Uttermost West . . . ," he lamented.

Walk down three sections of the stairway. You will be on a small platform with the enormous Yeshivat Hakotel-Hechal Wohl looming on the right. A window with a flat arch sits in the *yeshivah*'s wall just above ground level. If you look in you see a group of dwellings, remains from the Second Temple Period. They are now covered up in part by boards to protect them from the construction activities. The site will be open to the public, eventually.

Continue down the steps and after the eighth section of stairs you will see, on the left, another entrance to the lower section of St. Mary's. Enter the garden through this opening—where the wide banister ends—it's an enchanting spot. Rich deep violet bougainvillea magnificently sprawl across white walls. The floor of this former German hospital is now covered with red clay pottery shards, of which there seems to be an endless supply in Jerusalem. The shards were put here to relieve the monotony of the white stone, says archaeologist Meir Ben Dov, who was in charge of the restoration work. If you look closely you might even find broken spouts or cracked pot-handles that are probably Late Turkish or Early British, circa 1917 A.D.

Three piers divided this hall into two aisles. The westernmost pier—farthest from where you entered—and the two ribs of the groin vault have been reconstructed to give an idea of the scale of the building. If you stand under the rebuilt arches with the pier on your right and look up at the southern wall of the church above, you can see, to the right of the reconstructed arch, the remains of a capital with a broad leaf motif. A second story stood above the hospital. The whole building was modest, with little ornamentation.

Return to the Yehuda Halevi steps. The second massive building on the southern side of the steps is the Porat Yoseph Yeshivah. The original building, completed in 1923, was named after Yoseph Avraham Shalom of Calcutta who gave the money to build it and provided an endowment to maintain it. It was a Sephardic center of learning until its destruction in 1948. The new building was designed by Moshe Safdie, who discusses his ideas for this structure in his book *For Everyone a Garden* (Cambridge, 1974).

Where the steps of Yehuda Halevi veer sharply to the left a small platform is formed. Stand here for a minute, or, better yet, sit on the wide stone banister and look ahead. Here, against the Mount of Olives, is the heart of the Holy City, the fountainhead of dreams, prophecies, and conflict—the Temple Mount.

The Temple was called Beit Hamikdash in Hebrew, the "House of Sanctuary," the "Holy House," and it inspired the Arabs' name for Jerusalem, Beit el-Maqdis or simply el-Quds, "The Holy." Now the golden Dome of the Rock, one of the most splendid buildings in the world, stands on the site of the Temple. Beneath it lies the rock on which, according to tradition, Abraham tied his son to sacrifice him. Later, King David bought the site from Araunah the Jebusite, and Solomon built the First Temple on it. This is where the miracle of Hanukkah occurred after the Hasmonean revolt. Herod enlarged the enclosure here and adorned the Temple—the Royal Portico alone was the largest structure in the land. Wrote Josephus:

> Viewed from without, the Sanctuary [Temple] had everything that could amaze either mind or eye. Overlaid all around with stout plates of gold, in the first rays of the sun it reflected so fierce a blaze of fire that those who endeavoured to look at it were forced to turn away as if they had looked straight at the sun. To strangers as they approached it seemed in the distance like a mountain covered with snow; for any part not covered with gold was dazzling white.

This was the Temple that Jesus knew, destroyed by the Romans in 70 A.D. When the Temple was burned and Jerusalem was captured the Jews were dispersed and did not become an independent nation again until 1948.

Since the seventh century the shrines on the Temple Mount have been sacred to the Moslems. For nineteen centuries the Jews have prayed daily to return to a restored Temple in Jerusalem: "May we be privileged to worship Thee in our restored Sanctuary in splendor and in awe, as in ancient days."

On June 7, 1967, Colonel Motta Gur announced: "The Temple Mount is ours!" Three hours later Defense Minister Moshe Dayan ordered the Israeli flag removed from the Dome of the Rock and the withdrawal of the paratroopers from the area. The protection of the Mount was given back to the Moslem guards. On June 17 Dayan returned the Temple Mount to the Arabs in a most noble political gesture.

So today the Temple Mount is in Arab possession. Visitors are allowed to enter the area if properly clad. As they enter they are inspected for weapons by the Arabs. When they return they are searched by the Israelis. Extremely Orthodox Jews believe that the rebuilding of the Third Temple has to be left in the hands of the Almighty, and will probably not happen in our generation. One less conflict!

Under Robinson's Arch there is an inscription that was carved in the fourth century A.D., a quote from Isaiah (66:14): "And when you see this, your heart shall rejoice, and your bones like young grass [shall flour-

At the Western Wall

ish]." Under the rule of Roman Emperor Julian ("the Apostate," 361–63 A.D.) permission was given to the Jews to rebuild the Temple but upon his death the project came to naught. The inscription may indicate the hopes of the Jew who engraved it onto the Wall.

When Professor Mazar's excavations reached the level of the Herodian street that was parallel to the Wall, to the right of Robinson's Arch, near the corner where the western and southern walls of Herod's platform meet, some large stones were found. They had fallen from the top of the wall when the Temple was destroyed in 70 A.D. Inside one stone was inscribed, in Hebrew, *L'beit Hatkiah* . . . , "To the Place of Trumpeting." Josephus relates that a tower stood at this corner, and from it a *cohen*, a priest, used to blow the trumpet every Friday afternoon to announce the approach of the Sabbath. The fallen stone came from the spot where he stood, almost two thousand years ago. Today, in front of the Western Wall, the same tradition continues, and if you are here on the eve of the Sabbath you can hear the call of the *shofar* and see hundreds of Jews pouring down to the ancient Wall.

At the bottom of the steps turn right and walk to the Dung Gate, where the walk ends.

Restaurants and Shops

Restaurants

Read the "Food and Drink" section on page 10 before you embark on the quest for local delicacies. A man once told me that he was very disappointed because the Chinese restaurants in Jerusalem were not up to his standards. "How is the Israeli food in Hong Kong?" I asked. If the pizzas, steaks, and wonton soups are not to your liking, try the local specialties here that have been influenced by the cuisines of the Middle East and North Africa. There is also an established tradition of middle-European cooking: goulash, schnitzel, and even *kishkeh* (stuffed derma) can be found, done to perfection. At the large hotels, most of which keep kosher, the food tends to be fairly standard, prepared in a modified French manner.

The list of my favorite restaurants is purely subjective; the "Out of Town" eating places were chosen because of a special feature, the view, or the atmosphere. The main list does not include all the restaurants in the city and you may wish to consult the weekly tourist publication for others. The categories—expensive, moderate, inexpensive—are, of course, relative and subject to change, as is the quality of the food and the service. Call for reservations and credit card information. Some places are not open for lunch; many are closed on Friday nights and during the day on Saturdays.

A word about Israeli waiters: they have yet to perfect the art of serving, but they make up for it by constantly urging you to eat more, and by becoming your bosom buddy before you've had dessert.

SOME SPECIAL PLACES

American Colony Hotel, Nablus Road, tel. 282421. Owned by the descendants of the Spaffords, who founded the American Colony in 1881, the hotel is set in a mid-nineteenth-century Arab villa, a classic example of local construction for an elegant private residence: domed ceilings, tiled floors, glazed tiles on the walls, and a restful central courtyard. The hotel and restaurant are now operated by a Swiss chain, Gauer, and the chef is also Swiss. The cuisine is International with a few Oriental selections. In summer, on Friday nights, the hotel features barbecues and belly dancers by the poolside. At lunch on Saturday eat as much as you can at the elegant buffet. On any summer afternoon the garden merits a visit; you can have a cup of coffee, tea, or more serious stuff. The indoor bar is lovely too. Dining is expensive.

(Sea) Dolphin, Rashid Street, tel. 282788. Co-owned by an Arab and a Jew, one of the first post-1967 joint ventures, this has become a most popular and well-known restaurant. At times you have to stand and wait, so be sure to make a reservation or get here early. The food is excellent, and even people who don't like fish come here. You can have fresh trout cooked several ways: with almonds or orange juice or olives—my favorite, made with the local tangy, bitterish olives. The shrimp defies description. Remember not to ruin your appetite on the salads. Portions are generous, prices moderate.

Hamarakiah Haktanah, 10 Bezalel Street. This "Little Soup Place" is favored by students because of its low prices and good food. A meal consists of salad, bread, beer or wine, and the main attraction: one of several homemade soups filled with meats, vegetables, and other surprises. Service is very casual, as is the decor. Inexpensive.

Hen, 30 Jaffa Road (Walk 3, page 145), tel. 227317. No linen tablecloths here, but the food, and the prices, make this tiny place worthwhile. It is owned by a Kurdish family, and they do most of the cooking and the serving. If you are baffled by the menu, consult your waiter. Some soups are almost a meal by themselves, the salads are standard Israeli. The pièces de résistance are the *memulaim*, all kinds of vegetable shells stuffed (*memula*) with meats, rice, and other good things. Come early—at lunchtime the place is packed. Inexpensive.

Israel Museum Cafeteria. No meat dishes, but very good *gefilte fish*, blintzes, and an array of salads, cheeses, cooked vegetables, and fresh fruits. The selection varies with the seasons. Inexpensive.

Katy, 16 Rivlin Street (Walk 3, page 142), tel. 234621. Elegant dining in a remodeled nineteenth-century dwelling. The small and intimate restaurant is named for one of its owners, a charming, former nurse from Casablanca who adds to the warmth of the place. The cuisine is basically French with an occasional hint of North African influence. The bar is also pleasant. Make a reservation. Expensive.

Mifgash Bavly, 54 Hanevi'im Street (Walk 5, page 218), tel. 222195. Open only between 9:00 A.M. and 4:30 P.M. Don't be put off by the word *vegetarian*—the selection of both hot and cold dishes is unique, from avocado, beet, or eggplant salad to Russian eggs, soup, or fish. You can try a little of each at the buffet, where you'll be greeted by Mr. Bavly. The restaurant is located in a former, late-nineteenth-century private house, on what used to be known as Street of the Consuls. Inexpensive.

Philadelphia, Az-Zahara Street (off Rashid), tel. 289770. Formerly called The City Restaurant which was located just within Herod's Gate, this establishment has maintained its high quality in this more spacious location. If you ask for "a few salads" to begin with, you'll end with fifteen dishes filled with a fantastic variety of chopped, blended, and pickled vegetables, so try to be specific. Anything off the grill is good, but it's the lamb chops that made Philadelphia famous. Moderate.

Taj, 27 Jaffa Road (Walk 3, page 144), tel. 241515. Persian dishes are basically similar to Near Eastern food but the herbs and spices are different, explains chef Rachel, who is the sister of the owner, Mr. Kermasha. Good eggplants, pickles in red vinegar, stuffed grape leaves like you've never had before. *Chorsht sabsi* is a heavy soup filled with meat and beans. There is also grilled food for the less adventurous. Friendly, kosher. Moderate prices.

OUT OF TOWN

Goulash Inn, Ein Kerem, tel. 419214. When the door shuts behind you, you are transferred from the Judean hills to a Hungarian country inn. The service is pleasant and warm and you might even be shown the famous albums with the "Who's Who" photos of people who have dined here in the past. Goulash, dumplings, and mixed grill are all good. If you have room, try Sweet Elizabeth for dessert. Expensive.

Intercontinental Hotel, Mount of Olives, tel. 282551. A wonderful view of Jerusalem from the east—Wall, domes, Temple Mount, minarets, church cupolas, and bell towers. The bar is pleasant, and lunch (basically Oriental) is very good.

Mei Naftoah, Lifta Tahtit 11, tel. 521374. In an old Arab house overlooking the hills west of the city. The restaurant serves basically Oriental and Israeli food. The garden café is especially pleasant on a hot summer afternoon. Moderate.

Mishkenot Haroim, East Talpiot, behind United Nations, tel. 717666. The food is listed as Israeli, Oriental, Continental, with South American specialties from the grill. The main reason to come here is the view, even if you have only coffee and cake. You see Jerusalem from the south, and can understand why people always "went up" to Jerusalem and to the Temple. Spectacular at sunset. Moderate.

Motza Inn, on the main road to Tel Aviv, tel. 531713. Five kilometers west of the city, in an old house in a small village, the restaurant has an intimate atmosphere, simple decor, and good Moroccan food. Try the couscous. Prices are moderate.

OTHER RESTAURANTS

Expensive

Au Sahara, 17 Jaffa Road (Walk 3, page 115), tel. 233239. Pungent Moroccan food and decor.

Chez Simon, 15 Shamai Street (second floor), tel. 225602. Fine French and Continental cuisine, elegant service.

Cow on the Roof, the Plaza Hotel, tel. 228133. Award-winning, interesting kosher *à la* Israel food.

Gondola, 14 King George Street, tel. 225944. A popular place for good Italian cooking.

La Regence, King David Hotel (Walk 4, page 156), tel. 221111. Elegant food, setting, service. Kosher.

Mishkenot Sha'ananim, below Montefiore's windmill (Walk 4, page 169), tel. 226746. Very expensive, good kosher French cooking. Glorious view.

Venezia, corner of Ben Shetah and Hassoreg streets, tel. 231793. Good cannelloni, calamari, and other Italian delicacies.

Moderate

Dagim Beni, 1 Mesilat Yesharim, tel. 222403. Variety of fish dishes and soups. Kosher.

Europa, 42 Jaffa Road (Walk 3, page 142), tel. 228953. Leah Brummer's fine Hungarian home cooking. Kosher.

Fefferberg, 53 Jaffa Road, tel. 224841. Traditional Eastern European Jewish cooking.

Fink's Bar, 13 King George Street, tel. 234523. Famous for its goulash soup since the days of the British Mandate. A must!

Hassan Effendi, 3 Rashid Street, tel. 283599. Pleasant Oriental food, atmosphere, and service.

Hatzrif (Pie House), Horqenos Street (Walk 3, page 134), tel. 222478. Various meat, vegetable, and fruit pies in rustic setting. Interesting, often crowded.

Hesse, 5 S. Shetah Street, tel. 226893. A good French restaurant and coffeehouse.

Jerusalem Oriental, Rashid Street, tel. 284397. "Arabian nights" atmosphere and food.

Jerusalem Theatre Restaurant, 20 Marcus Street, tel. 630078. International, especially South American food. Big steaks.

Kfir, 25 Saladin Street (second floor), tel. 280555. Oriental food, *cholnet* on Saturdays.

L'Entrecôte chez Desire, 6 Hillel Street, tel. 245515. French steak house. Set menu with salad and wine.

Leviathan, 11 Rashid Street, tel. 283655. Variety of fish and seafood specialties.

Mandarin, 2 Shlomzion Hamalka (Walk 3, page 144), tel. 222890. First Chinese restaurant in Jerusalem.

Palmachi, 13 Shamai Street, tel. 234784. Oriental and Israeli dishes. Pleasant service. Kosher.

Rondo, 53 King George Street, tel. 232223. Dairy food, served outdoors in Independence Park.

Shemesh, 21 Ben Yehuda Street, tel. 222418. Oriental and European cooking. Popular spot. Kosher.

Inexpensive

Abu Shukri. (Enter Damascus Gate, bear left at first main fork, and just keep walking; it's approximately three hundred yards beyond the Armenian Catholic Patriarchate and the Government Hospital of Jerusalem, on your left.) Perhaps the best hummus in the city.

Abu Tor Observatory, 5 Ein Rogel Street, tel. 718842. Self-service, tasty dairy food.

Alpin, 25 King George Street, tel. 226626. Vegetarian dishes. Good salads, soups, blintzes.

Gino, Christian Quarter Road. Excellent pasta and pizza.

Mama Mia, 5 Hillel Street, tel. 248080. Rustic decor, home-made pasta. Kosher.

Oftagun, 36 Jaffa Road, tel. 222217. Self-service. Southern—kosher—fried chicken.

Oneg, off Zion Square behind 42 Jaffa Road (Walk 3, page 141). Claims to have the cheapest food in town.

Rasputin, Rivlin Street. Pleasant food and setting.

Sova, 3 Hahistadrut Street, tel. 226626. Self-service, inexpensive, kosher.

The Tavern, Rivlin Street (Walk 3, page 142), tel. 224500. Draught beer, hamburgers, light meals.

Uncle Sam, 7 King George Street, tel. 224228. Hot dogs, hamburgers, and everything else the name implies.

Shops

For centuries Jerusalem lived off the pilgrims' trade and to this day part of the city's commerce is still oriented toward the tourist. There are several main shopping districts. One is along David Street (Suq el-Bazaar) and Christian Quarter Road. It is a good place for buying inexpensive gifts; there is also an endless supply there of *objets de piété* for Christians. The Triple Bazaar, farther east, is the place where most Arabs buy their foodstuffs. Outside the Old City, you will find most shops on Jaffa Road, Ben Yehuda Street, and King George Street. For Jews, Mea Sha'arim offers a wide selection of religious items. Read the section on shopping in "Information and Advice"; bargain at the bazaar, don't bargain in western Jerusalem, and try your luck at Mea Sha'arim—sometimes you may get a discount. Most guides in Israel are not only well informed but pleasant and honest as well. Still, you must beware that there are people who will take you to a certain shop because they will get a cut from the owner.

The following suggested shops are a small part of a very long list of possible places. You are best off to walk into several places and make your own comparisons.

Antiques: King David Antiques, 10 King Street; Barakat, David Street (Suq el-Bazaar).

Books: Ha'atid, 2 Hahavazeleth Street; Jordan, 42 Jaffa Road; Ludwig Mayer, 4 Queen Shlomzion; Steimatzky, 39 Jaffa Road. (All of the bookshops are on Walk 3.)

Clothes: Chic Parisien, 1 Ben Yehuda Street; D'Or, 2 Ben Yehuda; Epstein & Felheim, 50 Jaffa Road; Hamashbir Latzarhan Department Store, corner Ben Yehuda and King George streets; Li & La, 15 Shamai Street; Rosenblum, 62 King George Street, and at the King David Hotel.

Cross-stitch Embroidery: Palestine Needlework Program, 79 Nablus Road.

Gifts, jewelry, and souvenirs: Charlotte, 4 Koresh Street; House of Quality (Ot Hamutzar), 12 Derech Hevron; Hutzot Hayotzer, Jerusalem Brigade Street; Idit, 16 Ben Yehuda Street; Wizo, 34 Jaffa Road.

Shoes: Comfort, 23 Ben Yehuda Street; Freiman & Bein, 50 Jaffa Road; Mautner, 9 Ben Yehuda Street—especially for Nimrod sandals.

Index

Index

Index

Index